COMMUNICATION AND INTERACTION

IN GLOBAL POLITICS

ADVANCES IN POLITICAL SCIENCE
An International Series
*Published in cooperation with the International
Political Science Association*

Series Editor

Richard L. Merritt
University of Illinois at Urbana-Champaign

Editorial Board

Helio Jaguaribe de Mattos, *Conjunto Universitário
Cândido Mendes*
Hans Klingemann, *Freie Universität Berlin*
Jean Laponce, *University of British Columbia*
Arend Lijphart, *University of California, San Diego*
John Meisel, *Queen's University, Kingston*
Marcel Merle, *Université de Paris I (Sorbonne)*
Elinor Ostrom, *Indiana University*
Vadim S. Semenov, *Institute of Philosophy, Moscow*
Michitoshi Takabatake, *Rikkyo University*

Volumes published in this series:

1. THE EMERGING INTERNATIONAL ECONOMIC ORDER: Dynamic Processes, Constraints, and Opportunities (edited by Harold K. Jacobson and Dusan Sidjanski)
2. MANAGING INTERNATIONAL CRISES (edited by Daniel Frei)
3. WHY GOVERNMENTS GROW: Measuring Public Sector Size (edited by Charles Lewis Taylor)
4. INNOVATION IN THE PUBLIC SECTOR (edited by Richard L. Merritt and Anna J. Merritt)
5. COMMUNICATION AND INTERACTION IN GLOBAL POLITICS (edited by Claudio Cioffi-Revilla, Richard L. Merritt, and Dina A. Zinnes)

COMMUNICATION AND INTERACTION
IN GLOBAL POLITICS

edited by

Claudio Cioffi-Revilla
Richard L. Merritt
Dina A. Zinnes

Published in cooperation with the International Political Science
Association and as part of the Merriam Seminar Series on Research
Frontiers

SAGE PUBLICATIONS, INC.
Beverly Hills   London   New Delhi

For information address:

SAGE Publications, Inc.
2111 West Hillcrest Drive
Newbury Park, California 91320

SAGE Publications Inc.
275 South Beverly Drive
Beverly Hills
California 90212

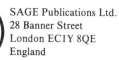

SAGE Publications Ltd.
28 Banner Street
London EC1Y 8QE
England

SAGE PUBLICATIONS India Pvt. Ltd.
M-32 Market
Greater Kailash I
New Delhi 110 048 India

Printed in the United States of America

Library of Congress Cataloging-in-Publication Data

Main entry under title:

Communication and interaction in global politics.

(Advances in political science; v. 5)
Includes index.
1. International relations—Research—Congresses.
2. Communication, International—Congresses.
I. Cioffi-Revilla, Claudio A., 1951– . II. Merritt,
Richard L. III. Zinnes, Dina A. IV. Series:
Advances in political science; 5.
JX1291.C54   1985   327′.072   85–14487
ISBN 0-8039-2532-8

FIRST PRINTING

CONTENTS

PART III: SOCIAL AND POLITICAL COMMUNICATION

FROM THE SERIES EDITOR

Advances in Political Science: An International Series reflects the aims and intellectual traditions of the International Political Science Association: the generation and dissemination of rigorous political inquiry free of any subdisciplinary or other orthodoxy. Along with its quarterly companion publication, the *International Political Science Review*, the series seeks to present the best work being done today (1) on the central and critical controversial themes of politics and/or (2) in new areas of inquiry where political scientists, alone or in conjunction with other scholars, are shaping innovative concepts and methodologies of political analysis.

Political science as an intellectual discipline has burgeoned in recent decades. With the enormous growth in the number of publications and papers and their increasing sophistication, however, has also come a tendency toward parochialism along national, subdisciplinary, and other lines. It was to counteract these tendencies that political scientists from a handful of countries created IPSA in 1949. Through roundtables organized by its research committees and study groups, at its triennial world congresses (the next of which takes place in August 1988 in Washington, DC), and through its organizational work, IPSA has sought to encourage the creation of both an international-minded science of politics and a body of scholars from many nations (now from more than 40 regional associations), who approach their research and interactions with other scholars from an international perspective.

Communication and Interaction in Global Politics, edited by Claudio Cioffi-Revilla, Richard L. Merritt, and Dina A. Zinnes, is the fifth volume in *Advances in Political Science: An International Series*. Like its predecessors, it comprises original papers which focus in an integrated manner on a single important topic — in this case, how quantitative approaches in international politics can help us understand aspects of communication and interaction among and within nation-states.

The papers in the volume were originally presented at a roundtable of the IPSA Research Committee on Global Communication, held in September 1983 at the Allerton Park conference center of the University of Illinois at Urbana-Champaign. Financial support for the conference came from the Merriam Laboratory for Analytic Political Research, the Office of International Programs and Studies, and the Department of Political Science, all at the University of Illinois, as well as the International Political Science Association. IPSA and the series editor are grateful to Robert B. Crawford, then director of the University's Office of International Programs and Studies, for encouragement and support; Judith Jones and Janie Carroll, who facilitated the Allerton Park roundtable; and Eileen Yoder, who produced the manuscript, and Geoffrey A. Merritt and Robert G. Muncaster, who carried out the art work.

—Richard L. Merritt

CHAPTER 1

COMMUNICATION AND INTERACTION IN GLOBAL POLITICS

CLAUDIO CIOFFI-REVILLA
RICHARD L. MERRITT
DINA A. ZINNES

Communication and interaction are at the core of global politics, in the complex world of today as inseparable as they are unavoidable. It is impossible to explain international political interaction without looking at the communication phenomena accompanying its many forms. Exploring international communication — the flow of messages and signals in a channel composed of senders, encoders, images, and other key components — also forces us to look at its underlying, dynamic interaction process. Communication gives meaning to interaction; interaction gives purpose to communication.

It is the contention of this volume that systematic analysis of communication and interaction will help us understand the complexities of global politics. The topics as such are not new. Political analysts since the time of Aristotle have with greater or lesser success inquired into their manifold dimensions. But certain aspects of modern social science offer new insights into the interplay of communication and interaction: the conceptual frameworks, models, and methodologies have the potential — in part fulfilled but in part still a challenge — to provide even greater understanding.

This volume explores some properties of communication and interaction in international political behavior. It presents an integrated set of papers that deal in varying ways with the central theme. This introductory chapter presents an overview of the half-score of papers — what they contribute to our main concern, how they fit into the general literature of the field, and how they fit together. The three parts of the chapter, which parallel the three parts of the volume, focus on increasingly specific aspects of the underlying theme, from the generic, more abstract, theoretical level to the more particular or specific dimensions of the nexus between international communication and interaction.

Global Interaction Dynamics

The first set of papers focuses on what we view as some of the broadest, generic, or contextual aspects of global politics: the enduring problem of developing international cooperation in an essentially "anarchic" political environment (Chapter 2); the pervasive probability of war in such an environment (Chapter 3); the important, sometimes determining, interphase between polity and economy in the global system (Chapter 4); and the notion of time within which all political phenomena in general, and interaction and communication in particular, are embedded (Chapter 5). These chapters touch on basic international political issues of cooperation and conflict, war and peace, riches and poverty, and time and space. Together with other such issues (freedom, security, spontaneity), they constitute the backdrop against which most global political dynamics take place. And they form the background for the more specific concerns addressed in subsequent sections of the volume.

The central problem for Dina A. Zinnes and Robert G. Muncaster in their "Transaction flows and integrative processes" is the development of cooperation among nations. Returning to the pioneering work of Karl Deutsch, they build a model of cooperation based on Deutsch's ideas about the relationship between interaction and the evolution of international political communities. Assumptions, extracted from propositions originally put forth by Deutsch, are stated in mathematical form. These assumptions suggest how interactions such as trade flows, mail flows, and tourist exchanges generate ties of friendship and even solidarity. The basic question for Zinnes and Muncaster is how and when these interactions produce sufficiently strong ties of cooperation to set the stage for an international community. Although the complexity of the model does not permit a complete answer to the question, the authors specify sets of conditions that produce integration and other sets that produce disintegration.

Claudio Cioffi-Revilla, analyzing "Crises, war, and security reliability," is similarly concerned with the interaction of nations. His study, however, is the flip side of the chapter by Zinnes and Muncaster. Where the latter seek to determine the relationship between positive forms of interaction and increasing ties of friendship and community,

Cioffi concentrates on the relationship between negative interactions (crises) and major forms of violence, including war. Using his theory of political reliability, Cioffi shows that a continuing sequence of crises, even if each individual crisis has a relatively low probability of resulting in war, can essentially "weaken" the system and eventually bring about war. Like Zinnes and Muncaster, Cioffi mathematically formulates the work of a major contributor to the study of international relations, Quincy Wright. But while Zinnes and Muncaster view cooperation and international community in the form of a deterministic model, Cioffi models crises and war totally within the framework of probability theory.

The models of both Cioffi and Zinnes–Muncaster either implicitly or explicitly make certain assumptions about how interaction proceeds and the relationship of that interaction to certain political outcomes, war or integration. In their chapter on "Modeling an international trade system," Brian M. Pollins and Grant Kirkpatrick present a broader, empirically based examination of the relationship between economic interactions and political interactions. Their long-range goal is to develop a computer simulation unit to incorporate into the broader GLOBUS computer simulation of the Science Center Berlin. Toward this end, they formulate an econometric model that links economic variables to political events. An extensive discussion of the problems and procedures inherent in estimating the model precedes the presentation of some preliminary results. While Cioffi's model is probabilistic and that of Zinnes and Muncaster deterministic, the model generated by Pollins and Kirkpatrick is more a blend of both probabilistic and deterministic assumptions.

The first three chapters of this section all develop models of interactions among nation-states. Each of these models is implicitly (as in Cioffi's study) or explicitly (as in the Zinnes–Muncaster or Pollins–Kirkpatrick chapters) a function of time. The processes being modeled take place through time. But what is time? Or, more correctly, what is the metric along which these interactions are being measured? This is the problem that Pierre Allan addresses in his chapter on "Social time." Social scientists in general, he argues, but more particularly those studying international phenomena, are too willing to accept the time scales developed in classical physics. Allan challenges the usefulness of this simple translation. He attempts to show that other time scales are more reasonable for the study of social phenomena, and that strict adherence to physical time can distort and obscure the kinds of social processes being modeled.

Information and Bargaining

Bargaining behavior is ubiquitous to international politics, even in war. The central theme of the second part of the volume is the interplay of information and bargaining. The linkage between them is a more specific aspect of the interplay between communication and inter-action. The three chapters in this section focus primarily on conflict. All three model inter-state politics as an interactive (bargaining) system in which the flow of information plays a vital role. Formally, all three models are cast in the mathematical language of games. This is natural. The mathematical language of game theory was invented precisely for analyzing, rigorously and with as little ambiguity as possible, those empirical social phenomena where choice, perceptions, estimates, outcomes, and chance interact in a system of actors.

Game-theoretic analyses have contributed substantially to our theoretic and practical knowledge of information processes in bargaining. An initial landmark study was Schelling's (1960) classic *Strategy of Conflict*, followed soon after by Iklé and Leites's (1962) formal model of the international bargaining process. Even in these early studies there was an explicit attempt to relate information and bargaining within a single framework. They saw the international bargaining process as an interplay of perceived policy *alternatives*, expected *outcomes*, *likelihoods*, and estimated *pay-offs*. Other seminal studies in this tradition include Singer's (1963) decision model of the *influence process* that is inherent in bargaining; Boulding's (1962) contribution to the theory of *threats*; Pruitt's (1969, 1981) innovative analysis of bargaining *reactivity*; Axelrod's (1967, 1970) conceptuali-zation and rigorous definition of *conflict of interest* in bargaining; and Rapoport's experimental work on games.

Just as information and bargaining have been central to past theoretic work in this area, the three chapters in this section demonstrate that these elements continue to remain paramount. The studies illustrate a principal focus of contemporary bargaining theory: the relationship between information and outcomes. Written by leading scientists in this area, the chapters are thus a sample of the current state of the art in the use of game models for the scientific understanding of decision making, negotiation, and bargaining, and the role that information plays in such dimensions of global politics. The studies are not, however, purely formal, abstract, or "content-free." They focus on important international problems, including deterrence, the arms race, and such regional conflicts as the Malvinas/Falklands war of 1982. Using the rigorous mathematical structure of games, the chapters illustrate how specific and politically relevant problems of contemporary international relations can benefit from formal treatment.

In his discussion of "Misperception and satisficing in international conflict," Michael Nicholson explores the specific case of the recent Malvinas/Falklands war between Argentina and Britain. It draws broad theoretical inferences about the crucial role that information plays in determining behavior. The study examines the impact of information about pay-offs, probabilities, alternatives, and expectations of outcomes.

Steven J. Brams and Morton D. Davis address the intricate problem of "The verification problem in arms control." This problem is notorious for the complications arising from the interaction of expectations, deception, and cheating. Simpler game-theoretic analyses of arms control issues rarely consider these factors. Yet these issues are crucial for a complete understanding of the difficulties inherent in verification. The analysis by Brams and Davis shows that the verification problem is not simply a technical one, as is so often assumed in the literature on national security. This chapter, like the other two in this section, demonstrates that bargaining behavior cannot be understood without considering the interplay of communication and interaction.

Using a remarkably simple set of mathematical tools (essentially only geometry and the algebra of inequalities!), Raymond Dacey explores the difficult problem of assessing "Ambiguous information and the arms race and mutual deterrence games." (That part of the study innovatively applying Jeffrey's probability kinematics to problems of arms racing and deterrence, however, cannot be grasped without more than just rudiments of probability theory.) From a purely methodological perspective, this study provides considerable theoretic insights using relatively simple mathematical ideas. From a substantive perspective, Dacey's analysis marks a noticeable advance in our current understanding of the effects of bribes and threats. It shows that bribes, threats, and "tit-for-tat" strategies are "risk-free" to the user when used probabilistically. Though treated in very formal terms, there is a significant amount of realism in the chapter that should not be overlooked. The probabilistic nature of bribes, threats, and most strategies in the real world makes Dacey's formulation and analyses of particular value for understanding international political processes.

The three chapters in Part II therefore differ in degree of generality as well as in level of mathematical sophistication. In all three the interplay of communication and interaction nevertheless plays a central role in explaining bargaining behavior.

Social and Political Communication

The third part of the volume focuses attention on international integration within the nexus of communication and interaction. Its three chapters also share the characteristic of being more empirically oriented than the previous ones.

An important thrust in the scientific study of international politics has been the search for international patterns based not on speculation, intuition, or anecdotal evidence, but on systematic theory grounded in data from the real world. This interest grew from frustration with the plethora of alternative and frequently contradictory hypotheses abundant in the literature on war, diplomatic behavior, communication, and other aspects of international life. Folk sayings and glittering generalities all too often passed for "inexorable laws." Concepts such as power and conflict were on many tongues but often meant something different to each one. It was in this setting that Pitirim Sorokin, Quincy Wright, Lewis Fry Richardson, and a handful of others began to look systematically and empirically at international phenomena. They thereby broke the path for still more detailed and sophisticated analyses based on data.

The 1960s saw a flowering of programs aimed at developing data for international (and comparative) research. The idea was to collect and make available in a standardized format data about the attributes and behavior of nation-states: data that were *reliable* in the sense of being replicable by researchers using the original analyst's definitions, sources, and methods; *valid* in the sense of being linked intimately and explicitly to the concept being "measured"; *functionally equivalent* across countries and time periods; and, where possible, *quantitative*. Among the early projects were the Yale Political Data Program under the direction of Bruce M. Russett, Rudolph J. Rummel's Dimensionality of Nations, and the Cross-Polity Survey of Arthur S. Banks and Robert B. Textor. Another important project, developed by J. David Singer and Melvin Small, focused on the Correlates of War for the century-and-a-half between 1815 and 1965.

Such projects had a manifold effect. For one thing, they facilitated at least preliminary studies that could subject old and new hypotheses to the test of quantitative data from the real world. Such studies in turn forced scholars to reconceptualize such general notions as power, interests, and capabilities. For another thing, these data programs and the projects they spawned emboldened still other researchers to generate new kinds of data, especially data that are hard to get at. And, of course, the availability of such data in the field of international relations and elsewhere led to increasing methodological sophistication on the part of analysts and the development of new methodological procedures to enhance the power of explanatory models.

An area of international political behavior that has benefited especially from such systematic approaches deals with aspects of integration and large-scale political community formation. As indicated earlier in this chapter, Karl Deutsch's work broke a number of conceptual logjams. His research on nationalism and social communication (Deutsch, 1953) and on political community at the international level (Deutsch, 1954), more specifically in the North Atlantic area (Deutsch et al., 1957), also pioneered new procedures for analyzing such processes. Others followed in his footsteps to refine the concepts, develop specific measures of integrative behavior, and lay the groundwork for further data-based research.

The three chapters in this section represent various data-based approaches to the study of international integration. Jean Laponce, in his "Language and communication: The rise of the monolingual state," examines an area in which data resources are underdeveloped. Language is a key element in both the integration of communities and the ability of people to express their separate identity. Some writers and thinkers have argued that enhancing the global population's ability to communicate in a common tongue will improve understanding and the prospects for peace. From this perspective the assimilation of minority language communities reduces uncertainty and potential conflict. From another perspective, however, it makes the world poorer by removing from it an element of diversity, languages in which people have traditionally expressed themselves in unique and often creative ways.

The remarkable thing is that social scientists have not developed adequate means for ascertaining whether we are moving toward or away from linguistic diversification. Moreover, while they have indicated some of the factors that seem to encourage or discourage such trends, there has been little effort to specify them in ways that enable us to assess their relative importance in various circumstances. Laponce makes a first step in this direction.

Cal Clark and Richard L. Merritt, in "European community and intra-European communications," examine developing communication patterns among the countries that later formed the European

Community. We would normally expect that, before some group of states takes formal steps toward economic or, eventually, political union, strong communication networks would characterize their interaction patterns. If so, then the worldwide flow of mail, as an indicator of global communications structure, should have revealed an incipient subnetwork among the Europe of the Six well before they signed the Treaty of Rome in 1957. To test this hypothesis, Clark and Merritt analyze data on international mail flows from 1890 to 1961 by means of a statistical model of transaction flows that indicates varying intensities of interaction between pairs of countries. Their data indicate that an emergent pattern did indeed exist, but also suggest that the concrete integrative measures enhanced the density of the intra-European communications network.

Alex Mintz and Philip A. Schrodt take a somewhat different approach to international patterns in their analysis of "Distributional patterns of regional interactions." Much of the literature in international relations posits relatively enduring patterns characterizing the interaction of nation-states. This should be particularly the case, according to the "common enemy" hypothesis in the field of international integration, among states allied in some common effort — such as members of the North Atlantic Treaty Organization, aimed at deterring possible Soviet aggression, or Arab states in the Middle East, united at least in their hostility toward Israel. Mintz and Schrodt find no such patterning. The interactions of these two sets of states, as seen in data on international events (1948–78) drawn from the Edward Azar's Conflict and Peace Data Bank (COPDAB), obey rather the Poisson law, a form of random distribution. This finding raises several interesting questions. It is possible, Mintz and Schrodt suggest, that different modes of temporal or event-typical aggregation might tease out some pattern; but we might also argue that scholars must pay more attention to their assumptions about patterned interaction.

Communication and Interaction in Global Politics

The chapters in this volume share three aspects worth highlighting. First of all, they make individual contributions to existing literatures. The study by Zinnes and Muncaster, for instance, further develops Deutsch's work by building a mathematical model capable of yielding deductions that were not apparent in Deutsch's original conception of integration. Similarly, Cioffi uses Wright's ideas about the relationship between crises and war to develop a model yielding conclusions not anticipated by Wright. Pollins and Kirkpatrick, by making explicit and rigorous the typically vaguely stated connections between polity and economy, show how it is possible to see more exactly how economic transactions "influence international political interactions." Allan's suggestion that the traditional concept of time must be revised holds great promise for advancing our understanding of laws of communication and interaction.

The three chapters of Part II develop further the current knowledge of bargaining. Thus, Nicholson looks at the consequences of information and misperception between a pair of countries in the contexts of optimizing vs. satisficing strategies; Brams and Davis discuss cheating and deliberate misinformation in negotiations on arms control; Dacey demonstrates the existence of a nontrivial set of previously unknown properties of bribes and threats common in the phenomena of arms races and arms control.

Finally, the three chapters of Part III provide gains for our empirical understanding of political phenomena. Laponce, in raising some concrete questions about global language trends that will have an impact on our daily lives, points to the need for a systematic collection and analysis of data that may be difficult to generate. Clark and Merritt apply transaction-flow analysis to interaction and communication patterns in the European Community system. (Perhaps Europeanists should examine studies such as these at least as often as they appear willing to read the EEC Commission's annual report on integration!) Mintz and Schrodt build on decades of data-gathering labor, applying previously developed techniques to tell us something new, at once surprising and problematic, about regional patterns of interaction. They show that in many instances the interactions of countries obey a Poisson law, a result also found concerning the incidence of war. Not all readers will be equally interested in the degree of cumulation achieved by these studies, but each chapter provides new insights that augment our previous knowledge.

Second, although the emphasis of every science is on general principles, most chapters in this volume make reference to, or are written within the context of, empirical, real (sometimes contemporary!) world problems. In the early years, when mathematical and quantitative approaches were first applied to the study of international relations, the relationship of these more formal approaches to real-world "substantive" issues was not always clear. In these earlier studies systems remained abstract, interaction processes were almost totally generic entities, and "games" were not usually played in "politically interesting ways." The chapters of this volume testify to the increasing concreteness and real-world "relevance" of scientific analyses of international politics. Many chapters (notably 4, 6, 10, and 11) concern very real actors in the global system. Their names are Egypt, France, Argentina, etc., and not just "the nth actor in the system."

Finally, it is interesting to note that the scientific study of international politics has gained the attention of scientists working outside the field of politics. This is particularly true of applied mathematicians, as witnessed by the participation in this volume of Muncaster, Davis, and Dacey. The fact that applied mathematicians recognize legitimate scientific questions in this area speaks well for the overall intellectual health of the discipline. Additionally, we may hope that certain properties of international politics will inspire mathematicians to develop new languages for stating political theories in more appropriate and satisfactory ways. This important interplay between abstract mathematical languages and the applications of these formal languages to real-world phenomena benefits both fields, as the development of probability theory and game theory amply demonstrates.

The scientific study of international relations is a young science. In recent decades we have achieved an increasing systematic understanding — the type of understanding science calls "nomological," or hypothetico-deductive — which permits an initial explanation of some forms of international behavior. International cooperation, communication, wars, and negotiation are far better understood today than was true even a decade ago. Science, however, is a never-ending and intricate game, in which careful and systematic measurement, creative theorizing, and disciplined willingness are needed to pursue questions of "how" (description) and "why" (explanation). We hope the studies collected here will challenge other scientists to continue where the present ones left off.

REFERENCES

AXELROD, R. (1967) "Conflict of interest: an axiomatic approach." Journal of Conflict Resolution 11 (March): 87–99.

——— (1970) Conflict of Interest: A Theory of Divergent Goals with Applications to Politics. Chicago, Ill.: Markham.

BOULDING, K. E. (1962) Conflict and Defense: A General Theory. New York: Harper & Brothers.

DEUTSCH, K. W. (1953) Nationalism and Social Communication: An Inquiry into the Foundations of Nationality. Cambridge, Mass.: MIT Press; and New York: John Wiley.

——— (1954) Political Community at the International Level: Problems of Definition and Measurement. Garden City, NY: Doubleday.

————, S. A. BURRELL, R. A. KANN, M. LEE Jr, M. LICHTERMAN, R. E. LINDGREN, F.L.LOEWENHEIM, and R. W. VAN WAGENEN (1957) Political Community and the North Atlantic Area: International Organization in the Light of Historical Experience. Princeton, NJ: Princeton University Press.

IKLÉ, F. C., and N. LEITES (1962) "Political negotiation as a process of modifying utilities." Journal of Conflict Resolution 6 (March): 19–28.

PRUITT, D. G. (1969) "Stability and sudden change in interpersonal and international affairs." Journal of Conflict Resolution 13 (March): 18–38.

———— (1981) Negotiation Behavior. New York: Academic Press.

SCHELLING, T. C. (1960) The Strategy of Conflict. Cambridge, Mass.: Harvard University Press.

SINGER, J. D. (1963) "Inter-nation influence: a formal model." American Political Science Review 57 (June): 420–430.

PART I

Global Interaction Dynamics

CHAPTER 2

TRANSACTION FLOWS AND INTEGRATIVE PROCESSES

DINA A. ZINNES
ROBERT G. MUNCASTER

In two recent papers (Muncaster and Zinnes, 1982–83, Zinnes and Muncaster, 1984) we have developed models of the dynamics of internation hostility that allowed us to understand and predict the occurrence of war. Those models focused on conditions that lead to war. In the present paper the focus is still war, or violent internation conflict, but we approach the problem from a very different perspective.

Our concern here is with Karl Deutsch's concept of a "security community," a community of nations among which there are "stable expectations of peace among the participating units" (Deutsch, 1954: 33). The focus of our current efforts is on those conditions that decrease the probability of war. We propose a model, based in large part on Deutsch's analysis of the evolution of security communities, that will allow us to assess the conditions under which security communities will or will not emerge.[1]

Deutsch's Analysis

Deutsch's arguments concerning "security communities" can be found implicitly and explicitly in a number of his works. However, the two volumes which appear to provide the most explicit treatment of this argument are *Political Community at the International Level* (Deutsch, 1954) and *Political Community and the North Atlantic Area* (Deutsch et al., 1957).[2] The first lays out most of the conceptual and theoretical bases for his argument; it is therefore, for our purposes, the more

AUTHORS' NOTE: This research was supported by a grant from the National Science Foundation (SES-80-24547 and SES-84-00877).

useful of the two. In the second volume, Deutsch and his collaborators analyze in summary form a series of historical cases that attempt to assess some of the ideas presented in the first volume; it is therefore useful as further documentation and an elaboration of points made in the first.

In his first volume, Deutsch approaches the concept of "security community" as a subset of a subset of another concept. A "security community" is a type of "political community" which in turn is one form of a "community." This can be seen through the following sequence of definitions. "All *communities* among people are characterized by the existence of a significant amount of transactions among them. Countries so isolated from one another as to have no significant dealings among their populations would not be members of one community" (Deutsch, 1954: 33). Thus, for any set of nations to be considered a *community*, there must be some minimal or threshold level of interaction or transaction among all possible pairs of nations. "A *political community* may be defined as a community of social transaction supplemented by both enforcement and compliance" (p. 40). A *political community*, then, is a community with three added requirements: (1) a set of decision rules or procedures, (2) an enforcement mechanism for marginal recalcitrants, and (3) predictable "habits of compliance sufficiently widespread." Finally, a *security community* is "more specialized than . . . [a] 'political community.'" It implies "stable expectations of peace among the participating units . . . " (p. 33). So a *security community* is a political community with the additional requirement that there be at least an expectation among the members that conflicts will be settled peacefully.

Deutsch proposes a set of factors and processes that attempt to explain the transitions between what might be called levels of "community-ness." Movement upward on the scale of "community-ness" is called *integration*: "The processes that create such unifying habits and institutions will henceforth be called *integration*, and the territories and populations among which such integration has taken place will be called a *security community*" (p. 33). But the concern is not only with upward movement on the "community-ness" scale. Deutsch is also interested in what takes the set of nations back down the scale. He notes that "a security community . . . may not prove stable" (p. 40), that is, may not endure, and he suggests some conditions necessary for stability and presents historical examples to exemplify how disintegration occurs when those conditions are not met. Thus the argument centers on two key issues: (1) What is the process that accounts for changing levels of "community-ness"? and (2) Under what conditions is that process stable; that is, under what conditions will the security community endure? These are the two questions that will be central to our analysis.

The definition of the security community concept (Deutsch's Chapter 2), together with a delineation of different types of security communities and the processes that lead to each, is followed in his Chapters 3 and 4 by a discussion of the factors that account for the integration process. One of the critical variables noted is the level of transactions or interaction among nations. A key attribute of such transactions is the total volume of activity. The definition of a "community" requires transaction volume to pass a threshold level before a set of states can be considered a community. In his Chapter 3 the importance of transaction volume is emphasized: "A primary focus of our study is the ways in which the institutions, processes, and habits of peaceful change and adjustment are developed in such a manner as to keep pace with the increasing volume of transaction" (p. 39). And in Chapter 4 the importance of transaction volume is further highlighted by the fact that integration is measured by determining whether or not the volume of transaction is significant, that is, whether it is greater than might be expected by chance.

Thus the volume of transactions among nations provides a basis for the development of a sense of community-ness. Deutsch explains that this is not only because nations are in contact with one another, but also because increasing volume enhances the need for decision rules to monitor and coordinate the flows. Agreement must be reached on these rules and their enforcement. The development of such agreement is the basis for the further development of community-ness. Transaction volume can, of course, be a two-edged sword, and Deutsch notes that: ". . . the volume of transactions . . . throws a burden upon the institutions . . . . What is of concern . . . is the race between the growing rate of transaction . . . and the growth of integrative institutions . . . . To be stable, . . . expectations must be geared not only to the current load of mutual transaction and potential conflicts . . . but . . . also . . . to any increase in the volume of such transactions and such possible friction among them" (pp. 39–40). Thus, transaction volume will be a positive factor for integration only to the extent to which it is accompanied by the development of appropriate institutional arrangements.

Clearly, however, transaction volume is not the only important variable in the integration process that produces a security community. In his Chapter 4 Deutsch notes that "political integration is a multidimensional process. No single measurement . . . can be expected to describe it completely" (p. 51). He then discusses 13 additional measures ("tests of integration") that might be used to "sense" the stages of the integration process. One of these "tests," which is directly related to volume, is the "balance of transaction flows." Deutsch argues that "a large and continued net one-way flow of valued assets . . . would tend to make . . . integration more difficult. On the contrary, a large area could be considered the more thoroughly integrated . . . the more nearly the different ranges of transaction tended to produce at least a rough balance" (p. 57). Thus the sense of community-ness will increase with volume provided (1) the trans-actions between nations are balanced and (2) the transactions are valued by both nations.

In *Political Community and the North Atlantic Area* these ideas are developed further. The examination of historical cases provides the evidence necessary for Deutsch to rank the factors along a scale of relative importance. "Values and expectations" (that is, "compatibility of the main values held by the politically relevant strata") are given top priority. However, transaction volume, or the amount of interaction between nations, is found in second and third place: "Another essential requirement for successful amalgamation was the presence of unbroken links of social communication . . . links . . . which provide effective channels of communication, both horizontally among the main units of the amalgamated security-community and vertically among the politically relevant strata . . . . Another condition . . . was the mobility of persons among the main units . . . . Full-scale mobility of persons has followed every successful amalgamated security-community in modern times" (Deutsch et al., 1957: 51, 53). Thus the volume of transactions or the amount of interaction between nations can be shown historically to have been critical in the evolution of security communities.

The second variable, balance in transactions, is in fourth place in this historical analysis, appearing in conjunction with the "multiplicity of transactions" ("successfully amalgamated security-communities require . . . a multiplicity of ranges of common communications and transactions" — p. 54). The authors note that among other conditions that "may well turn out to be essential for the success of amalgamation . . . the first . . . is . . . the balance in the flow of communications and transactions between the political units." It is, however, noted that it is "not essential that the flow . . . balance at any one moment . . . but the transactions should balance over some period of time" (pp. 55–6).

These two volumes, then, provide us with a basis for constructing a preliminary answer to Deutsch's first question: What is the process that accounts for changing levels of community-ness? Although Deutsch proposes a variety of factors for consideration, two that are of considerable importance are (1) the volume of valued transactions and (2) the balance in the exchange of those transactions. While we do not argue that these are the only two variables worth considering, we do feel that the arguments presented in the two volumes suggest that they are of sufficient importance to be worthy of initial consideration. Our philosophy is to begin with limited numbers of variables, describe their interrelationships, and then study the implications of those relationships. Having obtained a complete understanding of the simpler model, we can then move to more complex multiple-variable models. Our focus on these two variables, however, requires two key assumptions, if we are to be true to Deutsch's argument. First, we must assume that the transactions being considered are those valued by both parties. Second, we assume that increases in transaction volume are accompanied by the requisite development of institutions.

In the pages that follow we provide an initial, partial answer to Deutsch's first question by developing a formal model based on the key variables of sense of community-ness, transaction volume, and balance in transactions. The construction of the model, that is, the relationships between the variables, will be based to a large extent on the ideas presented above. Having developed the model, we then address Deutsch's second question: What are the conditions for a stable security community? As will become evident, however, even with only three variables the model will be sufficiently complex that we will only be able to provide partial answers to this question.

Translating the Security Community Argument

We simplify our analysis by focusing on only two nations. There is nothing inherent in the model to prevent its extension to a greater number, but the arguments will be clearer when phrased in terms of two nations. We are interested in the level or intensity of *good will* or the *sense of community* shared by these two nations toward one another. Although this sense of community can be considered a directional variable, that is, the amount of good will that A feels towards B, or vice-versa, the concern here is with the total shared sense of community on the part of all parties. We therefore define:

$C(t)$ = the intensity of feeling of community in a given set of nations at time t.

We assume that $C(t)$ is either equal to or greater than zero, that is, that the sense of community can never be negative. Some might argue that a negative $C(t)$ is meaningful, indicating hostility between the nations. In contrast, we believe that, while the concept of good will, friendship, or sense of community is certainly related to hostility, it is not reasonable to assume that one process is the inverse or negative of the other. While hostility and sense of community are indeed related, the processes that govern each can be quite different and the process that links the two complex. We prefer, therefore, to model the two processes independently of one another initially, and leave to later studies the investigation of possible ways in which the two might be combined.

The argument sketched above suggests that $C(t)$ is a function of the transactions or interactions between the two nations. We therefore define the *volume of transactions* between nations:

$V(t)$ = the total volume of valued transactions between the two nations.

The variable $V(t)$ can be interpreted as covering all forms of interactions between the two nations (e.g., social communication, mobility of persons, etc.), that both nations find valuable. Unlike the variable $C(t)$, however, it will be important to consider $V(t)$ from a directional perspective. It is thus necessary to define:

$V_A(t)$ = the transactions from nation A to nation B at time t.
$V_B(t)$ = the transactions from nation B to nation A at time t.

We are interested here only in the transactions that take place between the two nations under examination. But while attention is on the transactions exchanged between only these two nations, there is nothing in the definition that specifies how these transactions must be measured. The transaction literature suggests that the absolute amounts of interaction are of less interest than the "relative" scores, that is, that the transactions between nations A and B must be measured against the transactions that these two nations have with the rest of the world. There is nothing in the model that forbids this type of measurement.[3] In short, the model to be presented is independent of the way in which V is measured.

From the above it is clear that:

$$V(t) = V_A(t) + V_B(t).$$

Furthermore, we assume

$$V_A(t) \geq 0 \text{ and } V_B(t) \geq 0$$

for all t, that is, that transactions by definition can never be negative.

Consequently,

$$V(t) \geq 0.$$

The third critical variable in the argument is the *balance in transactions* between the two nations:

$$E(t) = V_A(t) - V_B(t).$$

If $E(t) = 0$, then there is complete balance between the transactions of the two nations. We assume in this construction that one nation's level of transactions will always be equal to or greater than that of the other. Since our model is applicable only over that period of time during which the volume of transactions of one of the nations exceeds that of the other, we adopt the convention that

$$V_A(t) \geq V_B(t).$$

Consequently,

$$E(t) \geq 0.$$

It is also important to note that

$$V(t) \geq E(t).$$

As $E(t)$ increases, the imbalance in the transactions between the two nations increases: the larger $E(t)$, the greater the *imbalance*. The limit of this imbalance is $V(t)$. When $E(t) = V(t)$, the transactions are in a state of complete imbalance. In this event one nation is sending all the transactions to the other. This can easily be seen by noting that, if $E(t) = V(t)$, then

$$V_A(t) - V_B(t) = V_A(t) + V_B(t),$$

and so

$$V_B(t) = 0.$$

In effect, then, there is one completely dominant nation. It is an interesting question as to which of the two nations should be considered dominant, the sending or the receiving nation. According to Deutsch's argument, the dominant nation is the recipient nation, that is, nation B in terms of the preceding definitions. This interpretation is consistent with much of the dependency literature. However, it should be pointed out that this labeling contains some latent problems or assumptions. Nation B is dominant if we assume that A's value for sending its transactions to B is considerably greater than B's value for receiving those transactions. This raises the question of what is meant by "valued transactions" and points to a difficulty in Deutsch's argument. The problem is that there are four, not two, "values" for the transactions that take place between two nations: A's value for being able to interact with B, B's value for receiving those transactions, B's value for its directed activities toward A, and A's value for receiving B's interactions. It is the total relationship between these values that is ultimately behind the labeling of a given nation as "dominant." For the purpose of our analyses, we adopt the standard assumption that nation B, as the recipient, is the dominant nation.

We are primarily interested in understanding how the variables C, V, and E affect changes in the variable C. That is, we wish to examine how the sense of community rises and falls as a function of the total volume of transactions, the balance between transactions, and previous levels of community feeling. But since transaction flows are anything but constant through time, it is also necessary simultaneously to consider how the total volume of transactions and the balance in transaction flow change through time. It is undoubtedly the case that the changes in the variables V and E may also be considered functions of the three variables C, V, and E. In short, then, we are looking for three functions of the variables C, V, and E which govern the changes in these variables over time:

$$
\begin{aligned}
\dot{V} &= F_1(E,V,C), \\
\dot{E} &= F_2(E,V,C), \\
\dot{C} &= F_3(E,V,C).
\end{aligned}
\tag{S}
$$

(Here and henceforth equations are denoted by suggestive symbols — (S) for system; (AS) for analytical system; (F1.1) for assumption 1 about force F_1; etc.)

The functions $F_1(E,V,C)$, $F_2(E,V,C)$, and $F_3(E,V,C)$, form the heart of our model. We develop explicit forms for them below by listing a set of assumptions, based largely on Deutsch's arguments, which should be met. While each assumption, taken by itself, is not complicated, collectively the assumptions, interrelating the behaviors of the three variables, are necessarily interlocked. Thus it is neither an obvious nor a simple process to find three functions which simultaneously and consistently satisfy them all. We shall not provide a detailed analysis for the specific functions we have found, though Appendix I contains an outline of some of the steps that are involved. Instead, following the list of assumptions, we simply specify the mathematical model and then proceed to demonstrate that the equations do in fact meet all the requirements proposed. Needless to say, the model is not unique.

Other sets of equations could be designed to meet our assumptions. Our specific model, however, is one of the simplest.

Basic Assumptions on the Total Volume, V
There appear to be five basic behaviors that must be captured by $F_1(E,V,C)$.

(1) The total amount of transactions between two nations must have a ceiling. This ceiling level may be very high, but for any pair of nations there must be a limit to the total amount of transaction that can take place between the two. Resources are limited. This means that, as V becomes increasingly large, that is, approaches ∞, the function $F_1(E,V,C)$ must decrease, that is, approach $-\infty$. To simplify the mathematical structure we assume that the decrease in $F_1(E,V,C)$ is uniform in E and C (that is, is similar for all levels of E and C). This first assumption can be stated as:

$$F_1(E,V,C) \rightarrow -\infty \text{ as } V \rightarrow +\infty \text{ uniformly in } E \text{ and } C. \quad \text{(F1.1)}$$

(2) Our second assumption concerns the impact that the balance in transactions will have on the volume of transactions: the more balanced the transactions, the faster the rate at which total volume will increase. When two nations exchange approximately the same amount of transaction, each, according to Deutsch's argument, is obtaining a comparable amount of value from the interaction. A basis is thus established for increasing the transactions between the two nations, which can be stated as:

$$\frac{dF_1}{dV}(E, V, C) \text{ increases as } E \rightarrow 0. \quad \text{(F1.2)}$$

(3) The third assumption proposes that, if there are (a) transactions between two nations, (b) some inequality in the balance of those transactions but not complete dominance by one of the nations, and (c) no sense of community, that is, no feeling of good will between those nations, then volume will decrease. In short, to conduct transactions two nations must have some feeling of community. This assumption can be stated as:

$$F_1(E,V,0) < 0 \text{ if } V \neq 0, E \neq 0, \text{ and } V \neq E. \quad \text{(F1.3)}$$

(4) Consistent with assumption (3), we postulate further that in the presence of feelings of good will the volume should increase. More specifically, the rate at which volume increases should be greater for increasing values of C and smaller for decreasing values of C. Thus, the volume of transaction will increase faster for ever higher values of C.

This can be stated as:

$$\frac{dF_1}{dC}(E, V, C) > 0. \tag{F1.4}$$

(5) Finally, if there is no interaction, so that $V = 0$ (note that $V = 0 \Rightarrow E = 0$), and no sense of community, so that $C = 0$, then nothing should happen; that is, transactions should remain fixed. We state this as:

$$F_1(0,0,0) = 0. \tag{F1.5}$$

Basic Assumptions on the Balance of Transactions, E

There are three important assumptions governing $F_2(E,V,C)$, the function that describes changes in transaction balance.

(1) If there are (a) transactions between two nations, (b) some feeling of good will, and (c) a complete balance in those transactions, then the equality in the balance of the transactions should not change. If both sides are equally receiving valued exchanges and there is already some sense of community, then the balance in the transactions should be preserved. This is stated as:

$$F_2(0,V,C) = 0. \tag{F2.1}$$

(2) Consistent with (F2.1), we argue that, when $E > 0$ but close to zero, if there are transactions and a feeling of good will, then the imbalance in transactions will decrease. Thus, when imbalances are slight, the sense of community helps to decrease the imbalance and make the exchanges more equal. This is stated as:

$$F_2(E,V,C) < 0 \text{ for } E \approx 0. \tag{F2.2}$$

(3) We consider next the rate at which imbalances in transactions change. Assumptions (F2.1) and (F2.2) indicate that when there is almost no imbalance in the transactions, that is, near $E = 0$, the rate of change dF_2/dE is negative. Thus $-dF_2/dE$ is a measure of the speed with which the system approaches complete balance. It is assumed that this rate of approach will be faster the higher the volume of transaction. When the volume of transactions is high, the system will move considerably faster toward a balance in those transactions, and when there are few transactions between the two nations, the transaction flows will move only slowly toward balance. When the volume of transactions reaches zero, this rate also goes to zero. Since increasing values of E reflect increasing levels of imbalance and an increase in $F_2(E,V,C)$ indicates a rise in imbalance, we state this assumption as follows:

$$\frac{dF_2}{dE}(E, V, C) \text{ decreases as } V \text{ increases;}$$

$$\frac{dF_2}{dE}(0, 0, C) = 0. \tag{F2.3}$$

Basic Assumptions Concerning Dependency
Recall that:

$$V(t) - E(t) = 0$$

is a situation in which one nation is sending all the transactions. In this sense, $V(t) - E(t)$ can be considered a measure of domination, or the extent to which one nation dominates the other. Since the transaction literature, as discussed earlier, suggests that it is the sender nation that is dominated, $V(t) - E(t)$ is a measure of *dependency*, or the extent to which the sender nation is dependent on the recipient nation. Two assumptions are made about the nature of this dominance. Since changes in dominance can be written as:

$$(V - E)^{\cdot} = F_1(E, V, C) - F_2(E, V, C),$$

the assumptions needed concern the relationship between $F_2(E, V, C)$ and $F_1(E, V, C)$.

(1) First, we assume that when there is total dominance, with one nation sending all the transactions, none of the variables in the model has the power to change this situation. This is not to say that total dominance cannot be changed. Rather, within the context of the present model such changes are not possible. Since total dominance occurs when $V = E$, this assumption can be written as:

$$F_1(V, V, C) - F_2(V, V, C) = 0. \tag{F3.1}$$

(2) Consistent with the first assumption, the second assumption proposes that when the system is near total dominance, that is, when $V - E$ is close to 0, the system tends to greater dominance. If one nation is highly dependent on the second, there is a tendency for that dependency to increase. Since total dependency is characterized by $V - E = 0$, for changes in dependency to move toward 0 this assumption must be stated by:

$$F_1(E, V, C) - F_2(E, V, C) < 0 \text{ for } V - E \approx 0. \tag{F3.2}$$

Basic Assumptions Concerning the Sense of Community, C
We come finally to the last set of assumptions, those that govern changes $F_3(E, V, C)$ in the sense of community or the feeling of good

will. We propose five assumptions that this function must meet in order to model adequately how the sense of community rises or falls in terms of our three basic variables.

(1) Deutsch's analysis provides the first clear assumption. If two nations have a significant amount of interaction, and there is complete balance in those valued transactions, then the sense of community should increase. Furthermore, when transactions are in balance, an increasing volume of transactions increases the rate at which the sense of community grows. That is, if two nations have balanced trans- actions, then their sense of community will rise faster the higher the total volume of interaction. These two assumptions can be stated as:

$$F_3(0, V, C) > 0 \text{ if } V \neq 0,$$

$$\frac{dF_3}{dV}(0, V, C) > 0.$$

(F4.1)

(2) Consistent with the first assumption, the second proposes that, when two nations are interacting and there is a balance in the trans- action flows, any sense of community already existing between those nations will not only increase, as suggested by (F4.1), but will also increase faster for higher levels of good will. When there is a balance in transactions the existing feelings of good will provide a basis for more good will and friendship. We state this as:

$$\frac{dF_3}{dC}(0, V, C) > 0 \text{ when } V \neq 0 \text{ and } C \neq 0.$$

(F4.2)

(3) Assumptions (1) and (2) require that some transactions exist between the two nations. Deutsch argues that there can be no sense of community in the absence of transactions. We know that $V = 0 \Rightarrow E = 0$, but Deutsch's argument further suggests that $V = 0 \Rightarrow C = 0$. We therefore postulate that, if $V = 0$ and $C = 0$, there will be no change in C; that is, a sense of community cannot develop. This is stated as:

$$F_3(0,0,0) = 0.$$

(F4.3)

(4) Our final two assumptions concern the impact of dependency $V - E$ on the feeling of community. First, we assume that a sense of community requires not only the existence of transactions but also the absence of total domination. Some might question this assumption. Deutsch (1954: 34, 38), however, suggests that, while a security community can be "created by subjecting . . . previously sovereign states . . . to a common government having its own superior armed forces . . ., thus far no record of any large-scale security community

established by means of this . . . approach alone has been uncovered. If one should become established it could hardly be expected to endure." While dependency and domination in our model are not completely similar to the type of domination referred to by Deutsch, there is nevertheless a sufficient parallel to provide a basis for our present assumption: the sense of community begins to develop when one nation is not totally dominant. Stated more formally, we have:

$$F_3(E,V,0) > 0 \text{ when } V \neq E. \tag{F4.4}$$

(5) As a corollary to the preceding assumption we assume that, when one nation is totally dependent on another (i.e. when $V = E$), then any feeling of community existing between those nations will decrease. Suppose, for example, that two nations had been interacting for some period of time and that, while the transactions were not completely balanced, one nation was not totally dominant. According to assumption (F4.4), a sense of community would begin to develop. Now suppose, however, that conditions change dramatically: One nation begins to send ever greater transactions to the other and these transactions are not balanced by a reciprocal flow in the other direction. Eventually one nation becomes totally dependent on the other. When this happens the sense of community will decline:

$$F_3(V,V,C) < 0 \text{ for } V \neq 0 \text{ and } C \neq 0. \tag{F4.5}$$

Specification of the Model

Our goal has been to put forth a set of assumptions that must be met by the changes in transaction volume, balance in the flow of transactions, and sense of community. The ultimate purpose is to develop a model that explains how and why a sense of community grows or declines, and the conditions under which that process is stable. Our assumptions in no way exhaust the possible restrictions that might be made. Some may wish to add to the set; others may feel that certain assumptions are wrong and should be deleted. We see this set of assumptions as a starting point.

The system (S), together with the restrictions (F1.1)–(F4.5), constitutes our model of the interaction among good will, transaction volume, and transaction balance. However, in its present form it is too general to deliver easily mathematical conclusions about the processes involved. Consequently, we refer henceforth to the preceding restrictions as composing our *abstract model* and turn now to the specification of an *analytical model*, a set of explicit equations that jointly meet all of the above requirements. The equations presented below are not unique, in that there could well be others that would also meet all of the assumptions. We have, however, attempted to work with the simplest set. The following system of equations represents our analytical model:

$$\dot{V} = (V - E)\left[\{\alpha E/2 + \epsilon C/(1 + C)\}(V - E) - \alpha VE - \beta E - \gamma V^2\right],$$
$$\dot{E} = -E(V - E)(\alpha V + \beta), \qquad\qquad\qquad\text{(AS)}$$
$$\dot{C} = (\rho V - \sigma E)C + \varphi(V - E),$$

where the parameters α, β, γ, ϵ, ρ, σ, and φ satisfy the restrictions:

$$\alpha > 0, \beta > 0, 0 < \gamma < \alpha/2, \epsilon > 0, \varphi > 0, \sigma > \rho > 0. \qquad\text{(R)}$$

The explicit expressions on the right-hand sides of (AS) were obtained by a combination of guess-work and mathematical analysis. While these calculations form an important component of the modeling process we employ, they are rather complex and not particularly central to the substantive theme of our study. (For details, see Appendix I.) It is nevertheless important to show that (AS) meets all the requirements (F1.1)–(F4.5) that embody our translation of Deutsch's ideas. We do this below. Those readers primarily interested in the consequences of the model may turn immediately to the next section.

First, we show that $F_3(E,V,C)$ satisfies the requirements (F4.1)–(F4.5). Comparing systems (S) and (AS), we see that this function is given explicitly by

$$F_3(E,V,C) = (\rho V - \sigma E)C + \varphi(V - E).$$

Condition (F4.3) is clearly true. Now we note, after some calculation, that:

$$F_3(0, V, C) = V(\rho C + \varphi),$$

$$\frac{dF_3}{dV}(0, V, C) = \rho C + \varphi.$$

$$\frac{dF_3}{dC}(0, V, C) = \rho V.$$

$$F_3(E, V, 0) = \varphi(V - E),$$
$$F_3(V, V, C) = -(\sigma - \rho)VC,$$

and so (F4.1), (F4.2), (F4.4), and (F4.5) are all direct consequences of the inequalities (R) and the fact that $0 \le E \le V$.

Next, consider the function $F_2(E,V,C)$. By (S) and (AS), it has the form:

$$F_2(E,V,C) = -E(V - E)(\alpha V + \beta).$$

Since $0 \le E \le V$ and, by (R), $\alpha > 0$ and $\beta > 0$, we see that (F2.1) and (F2.2) are satisfied. Also, since

$$\frac{dF_2}{dE}(E, V, C) = -(V - 2E)(\alpha V + \beta),$$

this derivative certainly decreases as V increases (since both factors separately increase) and vanishes when $V = E = 0$. Hence (F2.3) is true.

By a final comparison of (S) and (AS), we see that:

$$F_1(E,V,C) = (V - E)[\{\alpha E/2 + \epsilon C/(1 + C)\}(V - E) \\ - \alpha VE - \beta E - \gamma V^2].$$

To verify the dependency conditions (F3.1) and (F3.2), we note, after a simple calculation, that

$$F_1(E,V,C) - F_2(E,V,C) = (V - E)[\{\alpha E/2 + \epsilon C/(1 + C)\} \\ (V - E) - \gamma V^2].$$

This difference certainly vanishes when $V = E$, giving us (F3.1). Also, since the term here in square brackets reduces to the negative term $-\gamma V^2$ when $V = E$ (recall that $\gamma > 0$ by the inequalities (R)), (F3.2) is satisfied.

Finally, consider the requirements (F1.1)–(F1.5). Clearly (F1.5) is satisfied. Also,

$$F_1(E,V,0) = -(V - E)(\alpha E^2/2 + \alpha VE/2 + \beta E + \gamma V^2),$$

and so (F1.3) is true owing to the inequalities (R). If V is very large, the dominant term within the square brackets in our formula for F_1 is $-\gamma V^2$. Hence, since $-\gamma V^2(V - E)$ approaches $-\infty$ as V approaches $+\infty$, (F1.1) is satisfied. A simple calculation shows that

$$\frac{dF_1}{dC}(E, V, C) = \epsilon(V - E)^2/(1 + C)^2,$$

and since $\epsilon > 0$ we obtain (F1.4). Finally, (F1.2) is equivalent to the requirement that the second derivative $d^2F_1/dVdE$ be negative. A direct calculation gives us

$$\frac{d^2F_1}{dVdE}(E, V, C) = -2\epsilon C/(1 + C) - \beta - 2(\alpha/2 - \gamma)V,$$

and by the inequalities (R) we see this is indeed negative. Thus, (F1.2) is satisfied.

Consequences of the Model

The model we have developed characterizes the basic variables in the integration process, namely, sense of community C, transaction volume V, and transaction balance E, as solutions of the system of differential equations (AS). To draw conclusions about the development of a security community according to this model, we must learn how solutions of (AS) behave as time proceeds. The consequences of the model that we present shortly can best be described by reference to Figure 2.1, which shows the space defined by our three basic variables. In the C,V plane E is obviously zero. Thus, whenever the system is in this plane there is a complete balance in the transactions. The plane that bisects the region between the C,E plane and the C,V plane is defined by the condition $V = E$. Whenever the system is on this plane one nation is completely dependent on the other, the totally dominant nation. Implicit in the reasoning that led to the model were the restrictions

$$0 \le E \le V, 0 \le C. \tag{D}$$

Thus, we are interested only in the region in Figure 2.1 that lies between the plane of balance and the plane of dominance or dependence and above the horizontal plane $C = 0$ on which the sense of community vanishes. Each solution of (AS) can be viewed as a sequence of points, or more generally a curve, in this region, such as the one shown in Figure 2.1. The movement of the system along such a curve, as indicated by the arrows, tells us how sense of community, transaction volume, and transaction balance rise and fall in the course of time.

We present now three theorems that provide information about the qualitative behavior of solutions of (AS). The proofs, which are somewhat technical, appear in Appendix II. In part, the theorems confirm some of our expectations for the model, such as the inequalities (D), and hence give us confidence that the modeling process is sound. At the same time, they provide information about the integration process that is surprising and new. Our theorems concern in large part the behavior of the system on the two planes distinguished in Figure 2.1, namely, the plane of complete transaction balance and the plane of complete transaction dominance or dependence.

The first theorem may be stated as follows:

Theorem 1: Solutions that begin in the region defined by $0 \le E \le V$, $0 \le C$ always remain in this region. Moreover, the planes $E = 0$ and $E = V$ are invariant and asymptotically stable.

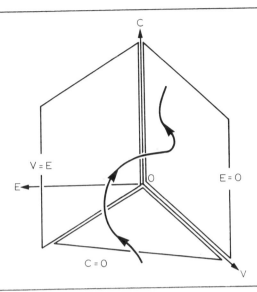

Figure 2.1 A Typical Trajectory in the Region of Motion Bound by the Plane of Balance ($E = 0$), the Plane of Dominance or Dependency ($V = E$), and the Plane of Null Good Will ($C = 0$).

Theorem 1 indicates that the system must always lie within the region bounded by the complete balance and complete dependence planes and the plane $C = 0$ of null good will. Such a conclusion may not be surprising, particularly in view of the restrictions (D) implicit in the modeling process, but it is important to realize that our final model consists only of the system (AS) and the parameter inequalities (R). Thus, at this stage the restrictions (D) are a matter for proof rather than assumption. Either solutions of (AS) satisfy them, or they do not. The first portion of Theorem 1 confirms that (D) does indeed hold, and so shows that the equations we have constructed have successfully met certain basic requirements inherent in the definitions of the variables V, E, and C.

The first theorem also shows that the planes of complete balance and complete dependence are invariant. If the system ever begins on one of these planes it is trapped there. It can never move off that plane. Thus, if the system is in complete balance (i.e. if $E = 0$), while transaction volume and the sense of community can change, the balance in transactions will be preserved. Similarly, if the system ever reaches a situation of complete dependence, volume and sense of community may change but total dominance remains fixed. This is also not a surprising result, since assumptions (F2.1) and (F3.1) propose that this is how the process operates. This conclusion, like the earlier one, simply indicates that our model successfully reflects the assumptions. Note, however, that, although Theorem 1 indicates that the planes capture the dynamics, we have yet to say how the system moves in either plane. This is given by later results.

Finally, Theorem 1 indicates that when the process is close to either plane the system's dynamics are pulled into that plane. The system is asymptotically stable in the regions near each plane. If the transaction flows are nearly balanced, the dynamics will push the system toward greater balance. Similarly, if one nation is almost completely dependent on the other, the process moves the system toward complete dependence.

The remaining two theorems describe what happens on the two invariant planes once the system is on one or the other. Consider first the plane of complete dependence. For it we have

> *Theorem 2:* For any solution on the plane $E = V$ of complete dependence, the transaction volume $V(t)$ is a constant and the good will $C(t)$ approaches zero exponentially fast as t tends to infinity.

Theorem 2 indicates that, if the system enters this plane, then the volume of transactions will cease to change and the sense of community will decline. When one nation is completely dominant the volume of transactions is "frozen" — it can neither increase nor decrease — and the feelings of good will and sense of community decline to zero. Total dependency not only leads to a decline in the sense of community, but also "stabilizes" or fixes the volume of transaction. Ultimately, whatever sense of community might have existed disappears. Since Theorem 1 indicated that whenever the system was close to this plane it would be pulled into it, and that once in it the system could never escape, then given our assumptions, we must conclude that severe imbalances (regions close to the imbalance plane) produce conditions that make integration and the development of a security community impossible. Furthermore, although Deutsch was not concerned with stability in this sense, and indeed might hope that such situations would be unstable so that the system could move away from these degenerate conditions, Theorems 1 and 2 show that the system is stable: it will move to a condition of absolutely no feeling of good will and stay there.

The last and probably most interesting theorem concerns the system's dynamics on the plane of complete balance. It may be stated as follows:

Theorem 3: For any solution on the plane $E = 0$ of transaction balance, either: (a) transaction volume $V(t)$ is zero and good will $C(t)$ is fixed, for all time, or (b) as t tends to infinity, transaction volume $V(t)$ approaches the level $V^* = \epsilon/\gamma$ and good will $C(t)$ tends to infinity.

From Theorem 1 we know that once the system is on this plane it remains there: transaction flows remain balanced. The question then is what happens to transaction volume and the sense of community as time proceeds. Theorem 3 shows that, in the plane of balance, transaction volume tends to some constant value while the sense of community continues to rise to infinity. Although the consequences for transaction volume appear to be similar in the two planes, an important difference between Theorem 2 and Theorem 3 must be noted. The combination of Theorems 1 and 2 indicates that, when the system gets close to the dependency plane, the level of transaction volume at the time at which the system is in this vicinity is the level at which the system is frozen. More concisely, the system has reached a certain level of transaction volume; it is pulled into the plane of dominance, and the transaction volume is fixed at that level. Something rather different happens when the system approaches a region near the balance plane. Once again, the system is pulled into the balance plane, but the volume of transactions is not fixed at the time of "entry." Indeed, it will continue to change even when the system is on the balance plane. Theorem 3 tells us that the volume of transactions will constantly change but that this change is moving the system toward some "optimal" asymptotic level of transaction. If the volume is "too high" it will come down; if "too low" it will increase.

The more important conclusion to be drawn from Theorem 3 is the fact that the sense of community will continue to grow. Theorems 1 and 3 together suggest that the optimal conditions for integration (though at this point we cannot claim that they are the only conditions) require that the system be close to the plane of balance. It does not matter whether the sense of community is minimal (C is small), or the volume of transaction is low (V is small). If there is nearly a balance in the flow of transactions, then the two nations have an optimal chance of moving toward a security community.

A detailed analysis of the system (AS) when $E = 0$ produces a pictorial representation of the dynamics in the plane of balance. This is shown in Figure 2.2. Each of the curves is a possible path that the system might trace, in the direction of the arrows, as we follow its progress in time. Along all curves the sense of community C for the system is forever increasing. The volume of transactions V increases if at some point it is small and decreases if at some point it is large. Moreover, for all of the curves this volume approaches in time the special level $V^* = \epsilon/\gamma$ indicated by the vertical line, regardless of the volume of transactions initially.

Deutsch was concerned with the stability of the integration process. Under what conditions could it be reversed? If the sense of community had begun to rise, what conditions would make it change direction and decline? Our analysis only allows us to provide a partial answer to this question. First, we know that, in a region close to the balance plane, the sense of community will always increase. It may do so slowly or at varying speeds, but, as indicated by Figure 2.2, the variable C in the C, V plane can never decrease. Under conditions of near balance, then, the integration process is very stable (in the sense of Deutsch). Second, we also know that in a region close to the plane of dependency, regardless of the level of C, the sense of community will always decrease. Thus, under conditions of severe transaction imbalance, whatever process of integration might have been at work will cease.

Deutsch's query, however, is more complex. He would like to know more generally, off the planes of dependency and balance, if and when an integration process can reverse itself. If C is initially increasing in the space delimited by the two planes, under what conditions will it ultimately decrease? Unfortunately, this question is considerably more difficult to answer mathematically, and we must leave it to a future study.

Summary and Conclusions

We have constructed and analyzed here a model describing the relationship of transaction volume, transaction balance, and the sense of community between two nations. Our intent was to capture a few of the basic ideas originally put forth by Deutsch as to how these variables might be related. We proposed a set of assumptions about the behavior of these variables that hopefully reflects Deutsch's analysis. A set of equations that describe the dynamics of each of the three variables was then constructed such that all the assumptions would be met simultaneously. The analysis of the resulting model allowed us to draw some conclusions about the integration process.

While the conclusions are only as valid and as useful as are the assumptions used to design the model, our hope is that the development of the model and this initial analysis provide some

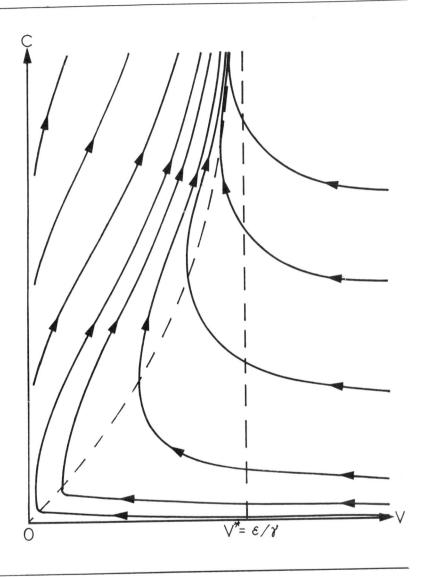

Figure 2.2 Time Trajectories of a System in the Plane of Balance

grounds for understanding the dynamics of integration. The study of integration dynamics and the development of security communities has been at a standstill in recent years. It has been argued that this was a consequence of some predictions not being substantiated. Perhaps the failure of the predictions has been due to an inadequate understanding of the assumptions that are made and an insufficient analysis of the interacting consequences of those assumptions. Perhaps the predictions were empirically wrong because they were also logically incorrect.

Appendix I

We describe here our construction of the functions F_1, F_2, and F_3 that appear in the analytical model (AS). The procedure is a semi-inverse one: forms of F_1, F_2, and F_3 are selected that are partly explicit and yet partly unspecified. The explicit parts are sufficiently special that some of the requirements (F1.1)–(F4.5) are satisfied trivially, and the unspecified parts are sufficiently flexible that we can proceed to deduce their form so as to satisfy the requirements that remain.

Since the dependency requirements (F3.1) and (F3.2) link F_1 and F_2, these two functions must be constructed at the same time, with the ten conditions (F1.1)–(F3.2) being considered simultaneously. This construction is too complex to present here in its entirety. We shall limit ourselves instead to an illustration: the derivation of the function F_3.

Condition (F4.2) would be most easy to satisfy if F_3 were linear in the good will variable C, so we try the semi-inverse form

$$F_3(E,V,C) = F_{31}(E,V)C + F_{32}(E,V).$$

F_{31} and F_{32} are new functions (the "unspecified" parts) which we leave arbitrary for the moment. Next we restate (F4.1)–(F4.5) as restrictions on these two new functions. (F4.2) implies that

$$F_{31}(0,V) > 0 \text{ when } V \neq 0. \tag{I.1}$$

(F4.3) is satisfied if

$$F_{32}(0,0) = 0. \tag{I.2}$$

(F4.4) requires that

$$F_{32}(E,V) > 0 \text{ when } V \neq E, \tag{I.3}$$

and (F4.5) is satisfied if

$$F_{31}(V,V) < 0 \text{ and } F_{32}(V,V) \leq 0 \text{ when } V \neq 0. \tag{I.4}$$

Finally, (F4.1) is satisfied if

$$F_{31}(0,V) > 0 \text{ and increasing in } V, \tag{I.5}$$
$$F_{32}(0,V) \geq 0 \text{ and increasing in } V. \tag{I.6}$$

The new condition (I.3) is most easily satisfied if $F_{32}(E, V)$ is proportional to $V - E$. Thus we try the additional semi-inverse form

$$F_{32}(E,V) = \varphi(V-E),$$

in which φ is the constant of proportionality. But now we see that with this form the requirements on F_{32} listed in (I.2), (I.3), (I.4), and (I.6) are all satisfied if only the constant φ is positive:

$$\varphi > 0.$$

Next we look for a function F_{31} that satisfies the remaining conditions by making the further specialization

$$F_{31}(E,V) = A(V)E + B(V),$$

in which $A(V)$ and $B(V)$ are functions we will now select. In terms of A and B, the conditions (I.1), (I.4), and (I.5) become:

$$B(V) > 0 \text{ when } V \neq 0, \tag{I.7}$$
$$B(0) = 0, \tag{I.8}$$
$$B(V) \text{ is increasing in } V, \tag{I.9}$$
$$A(V)V + B(V) < 0 \text{ when } V \neq 0. \tag{I.10}$$

Conditions (I.7)–(I.9) are easily satisfied by the function

$$B(V) = \rho V \text{ with } \rho = \text{constant} > 0,$$

and with this choice the last condition (I.10) is easily satisfied if A is a constant,

$$A(V) = -\sigma,$$

provided only that this constant is such that

$$\sigma > \rho.$$

Collecting together these results, we obtain an explicit representation of the function F_3 in the form

$$F_3(E,V,C) = (\rho V - \sigma E)C + \varphi(V - E),$$

in which ρ, σ, and φ are constants that satisfy the inequalities (R).

Appendix II

We prove in this appendix the three theorems that form the basis of our conclusions.

Theorem 1: Solutions that begin in the region defined by $0 \leq E \leq V$, $0 \leq C$ always remain in this region. Moreover, the planes $E = 0$ and $E = V$ are invariant and asymptotically stable.

Proof. The second equation of (AS) is satisfied identically if $E = 0$ for all time. By the theorem on the uniqueness of solutions of systems of ordinary differential equations (Hale, 1980: 18), we conclude that if $E = 0$ at any one instant then it must vanish for all time. Thus the plane $E = 0$ is invariant. Also, if $E \approx 0$ we see from the second equation of (AS) that $\dot{E} \approx -EV(\alpha V + \beta) < 0$. Therefore E is strictly decreasing here and so the plane $E = 0$ is asymptotically stable. Moreover, setting $E = 0$ in (AS), we see that solutions on this plane are governed by the simpler system

$$\dot{V} = V^2\{\epsilon C/(1 + C) - \gamma V\}, \qquad \text{(II.1)}$$
$$\dot{C} = V(\rho C + \varphi).$$

Define the new variable $Z = V - E$. Then when $Z = 0$ we are on the plane $E = V$. We may derive a differential equation for Z by noting that $\dot{Z} = \dot{V} - \dot{E}$, substituting for the derivatives of V and E using (AS), and then replacing E in all its occurrences by $V - Z$. After some simplification, we obtain

$$\dot{Z} = Z[\{\alpha(V-Z)/2 + \epsilon C/(1+C)\}Z - \gamma V^2].$$

We note that $Z = 0$ satisfies this equation identically, and for $Z \approx 0$ we have $\dot{Z} \approx -\gamma ZV^2 < 0$. Thus, by reasoning exactly as we have above, we conclude that the plane $Z = 0$, i.e. $V = E$, is invariant and asymptotically stable. Moreover, setting $V = E$ in (AS), we see that solutions on this plane must satisfy the system:

$$\dot{V} = 0, \qquad \text{(II.2)}$$
$$\dot{C} = -(\sigma - \rho)VC.$$

Finally, consider any solution that begins in the region $0 \le E \le V$, $0 \le C$. This solution cannot cross from one side of the plane $E = 0$ to the other. If it did, this solution would lie on the plane $E = 0$ at some intervening time, and so by invariance it must lie in this plane for all time. We conclude that $E \ge 0$ always. For similar reasons a solution cannot cross the plane $E = V$, and so $V \ge E$ for all time. Therefore a solution can leave the region specified in the theorem only by decreasing down through the plane $C = 0$. However, we see from (AS) that $\dot{C} = \varphi(V - E) \ge 0$ when $C = 0$, and so C is never decreasing on this plane. Thus $C \ge 0$ for all time, and the proof of the theorem is complete.

Theorem 2:   For any solution on the plane $E = V$ of complete dependence, the transaction volume $V(t)$ is a constant and the

good will $C(t)$ approaches zero exponentially fast as t
tends to infinity.

Proof. If $V(0) = V_0$ and $C(0) = C_0$, then the solution of the system
(II.2) governing solutions on the plane $V = E$ is

$$V(t) = V_0,$$
$$C(t) = C_0 e^{-(\sigma - \rho)V_0 t}.$$

Thus V is constant and $C \to 0$ exponentially fast as $t \to \infty$.

> *Theorem 3*: For any solution on the plane $E = 0$ of transaction
> balance, either: (a) transaction volume $V(t)$ is zero and
> good will $C(t)$ is fixed, for all time, or (b) as t tends to
> infinity, transaction volume $V(t)$ approaches the level
> $V^* = \epsilon/\gamma$ and good will $C(t)$ tends to infinity.

Proof. Introduce the new variable $Y = C/(1 + C)$. As C increases
from 0 to ∞, Y increases monotonically from 0 to 1, and so in terms of
the variables V and Y we are interested in the region $0 \le V, 0 \le Y \le 1$.
By noting that $C = Y/(1 - Y)$ and $\dot{Y} = \dot{C}/(1+C)^2$, we can transform
(II.1) into the following equivalent system for V and Y:

$$\dot{V} = V^2(\epsilon Y - \gamma V), \tag{II.3}$$
$$\dot{Y} = V(1-Y)\{\rho Y + \varphi(1-Y)\}.$$

In terms of these new variables, our theorem states that for this system
either (a) a solution is an equilibrium point of the form $V = 0$, $Y =$
const., or (b) the solution tends to $V = \epsilon/\gamma$, $Y = 1$ as $t \to \infty$.

To complete the proof we use a deep theorem on differential
equations concerning systems in two variables (Hale, 1980: 54). It
states that as $t \to \infty$ each solution of (II.3) must do one of three things:
become unbounded, approach a periodic solution, or approach an
equilibrium point. Since $0 \le V$ and $0 \le Y \le 1$, solutions can become
unbounded only if $V(t) \to \infty$. But (II.3) shows that $\dot{V} \approx -\gamma V^3 < 0$ when
V is large. Thus any solution for which V is large must be decreasing,
and so all solutions of (II.3) remain bounded.

We also note that our system has no periodic solutions. If this were
the case the variable Y would oscillate and so would increase at certain
times and decrease at other times. But (II.3) and the inequalities (R)
show that $\dot{Y} \ge 0$, and so Y can never decrease. Therefore there is no
solution that is periodic. We conclude that each solution of (II.3) is
either an equilibrium point or tends to an equilibrium point as $t \to \infty$.
To locate the equilibria we set the right-hand sides of (II.3) equal to 0.

We find that the only equilibria for which $0 \le Y \le 1$ are either

$$V = 0, \, Y = \text{constant}, \qquad (\text{II.4})$$

or

$$V = \epsilon/\gamma, \, Y = 1. \qquad (\text{II.5})$$

In every neighborhood of the equilibrium point $V = 0$, $Y = 0$, (II.3) shows that Y is strictly increasing, and so this point is unstable. In the neighborhood of every other equilibrium of the form (II.4), we see from (II.3) that V is strictly increasing. Hence all the equilibria (II.4) are unstable. We conclude that, apart from equilibrium points of the type (II.4), all solutions of (II.3) tend as $t \to \infty$ to the point given by (II.5); i.e., $V(t) \to \epsilon/\gamma$ and $C(t) \to \infty$. This completes the proof.

NOTES

1. Although the following analysis is based largely on the development of the security community argument presented by Deutsch, this research was originally stimulated by a seminar presented by Richard Merritt and by the paper by Clark and Merritt that is included in this volume (Chapter 10).

2. Some of the underlying framework is spelled out in Deutsch's (1953) study of nationalism.

3. Thus, V_A and V_B could both be considered RA (relative acceptance) scores, provided a transformation is made of those scores to force them to be positive.

REFERENCES

DEUTSCH, K. W. (1953) Nationalism and Social Communication: An Inquiry into the Foundations of Nationality. Cambridge: MIT Press, and New York: John Wiley.
———(1954) Political Community at the International Level: Problems of Definition and Measurement. Garden City, NY: Doubleday.
———, S. A. BURRELL, R. A. KANN, M. LEE Jr, M. LICHTERMAN, R. E. LINDGREN, F. L. LOEWENHEIM and R. W. VAN WAGENEN (1957) Political Community and the North Atlantic Area: International Organization in the Light of Historical Experience. Princeton, NJ: Princeton University Press.
HALE, J. K. (1980) Ordinary Differential Equations. New York: Krieger.
MUNCASTER, R. G. and D. A. ZINNES (1982–83) "A model of inter-nation hostility dynamics and war." Conflict Management and Peace Science 6 (Spring): 19–38.
ZINNES, D. A. and R. G. MUNCASTER (1984) "Hostile activity and the prediction of war." Journal of Conflict Resolution 28 (June): 187–230.

CHAPTER 3

CRISES, WAR, AND SECURITY RELIABILITY

CLAUDIO CIOFFI-REVILLA

Recent scientific research has attempted to establish a link between the behavior of states (or of a system of nations) during a period of crisis and the onset of war. However, in spite of significant progress in quantification and empirical testing (Eberwein, 1981), theoretical development — in the hypothetico-deductive tradition — still lags behind.

Using Wright's (1942) "crisis theory" of war as a point of departure, this study presents a rigorous theoretical foundation, extension, and generalization of Wright's conjectured link between crises and war. New concepts, models, and principles from the more general theory of political reliability (Cioffi-Revilla, 1983a) are applied to restate and derive Wright's equations from first assumptions, thereby providing a formal justification for Wright's model, and to derive a set of new theoretical and analytic insights. Analysis shows that, although the probability of war converges to 1.0 as the number of crises grows (as correctly predicted by Wright), the *speed* of convergence is actually quite faster than suggested either by Wright or by "some sort of intuitive reasoning" (as Lewis F. Richardson might have said). Moreover, the qualitative properties of the convergence process itself are not straightforward. These and other important properties are examined and compared with intuitive expectations about the probability of war over a historical period.

AUTHOR'S NOTE: This study was funded in part by grant SES-84-00877 from the National Science Foundation, and by the University of Illinois under grants from the Office of International Programs and Studies and the University Research Board. I am grateful to Raymond Dacey, Karl W. Deutsch, Richard L. Merritt, Robert Muncaster, and Dina A. Zinnes for their useful comments and suggestions.

First, some relevant aspects of current research on crises and wars, Wright's contribution, and the political reliability approach are reviewed. Second, Wright's original — but implicit — assumptions are stated explicitly and are then translated mathematically and used formally to derive a model for the probability of war as a function of crisis behavior. Third, the model is analyzed, with an emphasis on (a) quantitative and qualitative properties, and (b) sensitivity analysis.

Background

The empirical relationship between crisis behavior and escalation to war is far better understood today than it was in Richardson's or Wright's days. Not only are empirical crisis data more readily available (see, e.g., Singer, 1980; Eberwein, 1981; Casadio, 1983; Eckhart and Azar, 1978; Butterworth, 1978; Siverson and Tennefoss, 1982; Blechman and Kaplan, 1978; Kegley et al., 1975), but a considerable number of propositions have also been subject to empirical investigation and testing (see, e.g., Allan, 1979; Bremer and Cusack, 1980; Cusack and Eberwein, 1980; and reviews in Singer, 1981; Eberwein, 1981; and Zinnes, 1976: Part II). It is now known, for instance, that, "while only 13% of all major power militarized disputes [crises] since 1816 escalated to war, that figure rose to 20% when the parties were approximately equal in military terms, and to 75% if such parity was combined with rapid military buildup during the three years prior to the dispute" (Singer, 1981: 11). Purely empirical (or predominantly inductive) research has therefore already uncovered some valuable patterns that should be subject to further analytic study.

Nonetheless, most previous research has aimed at testing ad hoc hypotheses while theoretical progress — formally explaining empirical patterns — has been slower, particularly in developing hypothetico-deductive theory. On the linkage between crisis behavior and onset of war, recent theoretical contributions in the hypothetico-deductive tradition are not as numerous as inductive investigations (see, e.g., Cioffi-Revilla and Zinnes, 1983; Cioffi-Revilla, Zinnes, and Muncaster, forthcoming; Schrodt, 1981, 1983a). The ontology behind these theories often differs: some are deterministic, while others are stochastic. All nonetheless postulate a set of assumptions from which deductions (theorems) are derived. This is also the orientation of this study.

In *A Study of War*, Quincy Wright (1942) presented at least two theories of the onset of wars. The better known of these is "distance theory," which explains the onset of war as a function of changes in "peace expectancy, intellectual, legal, political, psychic, social, strategic, and technological distances" among states (1942: App. xliii). Distance theory has been subsequently developed by R. Rummel, J. Vincent, and others (cf. Zinnes, 1976: 149–157), but it is *not* the subject of this analysis.

Wright's other theory, here called his "crisis theory of war," was only briefly stated (1942: 1272). It views crises as episodes (or branching points, as is suggested below) during which wars may occur. Wright conjectured, but did not prove, that the onset of war over a period of time is a function of the probability of avoiding war during each of the crises occurring during that period. Unlike his distance theory, Wright's crisis theory of war has received only scant attention (e.g., Deutsch, 1978: 159). This is unfortunate, since the analytic implications of the theory are potentially richer than those of distance theory, and its deductive structure is generally more elegant.

In the approach of political reliability theory, wars are seen as instances of breakdown in the international security system (Cioffi-Revilla, 1983a, 1983c, 1985). The purpose here is to use the general political reliability approach to focus on Wright's crisis theory of war. In so doing, crisis theory is extended in two directions. First, a formal analytic derivation of Wright's conjecture is presented. Second, the analysis builds on Wright's work by applying new concepts, models, and principles from political reliability theory. Specifically, this paper (1) restates Wright's crisis theory from first assumptions—thereby providing a formal derivation for Wright's conjectured equations— and (2) presents a set of derived analytic results.

Theory

In *A Study of War*, Wright (1942: 1272) stated *without proof* a set of equations for the probability of war between states during a period of time:

$$P = 1 - (1 - p_1)(1 - p_2)(1 - p_3) \ldots (1 - p_n), \qquad (1)$$
$$P = 1 - (1 - p)^n, \qquad (2)$$

where p_i $(i = 1, 2, 3, \ldots, n)$ is the probability of the ith crisis escalating to war, n is the number of crises, and p is an average over the p_i. The substantive theoretical assumptions behind (1) and (2) were not made explicit in Wright's original presentation. Here, a set of three necessary and sufficient assumptions is presented and justified. Formal, rigorous derivation of (1) and (2) is demonstrated after translating these assumptions into a mathematical model. The model is then interpreted in light of political reliability theory and analyzed for implications.

THEORETICAL ASSUMPTIONS

Wright's theory focuses on the onset of wars over a period of history. Specifically, the theory states that "the probability of war between two states during a period of time is a function of the number of crises and the probability of avoiding war in each crisis" (Wright, 1942: 1272). The precise functional relation between the probability of war on the one hand, and the number of crises and the probability of war on the other, is given by (1) and (2). Both equations are now formally derived. Three assumptions are needed.

Assumption 1 (Behavioral Determination): The occurrence of war in the international system is determined by the behavior that states manifest during each of a set of n crises $C_i (i = 1,2,3,\ldots,n)$ taking place over a period of time in history.

As time goes by, a number of crises occurs among states, and the behavior of states during those crises crucially determines the probability of escalation to war. This theory does *not* explain the war phenomenon as a function of systemic attributes, or even as a function of the national characteristics of states (as in distance theory). Rather, the occurrence of war is explained as a function of inter-nation behavior, specifically during crises.

Assumption 2 (Crisis Prelude to War): Wars result only from crises; all wars are preceded by some crisis, even if the crisis is of short duration.

Here crises are seen as landmark "encounters" among states, or as branching points in inter-state relations. At every crisis juncture, states might peacefully resolve their conflict of interest or resort to war, as illustrated in Figure 3.1. This "historical branching tree" is akin to that put forth by Daniel Bernoulli to state the St Petersburg Paradox.[1] This view of crises as critical turning points in inter-state relations is in agreement with contemporary crisis theory (see, e.g., Snyder and Diesing, 1977; Hermann, 1972).

Assumption 3 (Independence of Crises): Crisis events C_i are (stochastically) independent of one another.

This important assumption, which can be relaxed in subsequent analysis, was not made explicit in Wright's original presentation. However, the equations proposed by Wright (1942: 1272, n. 38) make this assumption unmistakable, since (1) and (2) use "*the product* of the probabilities of war being avoided in each crisis" (italics mine). As is well known (see, e.g., Bittinger and Crown, 1982: 242), the product of

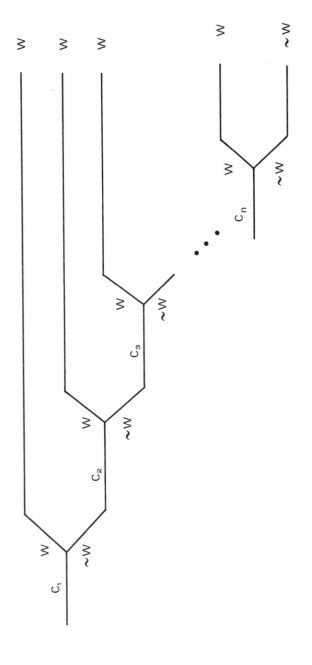

Figure 3.1 The Crisis-War Process as a Branching Tree
(C = crisis, W = war outcome, ~ W = no war outcome)

probabilities comes from the multiplication theorem for the probability of independent events. The assumption of independence is made explicit in this restatement of the theory.

In substantive terms the assumption of independence is equivalent to postulating that *crises arise from different causes*, or that different political, economic, and strategic factors are behind the occurrence of each crisis, making the genesis of each crisis idiosyncratic or *sui generis*.[2]

MATHEMATICAL MODEL

The above theoretical assumptions can be formalized as follows. Let P denote the probability that the event war will take place during a period of time containing n crises. In each crisis there is a probability p of escalation to war.[3] Then

$$P = \Pr[\text{war occurs during a period of } n \text{ crises}] \qquad (3)$$
$$= 1 - \Pr[\text{war is avoided during the period}].$$

However, since there are n crises, and crises are independent,

$$\Pr[\text{war is avoided during the period}] = \Pr[\text{war is avoided in crisis 1}]$$
$$\times \Pr[\text{war is avoided in crisis 2}]$$
$$\times \Pr[\text{war is avoided in crisis 3}]$$
$$\times \ldots \times \Pr[\text{war is avoided in crisis } n]. \qquad (4)$$

Now $\Pr[\text{war is avoided in the } i\text{th crisis}] = 1 - \Pr[\text{war occurs in the } i\text{th crisis}]$. Letting $p_i = \Pr[\text{war occurs in the } i\text{th crisis}]$, (4) can be rewritten as

$$\Pr[\text{war is avoided during the period}] = (1 - p_1)(1 - p_2)$$
$$(1 - p_3) \ldots (1 - p_n). \, (5)$$

Finally, substituting this last result into (3b),

$$P = 1 - (1 - p_1)(1 - p_2)(1 - p_3) \ldots (1 - p_n)$$

or

$$P = 1 - (1 - p)^n$$

where p denotes an average probability of war escalation. These last two formulas are those conjectured by Wright ((1) and (2)). QED.

The derivation just presented formally demonstrates the validity of Wright's conjectured equations. In particular, it renders explicit several key assumptions, such as the independence of crisis events, which had earlier remained only implicit in Wright's original formulation.

SECURITY RELIABILITY

Since P denotes the probability of war in the international system, its complement, $1 - P$, describes the probability of *no* war. But the absence of war is akin to the maintenance of international security. Therefore the probability $(1 - P)$ can be interpreted as a measure of the *security reliability* of the international system, or of the degree of confidence in war *not* breaking out, or security *not* breaking down. Formally,

> *Definition 1* (*Security Reliability*): The security reliability R of the international system is the probability that war will not break out over the period of n crises, each crisis having a probability p of escalating to war.

Formally,

$$R = 1 - P, \tag{6}$$

and, from (2),

$$R = (1 - p)^n. \tag{7}$$

Three aspects of the security reliability of the international system are worth noting.

Independence of Crisis Events

First, since this definition of security reliability is based on P, and since P is defined for independent crisis events, it follows that this concept of security reliability also assumes the independence of crises. In view of the frequency with which Poisson or near-Poisson distributions of international phenomena are reported in the literature (see, most recently, the study by Mintz and Schrodt in Chapter 11 below), this assumption is not unreasonable. For example, Allan (1979) reports near-Poisson results (with occasional contagion) in a study of onsets of crises using a variety of different crisis lists. Thus, the assumption of independence of crisis events is not without *empirical* justification, even if *intuitively* it might seem implausible.

Serial Structure of Security Reliability

Second, the reliability approach to the onset of war highlights an aspect of war which is not evident in Wright's equations (i.e. (4) and (5)): security reliability, as described by (9), is isomorphic to the reliability of a political system having a "serial" structure. In this interpretation, each serial component corresponds to the probability of a crisis escalating to war (Cioffi-Revilla, 1983a).[4] This can be shown as follows. The multiplicative structure to the nth power in (7) expands to

$$R = \underbrace{(1 - p)(1 - p)(1 - p) \ldots (1 - p)}_{n \text{ times}} \quad (8)$$

$$= \prod_{i=1}^{n} (1 - p_i).$$

But (8) is the same as

$$R = \Pr[\text{no war} \mid C_1] \times \Pr[\text{no war} \mid C_2] \times \ldots \times \Pr[\text{no war} \mid C_n] \quad (9)$$
$$= q_1 q_2 q_3 \cdots q_n$$
$$= q^n$$

where q_i denotes the probability of peacefully resolving the ith crisis. Equation (9c) is precisely the equation for the reliability of a political system having a serial structure with n components.

Generalized Concept of Crisis

The political reliability interpretation of Wright's theory, which hinges on the concept of security reliability, is wholly consistent with Wright's original account, but it is not evident from inspection of (4) or (5) alone. This interpretation, moreover, leads to a *generalized* view of what a "crisis" is. Indeed, a crisis can now mean any grave international problem, one not necessarily limited to episodes circumscribed in time and space. Thus we speak of the "energy crisis," "nuclear proliferation crisis," "world food crisis," and other systemic (i.e. "global") crises, *the inability to solve any one of which may cause war.*

This view of grave international problems as "crises" in the global system, consistent with the political reliability interpretation, is implicit in the following remark from a famous speech by Henry Kissinger (1980) to a NATO audience: "In the decade ahead we will face *simultaneously* (1) an unfavorable balance of power, (2) a world in turmoil, (3) a potential economic crisis, and (4) a massive energy problem" (italics mine).

The statement implies that failure peacefully to resolve any one of these international problems could result in war (McClure, 1980). For example, assuming that the four problems noted by Kissinger are independent, with $n = 4$ and $p = 0.5$ this yields a predicted security reliability of $R = (1 - 0.5)^4 = 0.0625$, or 6.25 percent for the decade in question. The explanation of this surprisingly low result, as well as other general properties of security reliability, are analyzed next.

Analysis

The preceding section stated Wright's assumptions explicitly, derived Wright's conjectured equations for the probability of war, introduced the concept of security reliability, and proposed a generalized interpretation of the concept of crisis in the global system. Two types of analyses, quantitative and qualitative, are now presented. Each illustrates several deductive properties of (1), (2), or (7), some of which are not quite evident from Wright's original statement or plain intuitive reasoning.

QUANTITATIVE ANALYSIS

In his brief analysis of (2), Wright (1942: 1272, n. 38) noted that, "even though p is very small, as n approaches infinity the probability of war approaches certainty." Formally stated:

> *Theorem 1* (*Wright's Theorem on Convergence*): $P \rightarrow 1$ as $n \rightarrow +\infty$, *regardless* of the value of p.

Although this result can easily be shown to be true (by taking the limit of P for $n \rightarrow +\infty$), a quantitative analysis of (2) is nevertheless useful for obtaining a deeper understanding of the *rate* or *speed* with which P in fact converges toward certainty. Wright's reference to n "approaching infinity," while *formally* exact, has the unfortunate effect of making it appear as if n must be *very* large, or "almost infinite," for P to be virtually 1. As shown below, however, this is a misleading interpretation *from a substantive viewpoint*.

Before analyzing P's speed of convergence to unity, or R's convergence to zero, the concept of *sensitivity* should be rigorously defined:

> *Definition 2* (*Sensitivity of P with respect to p*): The sensitivity of P with respect to p is equal to the ratio of the percentage change in P with respect to a percentage change in p.
>
> $$s_p(P) = \{(\Delta P/P)100\}/\{(\Delta p/p)100\} = (\Delta P/p)(P/\Delta p) \qquad (10)$$
> $$= (\partial P/\partial p)(p/P)$$
> $$= \{np(1-p)^{n-1}\}/P.$$
>
> *Definition 3* (*Sensitivity of P with respect to n*): The sensitivity of P with respect to n is equal to the ratio of the percentage change in P with respect to a percentage change in n.
>
> $$s_n(P) = \{(\Delta P/P)100\}/\{(\Delta n/n)100\} = (\Delta P/n)(P/\Delta n) \qquad (11)$$
> $$= (\partial P/\partial n)(n/P)$$
> $$= -\{(1-p)^n \ln (1-p)^n\}/P.$$
>
> *Definition 4* (*Sensitivity of R with respect to p*): The sensitivity of security reliability R with respect to p is equal to the

ratio of the percentage change in R with respect to a
percentage change in p.

$$s_p(R) = \{(\Delta R/R)100\}/\{(\Delta p/p)100\} = (\Delta R/p)(R/\Delta p) \quad (12)$$
$$= (\partial R/\partial p)(p/R)$$
$$= -\{np(1-p)^{n-1}\}/R.$$

Definition 5 (*Sensitivity of R with respect to n*): The sensitivity of
security reliability R with respect to n is equal to the
ratio of the percentage change in R with respect to a
percentage change in n.

$$s_n(R) = \{(\Delta R/R)100\}/\{(\Delta n/n)100\} = (\Delta R/n)(R/\Delta n) \quad (13)$$
$$= (\partial R/\partial n)(n/R)$$
$$= \{(1-p)^n \ln(1-p)^n\}/R.$$

These equivalent definitions of sensitivity for P and R are helpful for
understanding the nature of the dependence of P and R on both p and
n. Note that, without exception, the specific sensitivity functions (i.e.
(10c)–(13c)) are neither simple nor intuitive from plain inspection of
(2) or (7). Moreover, it is clear from comparing (10c) with (11c), and
(12c) with (13c), that changes in p and n induce quite different changes
on P and R, respectively. In particular, the following theorem holds:

Theorem 2: P is *more* sensitive to change in the probability of crisis
escalation p than to change in the number of crises n.

$$s_p(P) > s_n(P). \quad (14)$$

Corollary 1: $s_p(R) > s_n(R)$.

Proof. By definition,

$$s_p(P) = \{np(1-p)^{n-1}\}/P,$$
$$s_n(P) = -\{(1-p)^n \ln(1-p)^n\}/P.$$

Equating the right side of these two expressions and simplifying both
sides of the equality algebraically yields

$$p = \ln\{1/(1-p)^{1-p}\}.$$

Since the right side of this last expression is always strictly greater than
p (this lemma can be easily verified), it follows that $s_p > s_n$. QED.

Theorem 2 holds particular significance in light of Wright's (see also
Deutsch, 1978: 159) emphasis on the importance of n. Interestingly,
Wright looked exclusively at n when discussing P's convergence to 1.
By contrast, Theorem 2 *guarantees* that changes in p have greater effect
on P. Thus, Theorem 2 runs counter to Wright's original intuition.

TABLE 3.1 The Probability of War in the International System as a Function of Escalation Probabilities and the Number of International Crises

Escalation Probability (*p*)	*Number of Crises in the Period*					
	n = 2	*n* = 5	*n* = 10	*n* = 20	*n* = 50	*n* = 100
0.0	0.00000	0.00000	0.00000	0.00000	0.00000	0.00000
0.1	0.19	0.40951	0.65132	0.87843	0.99485	0.99997
0.2	0.36	0.67232	0.89263	0.98847	0.99999	1.00000
0.3	0.51	0.83193	0.97175	0.99920	1.00000	
0.4	0.64	0.92224	0.99395	0.99926		
0.5	0.75	0.96875	0.99902	1.00000		
0.6	0.84	0.98976	0.99990			
0.7	0.91	0.99757	0.99999		$P = 1.0^a$	
0.8	0.96	0.99968	1.00000			
0.9	0.99	0.99999				
1.0	1.00	1.00000				

a. War is virtually certain (to within 0.99999) in this region of $R^2(p, n)$ space.
SOURCE: Calculated by the author.

(Equations (10c)–(13c) can be used for producing tables containing the exact value of sensitivity at points in the $R(p, n)$ space. Such tables can be computed but are not presented here in the interest of space.)

Table 3.1 lists the probability of war for ten different values in the probability of crisis escalation, and for six different numbers of crises over a period of time. If for each crisis the probability of escalation is 0.3, for example, then for two crises ($n = 2$) the probability of war is 0.51. Figure 3.2 illustrates values of P as a function of p, parametrized by values of n.

Examination of Table 3.1 indicates the following additional results.

Hyporeliability of Security. The probability of war is always higher, and the security reliability is always lower, than the probability p of any crisis escalating to war (except for the trivial cases when $p = 0$ or 1, in which case they are equal). This is an important global property of the crisis process when conceptualized, as Wright proposed, as a branching tree (Figure 3.1). Formally stated:

> *Theorem 3 (Hyporeliability of Security):* Whenever $0 < p < 1.0$ and $n > 1$ (i.e. in *all* empirically meaningful situations), the probability of war P is *always* strictly greater, and the security reliability R is *always* strictly smaller, than the probability p of crisis escalation to war.

This result is not obvious from common thinking about the odds for or

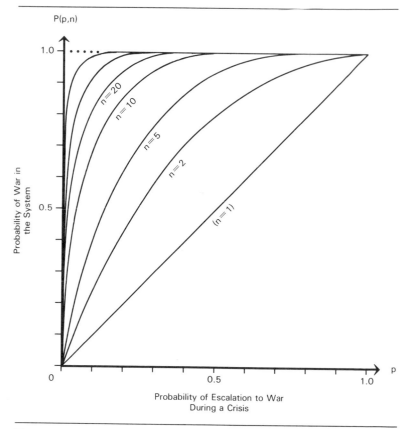

P(p,n)

Probability of War in the System

Probability of Escalation to War
During a Crisis

Figure 3.2 Graph of the Function P(p,n) Parametrized for Values of n.
      $(0 \le p \le 1, n \ge 1)$

against war over a period of war containing *n* crises; it means that the likelihood of war over a period of crises is *always greater* than the *individual* likelihood of any one crisis escalating to war. This is why security (for *n* crises) can be said to be *hyporeliable*; likewise, war is *hyperprobable*. (Proof of Theorem 3 rests on the lemma that the product of any set of numbers between 0 and 1 is always smaller than any of the numbers in that set.)

Sensitivity to n. Theorem 2 notwithstanding, the probability of war *P* over several crises is highly sensitive to change in the number of crises. In particular, an increase in the number of crises — or, as in the generalized interpretation of crises, in the number of "grave international problems" — causes a *sharp* rise in the probability *P* of war, *even when the probability of escalation p is low.* Beyond 50 crises war is virtually certain, even when the probability of escalation is as low as 0.10. Conversely, from this result we can also infer that, if by the fiftieth crisis war has not occurred, then *p must* be very small.

Diminishing Marginal Effects of Escalation. As Figure 3.2 illustrates, for periods of history containing many crises (large *n*), the probability of war *P* is mostly sensitive to changes in *n when the probability of escalation p is low.* This means that, for periods of time with large *n*, a rise in the probability of escalation beyond the first few decimal places does *not* have much effect on increasing the probability of war. If crises are minimally volatile (i.e. with low *p*), then the probability of war may remain low. However, when *n* is large (*n* > 5), "moderately volatile" crises are virtually as dangerous as "highly volatile" ones.

Rapid Convergence of P. Most importantly, the probability of war *P* reaches very high levels even when *both p* and *n* are at seemingly low levels. For example, *P* reaches 0.89 when *p* is as low as 0.20 and *n* is only 10. Clearly, then, although it is mathematically true that *P* converges toward certainty as *n* "approaches infinity," in practice, *P* is already virtually 1.0 for low values of *n* such as those of historical interest. For example, if there has been one major crisis between the superpowers every other year (e.g., Korea, Angola, Cuba, Central America, Horn of Africa, Middle East, etc.) during the past 30 years, then the post-World War II period contains about 15 crises. When *n* = 15, the probability of war is very high, even though the probability *p* of escalation in any individual crisis remains low.

These results are in general contrast with the intuitive estimate of how fast or slow *P* converges toward certainty. In particular, Wright's remark on *P*'s rate of convergence ("for $n \rightarrow +\infty$") must be interpreted in a purely mathematical sense, not in empirical terms.

Security Reliability of Deterrence. Finally, the above analysis prompts the following speculation about the nuclear deterrence balance between nuclear powers. If war between such powers has been avoided, then the probability of escalation at any given crisis *must* have been very low, given the relatively large number of crises which have taken place during recent decades and the new theoretical insight that *P* rises *sharply* even for low values of *n*. In turn, if the probability of escalation to war has been very low, it might then be inferred that the security reliability of the deterrence balance has been quite high.

As an illustration of this inference, consider estimating an approximate historical value for *p*. Suppose there have been about 15 nuclear power crises (Bracken, 1983: 56, reports a much higher estimate for the frequency of NORAD nuclear alerts). *P* can be set at less than 0.5

(since nuclear power war has not occurred). Now, solving (5) for p yields

$$p = 1 - (1 - P)^{1/n}. \tag{15}$$

Hence, the probability of nuclear power war escalation (deterrence failure) must have had an *upper* bound of $1 - (1 - 0.5)^{1/15} \approx 0.045$, or a security reliability in the deterrence system greater than 95 percent. Since this estimate of p is for $P = 0.5$, whereas in fact nuclear war has *not* occurred, then most likely p has been even smaller than 0.045 and the security reliability of deterrence therefore much stronger than 95 percent.

COMPARATIVE STATICS (SENSITIVITY ANALYSIS)

Equations (2) and (7) are clearly nonlinear functions of p and n. Moreover, since each independent variable has a different functional location (n is exponential; p is not), it is also clear that each affects the probability of war (and the security reliability of the system) in *qualitatively* different ways. Beyond the quantitative results just presented, it is therefore useful to obtain general expressions for the behavior of the model (comparative statics) with respect to separate variations in each of the independent variables. Hence,

$$\partial P/\partial p = n(1 - p)^{n-1}, \tag{16}$$
$$\partial P/\partial n = -(1 - p)^n \cdot \ln(1 - p), \tag{17}$$
$$\partial^2 P/\partial p^2 = -n(n - 1)(1 - p)^{n-2}, \tag{18}$$
$$\partial^2 P/\partial n^2 = -2(1 - p)^n \cdot \ln(1 - p). \tag{19}$$

(The corresponding comparative statics for security reliability R can be easily derived using (7).) Equations (16)–(19) describe the general sensitivity of the probability of war P to separate variations in the probability p of war escalation and in the number of crises in a given era.

Recall that, by definition, $0 \leq p \leq 1.0$, and $1 \leq n \leq +\infty$. Empirically, however, *all* relevant conditions are contained within the plane $0 < p < 1$, $n \geq 2$. Using (16)–(19), the following results can be derived.

Concavity of the First Partials. $\partial P/\partial p$ and $\partial P/\partial n$ are positive, upward-concave functions. Therefore the larger the value of the two independent variables, the higher the value of the probability of war, and the lower the security reliability of the system. However, as the form of (16) and (17) indicates, the specific relationship is different for each variable.

Convexity of the Second Partials. $\partial^2 P/\partial p^2$ and $\partial^2 P/\partial n^2$ are negative, downward-convex functions. Therefore, changes in the value of either independent variable have marginally diminishing effects on the probability of war. Once again, however, the specific behavior of this marginally diminishing effect varies from one independent variable to another, as shown by (18) and (19).

Total Variation (Gradient) of P. Finally, the first-order partial derivatives of $P(p,n)$ can be used to define the following quantity.

> *Definition 6 (Total Variation of P):* The total variation of P with respect to both p and n is defined by
>
> $$\overrightarrow{\nabla P} = n(1 - p)^{n-1}\hat{e}_p - (1 - p)^n \ln(1 - p)\hat{e}_n, \qquad (20)$$
>
> where $\hat{e}_p$ and $\hat{e}_n$ are orthogonal versors (unit vectors) in $\mathbb{R}^2(p,n)$ space.

While P is a *scalar* quantity, the quantity $\overrightarrow{\nabla P}$ is a *vector*. Using a well-known property of the ∇P (del) operator (see e.g. Kaplan, 1952: Chs. 3, 5), the following theorem can be stated:

> *Theorem 4 (Direction of grad P):* The quantity $\overrightarrow{\nabla P}$ always points in the direction in which the probability of war $P(p,n)$ changes most rapidly, i.e., the direction in which the derivative of P has its maximum. Moreover, the length of $\overrightarrow{\nabla P}$ is proportional to the amount of change in $P(p,n)$.

This last theorem, while seemingly of only formal interest, in fact provides a useful substantive result since it guarantees that, by evaluating (20) at any point (p,n), we can know in which direction on the (p,n)-plane the probability of war will undergo the most rapid change. Such insight is necessary when comparing different historical periods, or when evaluating alternative futures in terms of changes in p and n, or in decision-making about trade-offs between p and n. Such calculations are hardly accurate when using tables such as 3.1, and are surely impossible using common instinctive reasoning.

Several other aspects should be explored in future research. Among these, it would be interesting to revise and expand the model once further *empirical* progress (e.g. Allan, 1979; Cusack and Eberwein, 1980; Bremer and Cusack, 1980) has been made with the distribution function for the probability of escalation. For example, given the form of (2) and (7), P and R are likely to continue to exhibit different properties from p. In addition, p might be linked to n itself, since after many crises perhaps p undergoes some change, particularly for the same dyad.

For instance, if p (for dyads) decreases in proportion to n ("pacifying influence of war avoidance"), then P and R are mostly determined by the first few crises only. Conversely, if p is imagined to rise as a function of n (perhaps because of the accumulation of unresolved grievances), then clearly the risk of war will rise sharply and (by Theorem 3) in fact *much faster* than p. These and other questions concerning the link between crises and war will undoubtedly benefit from further empirical as well as hypothetico-deductive analysis.

Summary

In *A Study of War*, Quincy Wright (1942) advanced the hypothesis that the probability of war in the international system is a function of the number of international crises over a period of history, and the probability of escalation to war at any given crisis. Wright's conjecture derives its importance from the fact that it focuses explicitly on the probability of war escalation and proposes a formal statement.

In this study the more general theory of political reliability is used to provide a formal derivation for Wright's conjectured equations and to obtain a set of extensions and analytic results (theorems and other theoretical insights) stemming from the basic model. Specifically, the equation for the probability of war is derived from three assumptions. Analysis shows that, although the probability of war converges toward certainty, as correctly noted by Wright, the rate of convergence is much faster than he suggested. Even for relatively small numbers of crises, the probability of war can be very high if the probability of war escalation is moderate.

Analysis also shows other important properties of security reliability which are at variance with intuitive views and estimates. In particular, changes in the probability of escalation, from one era to the next, and changes in the number of crises contained in each era, have vastly different effects on security reliability and the probability of war in the system. Exact expressions for the sensitivity of security reliability are provided. Contrary to Wright's impression, analysis of the model rigorously shows (Theorem 2) that security reliability — and hence also the probability of war — is more sensitive to the probability of escalation than it is to the number of crises.

NOTES

1. I am grateful to Raymond Dacey, University of Idaho, for pointing out the isomorphism between this view of the crisis-war process and the St Petersburg Paradox. He correctly points out (Dacey, 1983, personal communication) that in this study "the occurrence of war, like the occurrence of tails in Bernoulli's game, terminates the process." Bremer and Cusak (1980: 1) also seem to take a similar, although not identical,

approach when they note that "The road leading from world peace to world war is often portrayed as having a number of major forks, where a turn in one direction makes war more likely and a turn in the other direction makes war less likely."

2. Note that the key assumption here refers to the independence of *crisis events* C_i; *not* to the occurrence of war. (This theory is silent about the relationship between different wars.) Moreover, the assumption of independence always refers to *the occurrence of events* (in this case crises), *not* to the probabilities p_i (or p) of escalation to war. (The latter might well be conditional probabilities.)

3. Cusack and Eberwein (1980) report a set of actual, historical estimates of p.

4. Cioffi-Revilla (1983a, 1983b) illustrates schematic diagrams for the graphic representation of structural reliability in political systems.

REFERENCES

ALLAN, P. (1979) "The occurrence of international conflict in time." Geneva: Graduate Institute of International Studies (mimeographed).

BITTINGER, M. L. and J. C. CROWN (1982) Mathematics. Reading, Mass.: Addison-Wesley.

BLECHMAN, B. M. and S. S. KAPLAN (1978) Force Without War. Washington, DC: Brookings Institution.

BRACKEN, P. (1983) The Command and Control of Nuclear Forces. New Haven, Conn.: Yale University Press.

BREMER, S. and T. R. CUSACK (1980) The Urns of War: An Application of Probability Theory to the Genesis of War. Berlin: International Institute for Comparative Social Research, Wissenschaftszentrum Berlin, West Berlin, IIVG/dp 80–128 (mimeographed).

BUTTERWORTH, R. L. (1978) Managing Inter-State Conflict, 1945–1974. Pittsburgh, Pa.: University of Pittsburgh.

CASADIO, F. A. (1983) Conflittualitá mondiale e relazioni internazionali: 1945–1982. Padua: CEDAM.

CIOFFI-REVILLA, C. (1983a) "Political reliability in international relations," pp. 11–45 in D. A. Zinnes (ed.), Conflict Processes and the Breakdown of International Systems. Denver, Colo.: University of Denver, Monograph Series in World Affairs.

——— (1983b) "A probability model of credibility: analyzing deterrence in strategic nuclear systems." Journal of Conflict Resolution 27 (March): 73–108.

——— (1983c) "Political reliability theory of international conflict." Unpublished paper presented at the 1983 Summer Institute for the Study of Conflict Theory and International Security, University of California, Los Angeles, June 23–25.

——— (1985) "Political reliability theory and war in the international system." American Journal of Political Science 29 (February) 47–68.

——— and D. A. ZINNES (1983) "The collapse of inter-state relations: a political reliability theory of crisis." Unpublished paper presented at the 24th Annual Convention of the International Studies Association, Mexico City, March.

———, D. A. ZINNES, and R. G. MUNCASTER (forthcoming) "The collapse of inter-state relations: a political reliability theory of crises."

CUSACK, T. R. and W.-D. EBERWEIN (1980) A Descriptive Analysis of Serious International Disputes During the Twentieth Century. Berlin: International Institute for Comparative Social Research, Wissenschaftszentrum Berlin, IIVG/dp 80–116 (mimeographed).

DACEY, R. (1983) Personal communication to the author.

DEUTSCH, K. W. (1978) The Analysis of International Relations (3d ed.). Englewood Cliffs, NJ: Prentice-Hall.

EBERWEIN, W.-D. (1981) "The quantitative study of international conflict." Journal of Peace Research 18, 1: 19–38.

ECKHART, W. and E. A. AZAR (1978) "Major world conflicts and interventions, 1945 to 1975." International Interactions 5 (September): 75–110.

HERMANN, C. F. (ed.) (1972) International Crises. New York: Free Press.

KAPLAN W. (1952) Advanced Calculus. Reading, Mass.: Addison-Wesley.

KEGLEY, C. W. et al. (1975) International Events and the Comparative Analysis of Foreign Policy. Columbia: University of South Carolina Press.

KISSINGER, H. (1980) Address to the conference on "NATO—The Next Thirty Years." (September, 1) Brussels: NATO.

McCLURE, D. H. (1980) "Why World War III seems unavoidable." South Africa International 11 (October): 102–109.

SCHRODT, P. A. (1981) "A mathematical model of the persistence of conflict. International Interactions 8, 4: 335–348.

———(1983) "A model of sporadic conflict," pp. 101–118 in D. A. Zinnes (ed.). Conflict Processes and the Breakdown of International Systems. Denver, Colo.: University of Denver Monograph Series in World Affairs.

SINGER, J. D. (ed.) (1980) The Correlates of War II. Beverly Hills, Calif.: Sage.

——— (1981) "Accounting for international war: the state of the discipline." Journal of Peace Research 18, 1: 1–18.

SIVERSON, R. M. and M. TENNEFOSS (1982) "Interstate conflicts: 1815–1965." International Interactions 9, 2: 147–178.

SNYDER, G. H. and P. DIESING (1977) Conflict Among Nations. Princeton, NJ: Princeton University Press.

WRIGHT, Q. (1942) A Study of War. Chicago, Ill.: University of Chicago Press.

ZINNES, D. A. (1976) Contemporary International Relations Research. New York: Free Press.

CHAPTER 4

MODELING AN INTERNATIONAL TRADE SYSTEM

BRIAN M. POLLINS
GRANT KIRKPATRICK

Since the publication of *The Limits to Growth* (Meadows et al., 1972), a number of research groups have undertaken the construction of large-scale computer simulations to study the long-term global consequences of economic and demographic growth. The set of problems which provides the focus of this research has come to be known as the "global problematique." As formulated by the Club of Rome and other groups working in the same area, the global problematique envisions economic and demographic growth processes as ultimately lethal (Meadows et al., 1972). Demands created by exploding populations and rising industrial production in the context of finite natural resources were seen as the cause of an "over-shooting" of the earth's environmental carrying capacity and societal collapse through pollution, starvation, and scarcity of raw materials.

While several scholars criticized the economic and demographic assumptions of these models (Kaysen, 1972; Cole et al., 1973; Nordhaus, 1973), the research group in which the authors participated at the International Institute for Comparative Social Research, Science Center Berlin, was founded on the premise that the "limits to growth" debate could not meaningfully be resolved without consideration of the political causes and political implications of the processes included in the global problematique. Simply put, whether or not limits to growth existed, the consequences of economic and demographic growth processes, in our view, would manifest themselves in national and international political arenas long before any material exhaustion was reached. At the same time, if the negative consequences of these same processes were to be ameliorated, political action at the national and international level would be required. Accordingly, the global model which is currently being constructed — entitled GLOBUS — explicitly represents many macro-political processes and their connections to the economy.

Previous global models characterized the world either as a single unit or as comprising geographical regions. To model political processes relevant to the global problematique, however, it is essential that nation-states be explicitly represented, because the nation-state is the single most salient and efficacious actor in the global arena. Proceeding from this premise, our conceptual approach envisions national governments as operating in four environments: the international economic environment, the international political environment, the national economic environment, and the national political environment (Bremer, 1981). National leaders have objectives in each of these environments (e.g. to secure the nation against foreign threats, to stabilize the national economy, and to minimize unemployment and inflation), and they must also react to developments in these same four environments (e.g. strikes or demonstrations at home, or a rise in the world oil price). Given this conceptual approach, the GLOBUS model is divided into five interrelated sectors. A domestic economic sector models major relationships in "open" national economies (hence taking account of cross-national financial ties and other external influences upon national growth and development.) A domestic political sector simulates the processes of national political institutionalization and instability. The international political sector traces relations of conflict and cooperation among the 25 nations in the GLOBUS model. An international economic sector models commodity trade flows between each pair of GLOBUS countries. And a government sector simulates budgetary processes of revenue generation and resource allocation. Hence, the overall model may be characterized as a representation of national governments operating within the four aforementioned environments.

This chapter concentrates entirely upon the description and theoretical specification of the trade algorithm within the international economic sector of GLOBUS. We proceed from a statement of world problems in the area of international trade, and develop a conceptual construct for the study of such questions employing a formal model. At the same time, this conceptualization takes account of the fact that the trade model must be integrated with all other GLOBUS sectors. We then present the formal specification of the model, including its grounding in international trade theory as well as the incorporation of political determinants. Next, the derivation of the estimatable form of the model is put forward. Only preliminary estimation results are presented, as these tasks are just now being undertaken. In sum, this chapter is meant to illustrate how complex global political and economic problems can be represented in a formal model, how the parameters of such a model may be estimated from observed data, and what preliminary parameter estimates are for one nation in our larger study.

Again, the key characteristics of the GLOBUS model include the explicit representation of nation-states as acting units, the incorporation of political variables as determinants of economic processes, the representation of political processes (such as conflict, cooperation, instability, and budget determination), and the tracing of the political consequences of the interrelationships.

These unique characteristics of our group's approach require that the trade model have certain basic characteristics. A representation of national (rather than regional) imports and exports is obviously necessary. And more specifically, because political relations among nations (such as conflict, cooperation, and alignment) occur on a bilateral basis, so must our representation of trade flows. Our substantive interest in the reciprocal influence of political and economic relations on one another places further demands upon us. For example, economic exchanges in specific areas such as food, energy, or armaments may have major implications for the strategic strength or vulnerability of particular states or alliance groups. And the current development debate between North and South is significantly focused upon the potential which current or alternative world orders offer to Third World countries to alter the commodity content of their trade. Specifically, developing countries seek to shift away from the production and export of primary commodities and to capture larger shares of global markets in manufactured goods. They view the international trade regime as a vehicle through which their own interests in development and the distributional (terms-of-trade) implications of exchange may be enhanced. Therefore, to capture adequately the stresses and strains which the world will confront during the coming decades in the area of international trade, it is equally clear that our simulation model must represent specific commodities and the terms of their exchange.

Our demands, then, are formidable: our model of international trade must be nation-specific, dyad-specific, and commodity-specific. And the structure of international trade (in terms of who trades with whom and in what relative volume, the commodity content of trade, and the terms of the exchange) must be modeled as having political determinants as well as political consequences.

Global Stresses and Strains Relating to International Trade Relations

We have identified three major international issue areas pertaining to trade relations which define likely areas of global stress during the coming decades. The first pertains to the resurgence of *protectionism* during the past decade and its possible continuation. Which countries might be most hurt by increased barriers to trade? By contrast, do all participants in an open system benefit equally? Relations among the industrially advanced nations of the West are most directly (but by no means exclusively) affected by the issue. These nations have provided the impetus behind the liberalization of the postwar trade system. By the same token, protectionist political response by these same countries — either to domestic pressure from beleaguered industries and unions, or as international retaliation to barriers erected by others — could destroy this same system. The extent to which the trade system becomes increasingly open (liberal) or increasingly closed (protectionist) will likely be a major point of political contention with significant economic consequences.

A second source of stress pertains to the issue of *distribution*. The North–South debate on a New International Economic Order addresses itself both to the distribution of the benefits generated by trade (terms of trade) as well as to the global distribution of economic activity (the division of labor). Different strategies have been proposed to restructure trade relations in a way that would foster Third World development. Commodity stabilization plans, tariff preference schemes, and self-reliance policies have widely different implications for North–South politics. What we do not yet have is a comprehensive picture of the consequences or feasibility of these strategies.

The third major area of stress involves *East–West relations*. Will the West choose confrontation or conciliation in its foreign economic policy toward the Soviet Union? Will increasing Western European dependence on Soviet energy undermine the Atlantic Alliance? Can the Soviet Union continue to meet the energy needs of Eastern Europe? Will the Eastern European and Soviet need for hard currency engender trade ties with the West that undermine COMECON? These questions highlight the fact that trade flows are significantly affected by relations within and between East and West blocs and that trade will likely remain an instrument of foreign policy.

To apply our simulation model to the study of questions in these three issue areas, we shall aggregate the individually specified bilateral commodity flows to provide information on six trade indicators:

(1) export baskets: the percentage breakdown of the total exports of each country by commodity;
(2) market shares: the percentage of world exports in each of the six commodity markets held by each country;
(3) partner and commodity concentration: separate indices varying between 0.0 (perfect diversification of trade) and 1.0 (total concentration of trade in one good or with one partner);
(4) group patterns: a description of the relative volume of trade (on a commodity-specific basis where relevant) within and between members of the OECD, COMECON, and the Group of 77;
(5) trade volume: total imports and exports, in real money terms, for each of the 25 modeled countries;
(6) distribution indicators: selected indices of changing relative prices between specific commodities (such as primary goods vs. manufactures), and a measure of trade "gain" relating to the increase in goods available for consumption due to trade.

Table 4.1 displays selected questions relating to six trade indicators to the three major issue areas we have identified.

Relevant Economic Literature and Trade-Theoretic Foundations of Our Model

We are presently constructing a dynamic simulation model of bilateral trade flows among 25 countries in six commodities plus services. The determinants of these trade flows include political as well as economic factors, and the values of these variables will vary during model runs according to developments in other model sectors. Since a model with these characteristics has never before been constructed, we cannot base our work upon any single research tradition or body of literature. Nor will our final product closely resemble existing efforts in empirical trade theory and modeling. Nevertheless, we are basing our work as much as possible upon the conventional economic wisdom in this area, while drawing upon diverse efforts in political science concerned with the relationship between trade and politics. Subsequent sections of this paper will discuss the incorporation of political determinants, and so we will presently comment upon economic literatures which inform our efforts.

The large majority of trade models specify the flow of goods as a function of income (or demand) and relative prices. Several models sharing this common approach have been quite comprehensively

TABLE 4.1 Sample Questions Relating Model Output to Substantive Issue Area

	Output Variables					
Trade Issue Area	Export Baskets	Market Shares, Market Structure	Partner and Commodity Concentration vs. Diversification	Group Patterns	Trade Volume	Distribution (gain from trade and terms of trade)
Open vs. Closed Trade System (Liberalism vs. "New Protectionism") (mainly North–North stress)	—Increasing market specialization in production and trade under an open system?	—Increasing market concentration with specialization?	—Does an open system have higher concentration than a closed system? —Is a global division of labor thrown into higher relief?	—Diversion of trade flows according to sphere of influence under a closed system?	—Volume decline through protectionism esp. FRG and Japan?	—Welfare effects of New Protectionism?
NIEO Proposals —Engagement —Disengagement (mainly North–South stress)	—Can South decrease dependence on primary commodity exports? —Are export earnings more stable with a diversified export basket?	—Are Lima targets attainable? Desirable?	—Can both forms of trade concentration be decreased as desired?	—Can South redirect its own trade?	—Which LDCs increase exports? —Do certain strategies significantly affect global volume?	—How will NIEO "gains" be distributed to members? —Do North–South terms of trade follow desired pattern?
Political Alignment and Tension (mainly East–West stress)	—How does commodity composition of exports vary with polarity?	—How does alignment relate to market structure in selected commodities (e.g. arms)?	—Partner concentration increase, commodity concentration decrease, as alignment and tensions rise?	—Under what conditions are either the WTO or NATO weakened? —Does world trade system dissolve along blocs lines as polarity increases?	—Are alignment and tension more a barrier to trade for some than for others?	—Can we assess trade "costs" of alignment?

reviewed by Magee (1975). Meanwhile, related econometric and simulation representations of international trade networks have been summarized, compared, and reviewed by Fair (1979) and Pollins (1982). These reviews reveal some relevant points for our own modeling work. First, very few models represent the gross flow of imports and exports for each state or region in the system. Instead, trade is viewed in residual terms; that is, domestic demand for a particular good is subtracted from the domestic production of the same good, and the remainder is deemed the *net* export of the particular state in question. The global marketplace is then represented as a pool to which net export supplies are sent and from which net import demands are filled. However, by aggregating all supply and demand at the global level, the pooled-market design precludes the tracing of bilateral trade flows (i.e., we do not know who is importing from whom). And by treating trade in net or residual terms, we can capture only a part of the picture. This is a particular liability in modeling trade in manufactured goods where a great deal of "intra-industry" trade takes place (i.e., countries may have high imports as well as exports of a good such as automobiles or machinery). The dominant approach to operationalizing the "income and relative price" models, therefore, does not meet our present needs.

Of course, the aforementioned reviews also reveal significant sections of the literature which do not employ net trade, pooled-market operationalizations. And a few examples here merit special attention.

In the early and mid-1960s, Tinbergen (1962), Pöyhönen (1963), and Linnemann (1966) employed a "Gravity" design to model gross, bilateral flows. As the name implies, the trade volume between any two countries was specified as a function of the "size" of each country and the "distance" between them. Size was typically indicated by gross national product and distance was operationalized not only by geography or transportation costs, but by several dummy variables indicating particular political ties between pairs of countries. (Was one a former colony of the other? Do both belong to the same customs union?) This particular work departs from the mainstream not only in its design, but also in its exclusion of prices as a determinant of trade flows.

A more recent example of a gross bilateral trade flow model incorporating both economic and non-economic determinants is the work of the Systems Analysis Research Unit. This model, entitled SARUM (see Parker, 1979) conforms somewhat more closely to existing trade theory in that relative prices as well as income affect bilateral trade flows. It also incorporates non-economic effects such as historical, cultural, and political ties with other economic determinants such as transportation cost and commercial policy in an empirically measured component of trade "bias." The SARUM effort, in our opinion, was a significant advance in the field of global modeling in general, and trade modeling in particular. And the design employed by SARUM meets many of the key needs of our own problem focus. But the political content of "bias" coefficients was never specified or modeled, and the linkages to existing trade theory have been left unidentified.

In the context of the existing designs which have been briefly discussed, let us now consider our own approach in greater detail. As we have set for ourselves the task of modeling bilateral trade flows in six commodities between 25 countries, one potential approach would be to specify each possible flow as a separate equation. The specification of Japanese oil imports from Saudi Arabia, for example, could look very different — in variables as well as parameters — from an equation specifying Japanese oil imports from Venezuela. Because the representation of bilateral trade flows is a complicated business, approaches similar to this have indeed been employed (Linnemann, 1966; Onishi, 1978; Ranuzzi, 1981).

However, for reasons of theoretical parsimony (as well as later computational simplicity), we wish to impose a common structural specification upon the 3,600 commodity flows ($= 25 \times 24 \times 6$) in our model. Furthermore, whatever independent variables we choose to explain these flows, they should be unambiguously divisible into economic and non-economic (including political) determinants for analytic reasons.

One further problem must be mentioned. While existing trade flow models typically identify (1) a specific good, (2) the buyer (or importing country), and (3) the seller (or exporting country), the specific good of any seller is usually considered by economists to be a perfect substitute for the same good offered by any other seller in the market. In other words, goods are not really differentiated according to their country of origin, and the implicit elasticity of substitution is infinite. But given our ultimate interest in the influence of political relationships upon trade flows, we must now contend on a priori grounds that the goods offered by our 25 sellers in any particular market are not perfect substitutes for one another (e.g., to a Soviet buyer, Chinese manufactured goods will not be viewed as a perfect substitute for East German manufactured goods). In one sense, we are introducing a "market imperfection" of a very specific kind. We are contending at the outset that dyadic political (as well as historical, cultural, geographical, and perhaps contractual) relations will lead each buyer to discriminate between goods in a particular market according to their country of origin. Our rejection of the assumption of perfect substitutability requires a different general theory of demand for our trade model than those which are more commonly used. And this point deserves careful consideration.

A theory of demand which does meet our requirements has been constructed by Paul S. Armington (1969), and this formulation provides the cornerstone for the model we are presently constructing. Armington's work addresses two major problems in the international trade literature, one theoretical and one applied. The theoretical problem is to derive demand functions which assume that all products in a particular market are not perfect substitutes for one another. The applied problem is to construct the formulation in a way which does not require the unique specification of each bilateral flow in a commodity-specific, dyadic trade model. Armington accomplishes this by beginning with a general Hicksian model of demand in which the import demand of a particular country for a given good from a specific supplying country is made a function of income and relative prices. The key simplifying assumption made by Armington is a constant elasticity of substitution (CES) between potential supplying countries. This CES assumption reduces the number of parameters which must be estimated and, as we will later see, clarifies the role played by non-economic (including political) influences on bilateral trade flows. In equational form, Armington's demand function for any given importer is written:

$$M_{ij} = b_{ij}^{\sigma_i} M_i^{1,\sigma} \left(\frac{P_{ij}}{P_i^*} \right)^{-\sigma_i}, \tag{1}$$

where:

M_{ij} = real imports of country i from country j
M_i = total real imports by country i
P_{ij} = export price offered by country j to country i
P_i^* = average or "world" price seen by country i
σ_i = elasticity of substitution between suppliers
b_{ij} = constant term

(For a full derivation of this demand function, the reader is referred to Armington, 1969.)

The choice of an income variable (M_i) and relative prices as economic determinants of bilateral flows places this formulation in the mainstream of the empirical literature on trade (Warner and Kreinin, 1980: 2; Magee, 1975). But the CES assumption has two distinct advantages over more common formulations. First, only one elasticity per market must be estimated. Because the substitution elasticity is constant, we need now estimate only 150 (= 25 × 6) elasticities rather than 3,600 (= 25 × 24 × 6). Second, and more importantly for our theoretical construct, this formulation permits the relatively unambiguous isolation of non-economic influences upon trade flows in the following way: were we to follow the more common "brute force" method of estimating bilateral flows (where each possible flow is estimated individually, yielding unique parameters), the non-economic influences would potentially manifest themselves in all parameters in the equation (Ranuzzi, 1981: 163–165). Czechoslovakia's strong preference for Soviet arms, for example, would likely manifest itself in a *substitution* parameter which was highly inelastic. Similarly, the respective *income* elasticities between two members of the European Community could well reflect higher trade creation effects than those between any other pair of countries not sharing membership in an economic union. And finally, the *constant* term would possibly pick up other non-economic effects such as inertia or history (Choucri and North, 1975: 170). But in Armington's formulation the substitution elasticities are held constant for each commodity across all bilateral relations; we in effect "force" the non-economic variables to manifest themselves in the constant term alone. Meanwhile, the market-specific substitution elasticities may possibly be interpreted as an indicator of concentration or monopoly power in that market (Ranuzzi, 1981: 165). Hence, the foundation is laid for the identification of political determinants in two ways: goods are distinguished by their place of origin and recognized as imperfect substitutes for one another; and the effects of major economic determinants (income and relative prices) are unambiguously separated from political and other determinants.

Given the Armington formulation, we may think of the major economic variables as determining the *shape* of the demand curve while the non-economic (including political) determinants determine the *location* of the curve. In terms of Figure 4.1, then, we hypothesize that any given country would find its demand curve at D' rather than D if its relations with a specific exporter are particularly friendly. Likewise, the same country could find the demand curve at D'' if relations are hostile. And in this formulation, political relations have tangible economic consequences. As Figure 4.1 also illustrates, price offer p results in purchases of quantity q_1 for the "neutral" pair while the same price results in quantity q_2 for the "friendly" nation pair and quantity q_3 for the "hostile" dyad. Of course, a wide variety of factors determines the intercept in the Armington formulation. Linguistic and cultural

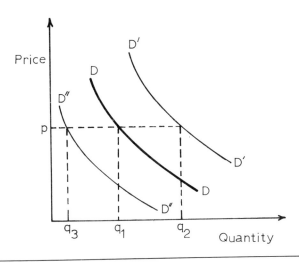

Figure 4.1 Armington-based Demand Curves Under Different Political Conditions

ties, geographic distance, and "supply-side" economic effects (such as the exporter's capacity and willingness to export) can play a role. It is simply our contention that political relations between an importer and exporter will be one significant determinant of the location of the importer's demand curve.

Specification of Political Determinants

To identify and measure the effects of political relations upon international trade flows, we may first turn to a wide-ranging literature which has approached this question from a variety of perspectives. None of this work has been concerned with modeling or explaining trade flows themselves (as we must), but the theoretical and empirical efforts to specify the effects of trade flows and political ties upon each other provide a solid starting point for our own efforts. The best known segment of this literature is concerned with the effects of trade ties upon political dependence. The seminal work in this area is A. O. Hirschmann's 1945 book, *National Power and the Structure of Foreign Trade*. Subsequently, Neil Richardson (1978) found limited evidence of foreign policy compliance among states which were trade-dependent. A second branch of this literature employs trade flows as an indicator of political integration (Russett, 1967). Earlier work on this question by Savage and Deutsch (1960) also constructed a "Relative Acceptance" indicator which bears conceptual similarity to our chosen means for measuring political determinants of trade flows. Of most direct relevance to the task at hand is a third segment of this literature, which examines political factors influencing trade flows. John Roemer (1977) found that hegemonic states tended to export a disproportionately high share of goods from their declining industries to recipients within their own political sphere of influence. Ruth Arad and Seev Hirsch (1981) have explored the theoretical effects of a cessation of hostilities between two countries upon trade creation and trade diversion. Finally, S. W. Polachek (1980) has attempted to measure empirically the reciprocal relationship between dyadic conflict and cooperation and trade ties using bilateral event flows contained in Azar's (1980) COPDAB data set.

Much of this work is highly suggestive, but we are left with the task of integrating it where possible, and linking those ideas to our model of bilateral trade flows. No one who has modeled international trade flows has attempted to specify their political determinants, and at the same time, no one who has theoretically or empirically attempted to link political variables to trade has modeled the trade flows themselves.

The unique character of our task requires us to carefully lay the foundation for the trade model which we integrate into GLOBUS. In this area, theoretical specification and empirical estimation is an iterative process, not a linear one. As our theory informs our empirical work, so will our results inform further specification and refinement of our model. The work we are now undertaking may be characterized as a multi-path and multi-method strategy. The first path involves the empirical "discovery" of political determinants in a well-defined economic model of trade, while a second path concentrates on the direct incorporation of selected political variables into a trade flow model. Before discussing estimation procedures and final model specification in greater detail, let us examine each of these two distinct tasks in turn.

As we saw above, the work of Armington provides us with a framework which separates key economic determinants of bilateral trade flows (i.e., relative prices and income or import demand) from other determinants. These other factors, which will determine the constant in Armington's equation, could include:

(1) friendly or hostile actions of one country toward another;
(2) the general political affinity or enmity between two countries;
(3) co-membership in an economic union such as the European Community, LAFTA, or COMECON;

(4) linguistic, cultural, or former colonial ties between countries;
(5) geographic distance separating them.

All of these characteristics of any given dyad are measurable, and the first three are of particular interest to us because they involve politically determined choices which remain policy-manipulable.

The first part of our strategy, then, is to estimate the parameters of Armington's equation for all possible pairs of GLOBUS countries. This will yield values for the constant term (which we may term "bias," following SARUM) for each dyad. These constants may then be employed as the dependent variable in an equation where the aforementioned non-economic determinants are the independent variables. This effort may be viewed as "unpacking" the constant in the Armington equation and "discovering" the role of political variables (the first three on our list) in determining the location of Armington's demand curve (*D*) in Figure 4.1.

Measurement of three of the aforementioned bias determinants is quite straightforward. Linguistic, cultural, or former colonial ties, as well as co-membership in an economic union, are treated as dummy variables. And geographic distance between states is measured as the great circle distance between their capital cities. The measurement of political affinity and political actions is designed to conform to the work of other GLOBUS team members. Political affinity will be measured as an index of similarity of the alliance patterns of the two countries in question. The USA and Britain, for example, would score high on the political affinity index since they are allied with many of the same countries; correspondingly, the West German–Soviet dyad would receive a low score. In GLOBUS, dyadic political interactions are measured as a quadripartite reclassification of events coded on Azar's 15-point conflict–cooperation scale. These event data are now recorded for each dyad as the quarterly accumulation of verbal cooperation, verbal conflict, non-verbal cooperation, and non-verbal conflict (see Ward, 1982b). In equational form, then,

$$b_{ij} = \beta_0 + \beta_1 PA_{ij} - \beta_2 NVC_{ij} - \beta_3 NNC_{ij} + \beta_4 EU_{ij} + \beta_5 CLC_{ij} - \beta_6 GD_{ij} + \epsilon_{ij} \qquad (2)$$

where:

b_{ij} = bias of nation i toward imports from nation j (i.e., the constant from the estimation of the Armington equation)

PA_{ij} = political affinity index (similarity of the alliance patterns of nations i and j)

NVC_{ij} = net verbal conflict (accumulation of verbal conflict events received by i from j minus the corresponding accumulation of verbal cooperative events)

NNC_{ij} = net non-verbal conflict (the similar net accumulation of dyadic non-verbal events)

EU_{ij} = economic union (a dummy variable indicating co-membership in organizations such as the European Community or LAFTA)

CLC_{ij} = cultural, linguistic, or former colonial ties (also a dummy variable)

GD_{ij} = geographic distance (inter-capital great circle distance).

This particular effort is important to the grounding of our model in two ways. First, it requires the estimation of Armington's equation, which to our knowledge has not yet been attempted (see Magee, 1975). Second, the unpacking of the bias coefficient should contribute to the small empirical literature associating political relations with trade flows. The distinguishing feature of our contribution in this area is that the major economic components are separated from the political determinants through Armington's formulation.

But this groundwork is not sufficient for our modeling needs. We cannot employ the simple single-equation specification of the unpacked bias coefficient directly in our model because it describes a static characterization of the relationship, while our model envisions a dynamic, continuous interplay between changing policies and political relations, and dyadic trade flows. In estimating the Armington equation itself (which will be discussed in greater detail in the next section) we will employ time-series data, and this implies, of course, that we will then have only one estimated value for the bias coefficient for each directed dyad over the estimation period. When the bias coefficient is then made the dependent variable, the time-varying determinants in equation (2) must be accumulated over an identical period. This part of the analysis, then, will not properly identify the role of political determinants in our overall trade model because we are really performing a cross-sectional rather than an intertemporal analysis. Our overall model, meanwhile, contends that political determinants must be specifically identified in a fully dynamic context.

This brings us to the second task in our specification and estimation strategy. Here, we will directly incorporate the key political aspects of a dyadic relationship into the determination of the trade flows between them. Specifically, we are speaking of the policy-manipulable variables relating to conflict, cooperation, affinity, and economic union co-membership. As our basic model of dyadic trade flows remains that of

Armington, what we propose here is the direct addition of political variables to Armington's formulation. To do so, consider again the full constant in Armington's original equation: $b_{ij}^{\sigma_i}$. We may again "unpack" this constant according to the types of components described above, yielding:

$$b_{ij}^{\sigma_i} = f(CC_{ij}, PA_{ij}, EU_{ij}, b'_{ij})^{\sigma_i}, \tag{3}$$

$$= f(CC_{ij}^{\sigma_i}, PA_{ij}^{\sigma_i}, EU_{ij}^{\sigma_i}, b'^{\sigma_i}_{ij}) \tag{4}$$

where:

$b_{ij}^{\sigma_i}$ = Armington's constant

CC_{ij} = dyadic conflict and cooperation indicators such as NVC and NNC

PA_{ij} = political affinity index, as in equation (2)

EU_{ij} = economic union dummy, as in equation (2)

b'_{ij} = all other components of bias (aforementioned "supply-side" effects, geographic distance, cultural, linguistic, historical ties).

We have thus unpacked the constant in a way which separates those components which are of particular interest to us, which are time-varying, and which are policy-manipulable from those non-economic elements (linguistic, cultural, historical ties, and geographic distance) which can be more meaningfully interpreted as true constants in a dynamic formulation.

We are now ready to bring politics directly into Armington's formulation. Let us succinctly state our maintained hypotheses in this regard. We contend that imports of any country from a particular exporter will respond to total import demand, relative prices, and particular political relations. More specifically, imports will covary with the number and salience of conflictual and cooperative events received by the importer from the exporter (as Soviet imports of US products rose during the period of détente and declined as hostility between these two powers increased again). Similarly, imports will vary with the level of, and changes in, the index of political affinity between two states (as Egypt's import pattern shifted from East to West with Sadat's post-1973 realignment). And a discrete change in membership in an economic union will result in a shift in the imports of the relevant states. In equational form,

$$M_{ij} = b'^{\sigma_i}_{ij} M_i \left(\frac{P_{ij}}{P_i} \right)^{-\sigma_i} CC_{ij}^{\sigma_i \beta_1} PA_{ij}^{\sigma_i \beta_2} EU_{ij}^{\sigma_i \beta_3}, \tag{5}$$

where:

M_{ij}	= real imports of nation i from nation j
M_i	= total real imports by nation i
P_{ij}	= export price offered to i by j
P_i	= average price offered to i by all
b'_{ij}	= effect of other economic variables, and "bias" variables which are not policy-manipulable (such as geographic distance)
σ_i	= substitution elasticity
CC_{ij}	= dyadic conflict–cooperation indicator as in equation (4)
PA_{ij}	= dyadic political affinity indicator as in equation (4)
EU_{ij}	= economic union co-membership dummy (1 = no, 2 = yes)
$\beta_1, \beta_2, \beta_3$	= elasticity of imports to changes in political relations.

Equation (5) then, is Armington's formulation (see equation (1) for comparison) with the constant unpacked in a very specific way, as illustrated in equations (2)–(4). Particular attention should now be given to the exponents on the three political terms in the equation ($CC_{ij}, PA_{ij}, EU_{ij}$). The beta term in the exponent defines the responsiveness of imports to a change in political relations (e.g. the decline in Soviet imports of US goods resulting from a hostile statement made by President Reagan). At the same time, however, the elasticity of substitution (σ_i) must be distributed over these political components as they have been "unpacked" from the original bias term in Armington's formulation, which was itself necessarily raised to σ_i in his derivation. This combination has a straightforward and elegant substantive interpretation: the "political response" (β_1) to a change in conflict relations will be tempered by the ease with which an importer may shift its purchases from one exporter to another (σ_i). The total effect depends upon the interaction of these two. Japan, for example, may shift very few oil imports away from Saudi Arabia despite receiving frequent hostile messages from the Saudis because of the relative inelasticity of substitution in the oil market. Similarly, the Chinese — assuming a similar barrage of hostility from the USA and a similar "sensitivity" to such hostility — might shift their imports of manufactured goods from the USA to Japan or West Germany quite readily owing to a relatively high elasticity of substitution in that market. The important point is that our formulation explicitly identifies the political as well as the economic determinants in trade flows, and does so in the parameters as well as the variables.

Our earlier interpretation of the Armington equation as a demand curve (see again Figure 4.1) may now be reconsidered. Our addition of three new determinants adds three dimensions to the definition of the overall demand surface. But any such *n*-dimensional surface may be viewed in two dimensions where one chosen variable defines the shape of the curve and all other variables act as shift factors, defining the location of the curve at a particular point in time. Hence, as before, we may view relative prices as determining the shape of the demand curve (*D*) in Figure 4.1, while changing political relations will, over time, move the curve outward toward *D'* or inward toward *D''*. In other words, instead of viewing the demand curve as fixed in one particular place for a given dyad, we may now view it as "floating" inward or outward as political relations change over time.

One important task remains before our model specification is complete. We must define the model in truly dynamic terms. Were we to declare equations (5) or (1) to be the fully dynamic representation of trade flows, we would be making important implicit statements about the dynamics of that system: namely, that each observation of the system captures the system "at rest," or in equilibrium. We would also be implicitly asserting that the system adjusts instantaneously to all changes. However, we believe precisely the opposite. That is, we assert that there is no instantaneous adjustment to change; the system is forever in flux and not at rest. And therefore, any observation we make is a "snapshot" of a system in continual movement. If our model specification does not explicitly take into account our assumptions regarding the nature of the dynamics, our estimations will not properly identify the parameters. For example, an estimation of equation (5) might show a particular country's imports to be highly price-inelastic, when in fact its imports could be highly responsive to price changes, but contractual obligations or lags in orders and deliveries might not allow that price reponsiveness to show itself until some length of time has passed; hence the actual price elasticity of imports would not be identified.

Since the above equations are implicitly written as continuous-time representations (the time subscript being excluded for simplicity), the dynamics are represented by differential rather than difference equations. The process itself is viewed as a partial adjustment mechanism. Equations (1) or (5) define the equilibrium or desired level of real imports by country *i*. If the actual level of imports differs from the desired level, this initiates a change which may be fast or slow depending upon the parameter α. For a number of reasons, we view the adjustment mechanism as a proportional one and so utilize a natural logarithmic representation:

$$D \ln M_{ij} = \alpha \ln \left(\frac{M_{ij}^*}{M_{ij}} \right), \qquad (6)$$

where M_{ij}^* is either equation (1) or (5), D is the differential operator, and ln is in the natural logarithm operator. The adjustment speed α also has a lag interpretation: $1/\alpha$ is the time needed for approximately 63 percent of the system's adjustment to take place. Unlike the parameters defining M_{ij}^*, the value of α depends upon our unit of time, for example, whether our time period is monthly or yearly. Some other implications of the chosen adjustment mechanism are discussed below.

Model Estimation

As mentioned earlier, we are undertaking a two-step research program. The first step is to estimate the parameters of the basic Armington model in continuous time. This is an important step in its own right, for, to the best of our knowledge, no one has ever empirically estimated an Armington system. More specifically, it is of central importance that we empirically test Armington's assumption of a constant elasticity of substitution (CES) between all potential trade partners in each importer's own trade system. As we discussed above, it is precisely this CES assumption which will later permit the proper identification of the effects of political variables in global trade relations.

The second step in our program, of course, will be the explicit incorporation of those political variables into our estimation equation. This paper will report upon our early results from step one.

As our paper is very much a progress report (but one with interest in its own right), we have decided to concentrate here on reporting estimates of a simple Armington system for the USA. Given the available data, we focus only on aggregate import flows rather than on six separate commodities. Moreover, in order to develop the estimation technique, we focus only on the more simple equation (1) representation. In other words, over the estimation period we assume that the political determinants are not time-varying.

The first point is to note that equation (1), defining desired imports, may be written in several ways. The equation represents a demand for a volume or quantity of imports. If we multiply both sides by P_{ij}/P_i, it represents the demand for nominal imports:

$$P_{ij} M_{ij} = b_{ij}^{\sigma_i} P_i M_i \left(\frac{P_{ij}}{P_i} \right)^{1 - \sigma_i} \tag{7}$$

Observe that equation (7) can also be written as a share equation since we may divide throughout by $P_i M_i$. In order to minimize data errors, we utilize this equation in our estimations.

Once we view equation (7) as a share equation, several other properties are apparent. As prices are always measured as indices, the ratio of prices will always be unity at the base period (1970 in our case). Hence the summation of the constants over all countries must equal unity; that is, all shares must add to the total:

$$\sum_{j=1}^{n} b_{ij} = 1.0.$$

Nothing is lost, therefore, by dropping the exponent on the constant.

Another feature is now apparent. Because import shares must add up to total imports, we are now dealing with a system in which all equations are linked *by definition*. Put another way, if we under-estimate the share of US imports held by one trade partner, we *must* overestimate the share held by another, for all shares must add to total US imports. Hence, if we add a disturbance term ϵ_i to equation (7), it is clear that:

$$\sum_{i=1}^{n} \epsilon_i = 0.$$

Not all equations of the system can, therefore, be estimated; at least one must be eliminated or the system will be determined. But something else is also implied: important information about the equations is now obtained by knowing how the disturbances covary across equations. In other words, we must estimate all the share equations for a given importer simultaneously as a system. The system for estimation can now be written as:

$$D \ln V_{ij} = \alpha \ln \left(\frac{V^*_{ij}}{V_{ij}} \right) + \epsilon_i$$

$$V^*_{ij} = b^{\sigma_i}_{ij} V_i \left(\frac{P_{ij}}{P_i} \right)^{1-\sigma_i}$$

(8)

where V represents the nominal equivalent of real imports (M) as in equation (1). (Note: because any given importer has N partners, system (8) will contain $N - 1$ equations.)

System (8) is a theoretical system, and as noted above is written in continuous time. Observations on the system, however, are discrete. Therefore, for estimation purposes system (8) must be carefully transformed into a discrete-time approximation of the continuous-time model. The distinction between the theoretical model and its estimating form is at the heart of "continuous-time econometrics" which is well described in Gandolfo (1981) and Bergstrom (1976). Very briefly, the equations of system (8) are integrated over a sampling period and the following approximations used:

$$\int_{t}^{t+\tau} D V_{ij} dt = \Delta V_{ij},$$

$$\int_{t}^{t+\tau} V_{ij} dt \cong M V_{ij},$$

where M is the moving average operator $\frac{1}{2}(1 + L)$ and L is the lag operator. Any single equation in system (8) is therefore approximated by:

$$\Delta \ln V_{ij} = \alpha \sigma_i \ln b_{ij} - \alpha M \ln V_i + \alpha(1 - \sigma_i) M \ln \left(\frac{P_{ij}}{P_i} \right) \qquad (9)$$

$$- \alpha M \ln V_{ij} - \eta_i.$$

Again, V represents nominal imports and M is the moving average operator. Note that η depends on ϵ and on the errors of approximation. If ϵ is serially uncorrelated then so is η. However, equation (9) holds only if variables are measurable at any given instant. Our data on imports, however, are not measured at an instant, but represent an accumulated flow over a period. Moreover, prices are actually measured as period averages. We therefore have to integrate the model a second time, and this introduces a moving average component into the disturbance term. However, unlike stochastic time-dependent pathologies, this moving average component is analytically derivable, and we can therefore appropriately transform our data in a manner equivalent to Cochran–Orchutt.

The estimating model is therefore represented by system (9) with the exception that the variables are transformed. All data transformations and estimates have utilized Clifford Wymer's Resimul package which is specifically written for continuous-time estimates. The package is described in Gandolfo (1981). Our data comprise yearly observations from 1960 to 1975, and data sources, etc., are described in Pollins (1984). In order to avoid an extremely complex and probably impractical estimation problem, the aggregate price variable P_i has been approximated by a share-weighted average of all prices (following Armington, 1969). This will have the effect of downwardly biasing the price elasticity, σ_i.

A final caveat regarding the data must be noted. System (9) must be estimated using a maximum likelihood estimator in order to incorporate the restrictions between and within equations (e.g., the same σ_i appears in all equations), in addition to the covariance matrix of the error terms of the equations. However, a maximum likelihood estimator is contingent on the number of observations being greater than the total number of variables (both predetermined and exogenous) entering the model. After data transformations we have 11 data points, and this would enable us to estimate only a very small system. As most of the interest is in the larger system, we have interpolated our data series quadratically and transformed our yearly observations into a larger number of quarterly observations. This procedure is merely statistical, since quadratic interpolation does not add any information to the yearly series as linear interpolation would. Within these restrictions, as many as 14 of the major trading partners of the USA were able to be included, thus obtaining a more realistic "global" picture of trade share developments.

Table 4.2 reports our full-information maximum likelihood (FIML) parameter estimates for the 14-equation system. One must be careful in using t-statistics since the standard errors of the parameters can be estimated only asymptotically. Nevertheless, the ratio of a parameter to its asymptotic standard error does reveal important information about the model. With this in mind, Table 4.2 indicates that the share of US imports held by a country is indeed sensitive to its relative price position. The elasticity of substitution (σ_i) between partner countries or nationally identified "goods" is higher than many empirical studies on price sensitivity in trade, and it is reasonable to expect that our estimate is downwardly biased by the high level of product aggregation in our data. This supports our contention that non-dynamic trade models have not properly identified the effects of changing prices in the world trade system. Moreover, the fact that the value of σ_i is greater than unity indicates that both real and nominal import shares are sensitive to relative prices, something which is very important for balance of payments and employment policy on the part of exporters. For those who might think that the value of our price parameter is not terribly novel, we would point to the great difficulties that all demand studies usually have in identifying significant price effects. There can be little doubt that relative prices are very important in our model. Another interpretation is also in line with our results. If, for example, South African exports were to decrease through measures other than a full embargo, then South Africa could restore its export position, ceteris paribus, by "changing" its relative price position. This is one

TABLE 4.2 FIML Estimates of Parameters for US Import Equation System, 1960–1975

General Parameter	Estimate	Mean Lag in Quarters	t-statistic: Ratio of Parameter to Asymptotic Standard Errors
σ_i	1.64		34.89
Canada			
α	0.049	20.4	4.50
b	−0.084		2.98
Mexico			
α	0.040	25.0	5.46
b	−0.353		7.69
Venezuela			
α	0.035	28.6	4.12
b	−0.281		3.45
Brazil			
α	0.074	13.5	14.60
b	−0.532		23.31
UK			
α	0.043	23.3	4.32
b	−0.312		8.74
France			
α	0.057	17.5	8.52
b	−0.428		16.60
Germany			
α	0.079	12.7	12.02
b	−0.302		15.70
Italy			
α	0.049	20.4	3.27
b	−0.355		7.32
Nigeria			
α	0.039	25.6	6.12
b	−0.413		2.90
South Africa			
α	0.075	13.3	13.96
b	−0.646		23.68
Iran			
α	0.061	16.4	9.06
b	−0.554		5.72
Saudi Arabia			
α	0.070	14.3	7.87
b	−0.633		6.61
Japan			
α	0.068	14.7	4.26
b	−0.173		5.76
Indonesia			
α	0.044	22.7	4.87
b	−0.471		5.51

Carter–Nager System $R^2 = 0.6299$
$X^2 = 29$; d.o.f. $= 1069$; significance <0.01

Note: the constants, b, are reported in their natural log form.

example of how the interaction of political and economic factors may be analyzed within our framework.

The next key feature of our results reported in Table 4.2 concerns the low but statistically significant adjustment coefficients, α, associated with each partner country. Import shares are indeed affected by relative prices but the lags are considerable. The mean lag for most countries, we find, is approximately 17 quarters, or more than four years. This seems to be long, and raises some suspicions that the growth rate of US imports is biasing the speed of adjustment toward this growth rate. However, the extent of such bias will not be dramatic, for we know that the quarterly growth rate of US imports over this period was only 0.7 percent. We shall return to this point below. Again, the values of our estimates of the adjustment coefficients, or mean lags, support our general approach, for they reveal a great deal of inertia in the trade system. Yes, the USA is responding to changing prices, but it takes a great deal of time to adjust fully. A trade model which is not specified in continuous time will confound these effects and fail to properly identify the role of prices as well as the partner preferences we have termed "trade bias."

The third set of parameters comprises the constant terms: b_{ij}. Being in logarithmic form, they should be negative since they must be less than unity. This is so in all cases, but when they are added (in antilog) they sum to greater than unity. A possible explanation of this problem is straightforward: if US imports are growing at a rate g and relative prices remain constant, then, ceteris paribus, each country's imports will grow at this rate. We could therefore write system (8) as:

$$D \ln V_{ij} = \alpha \ln \left(\frac{V^*_{ij}}{V_{ij}} \right) + g,$$

from which it follows that there are two constants in the equation, each individually unidentified. When we impose a plausible value for g, the summation of all b_{ij} is nearer to expectation, and indeed, they do sum to a value less than 1.0. We could also constrain the system estimation procedure to impose this adding-up condition, but such fine-grained polishing of our parameter estimates is not yet warranted, given that we must first bring the political variables into our estimations. This step alone should significantly affect estimation bias and efficiency.

Finally, we should consider the properties of the estimated system. Table 4.2 reports the system R^2, which is significant but, importantly, still leaves a great deal to be explained. Of course, it is our hope that the political variables we will soon directly introduce will improve our

TABLE 4.3 Armington Import Equation for the USA: Root Mean Square Errors (RMSE) in Static and Dynamic Forecasts

	Single-Period Forecast RMSE (%)	Dynamic Forecast RMSE (%)
Canada	0.26	0.53
Mexico	0.96	2.47
Venezuela	1.25	4.51
Brazil	0.81	3.04
United Kingdom	0.41	1.78
France	0.55	2.49
W. Germany	0.96	2.54
Italy	0.59	2.97
Nigeria	3.48	9.17
South Africa	1.09	4.87
Iran	3.83	11.17
Saudi Arabia	6.66	18.41
Japan	0.52	1.20
Indonesia	1.82	9.07

overall explanatory power. For present purposes, the system's properties are better illuminated by the forecasting statistics presented in Table 4.3. The system has been forecast over the period 1970–75, or 20 quarters. Given that the imports are in logarithmic form, the root mean square error can be interpreted as a percentage error. For static forecasts, the historical values of the lagged endogenous variables are utilized. Errors are in most cases around 1 percent, but in the case of Saudi Arabia, 6 percent. (Iran is, interestingly, only 3.8 percent.) However, the real test is dynamic forecasting, where only initial values of lagged endogenous variables are utilized. As we would expect, the errors are higher but tolerably so for most countries. The oil producers are clearly the exception, particularly Iran and Saudi Arabia.

The great discrepancy for these countries raises several interesting points. First, we know a priori that many of our "excluded" (i.e. political) variables have greatly changed over the period, thereby biasing our estimates which consider them fixed. However, the "background" (i.e. economic) variables were still important since the static forecasts were generally satisfactory; that is, it is the constant that was shifting, and it is this constant, we argued earlier in this paper, which will pick up all political effects in our formulation.

Second, it is in the nature of our model that changes in these variables for one country must influence all others. Thus, a decrease in willingness or desire to trade with Iran (since both the importer and the exporter are involved) must affect other countries, either positively or negatively, and we see this in the pattern of errors.

This is probably as good a point as any to close the discussion of our preliminary results, for it points to our future work: the incorporation into our estimation work of the political variables discussed above.

Conclusion

We believe that the specification of our trade model takes a significant step in theoretically integrating the trade flow modeling traditions in the fields of economics and political science. While political scientists have often attempted to model bilateral trade flows without taking account of trade theory, economists have rarely employed political determinants in their models. At the level of formal specification, we have now bridged that gap. While we are still far from claiming full success, our initial empirical results, as reported in this paper, appear to support our maintained hypotheses. More specifically, it appears that the Armington framework, which is central to the proper theoretical specification and empirical identification of political effects, is supported, and that specification in continuous time is indeed the proper approach.

Once we complete our estimation tasks, we will have at our disposal an analytical tool of considerable power. A model with such theoretical and empirical grounding, where the interplay of economic and political determinants is so extensively specified, should provide us with unique insights into the long-term hazards, pitfalls, and possibilities related to international trade relations. Knowing a little bit more about the possibility of avoiding a resurgence of protectionism, about the feasibility of restructuring trade relations to promote Third World development, and about the consequences of employing trade ties as a weapon in East–West rivalry must be considered worthwhile.

REFERENCES

ARAD, R. W. and S. HIRSCH (1981) "Peacemaking and vested interests: international economic transactions." International Studies Quarterly 25 (September): 439–468.

ARMINGTON, P. S. (1969) "A theory for the demand for products distinguished by place of production." International Monetary Fund Staff Papers 16: 159–176.

AZAR, E. E. (1980) "The conflict and peace data bank (COPDAB) project." J. of Conflict Resolution 24 (March): 143-152.

BERGSTROM, A. R. [ed.] (1976) Statistical Inference in Continuous Time Economic Models. Amsterdam: North-Holland.

BREMER, S. A. (1981) The GLOBUS Project: Overview and Update. Berlin: Science Center Berlin, International Institute for Comparative Social Research, Discussion Paper IIVG/dp 81–109.

CHOUCRI, N. and R. NORTH (1975) Nations in Conflict: National Growth and International Violence. San Francisco, Calif.: W. H. Freeman.

COLE, H. A. D., C. FREEMAN, M. JAHODA, and K. L. R. PAVITT (1973) Models of Doom: A Critique of the "Limits to Growth." New York: Universe Books.

FAIR, R. (1979) "On modelling the economic linkage in countries," pp. 209–245 in R. Dornbusch and J. Frenkel (eds.), Inter-Economic Policy: Theory and Evidence. Baltimore, Md: Johns Hopkins University Press.

GANDOLFO, G. (1981) Qualitative Analysis and Econometric Estimation of Continuous Time Dynamic Models. Amsterdam: North-Holland.

HIRSCHMANN, A. O. (1945) National Power and the Structure of Foreign Trade. Berkeley and Los Angeles: University of California Press.

KAYSEN, C. (1972) "The computer that printed out W*O*L*F." Foreign Affairs 50 (July): 660–668.

LINNEMANN, H. (1966) An Econometric Study of International Trade Flows. Amsterdam: North Holland.

MAGEE, S. (1975) "Prices, income, and foreign trade," pp. 175–252 in P. B. Kenan (ed.), International Trade and Finance: Frontiers for Research. Cambridge: Cambridge University Press.

MEADOWS, D. H., D. L. MEADOWS, J. RANDERS, and W. W. BEHRENS III (1972) The Limits to Growth. New York: Universe Books.

NORDHAUS, W. E. (1973) "World dynamics: measurement without data." Economic Journal 83 (December): 1156–1183.

ONISHI, A. (1978) "Technical details of the global macro-economic model." Unpublished paper presented at the Sixth IIASA Global Modelling Conference, Vienna, October 17–20.

PARKER, K. T. (1979) "Modelling inter-regional activity by use of trade biases," pp. 155–165 in J. M. L. Janssen et al. (eds.), Models and Decision Making in National Economies. Amsterdam: North-Holland.

POLACHEK, S. W. (1980) "Conflict and trade." Journal of Conflict Resolution 24 (March): 55–78.

POLLINS, B. M. (1982) "Modeling international trade flows: a survey and comparison of simulation approaches." International Political Science Review 3, 4: 504–533.

————(1984) Codebook for the GLOBUS Dyadic Trade Data. Berlin: Science Center Berlin, International Institute for Comparative Social Research, Research Documentation.

PÖYHÖNEN, P. (1963) 'A tentative model for the volume of trade between countries." Weltwirtschaftliches Archiv 90, 1: 93–100.

RANUZZI, P. (1981) "The experience of the EEC Eurolink Project in modeling bilateral trade linkage equations." Journal of Policy Modeling 3 (May): 153–173.

RICHARDSON, N. R. (1978) Foreign Policy and Economic Dependence. Austin: University of Texas Press.

ROEMER, J. E. (1977) "The effect of sphere of influence and economic distance on the commodity composition of trade in manufactures." Review of Economics and Statistics 59 (August): 318–327.

RUSSETT, B. M. (1967) International Regions and the International System. Chicago, Ill.: Rand McNally.

SAVAGE, I. R. and K. W. DEUTSCH (1960) "A statistical model of the gross analysis of transaction flows." Econometrica 28 (July): 551–572.

TINBERGEN, J. (1962) Shaping the World Economy: Suggestions for an International Economic Policy. New York: Twentieth Century Fund.

WARD, M. D. (1982b) A Model of Conflict and Cooperation Among Contemporary Nation States. Berlin: Science Center Berlin, International Institute for Comparative Social Research, Discussion Paper IIVG/dp 82–109.

WARNER, D. and M. E. KREININ (1980) Determinants of International Trade Flows. Stockholm: University of Stockholm, Institute for International Economic Studies, Seminar Paper No. 161.

CHAPTER 5

SOCIAL TIME

PIERRE ALLAN

In the social sciences we cannot claim to have discovered many regularities that consistently hold over time. A possible reason for this is our uncritical acceptance of calendar time to describe, measure, model, and theorize about social phenomena such as international conflict. This chapter will show, first of all, that our clocks and our time are concepts borrowed from physics. Pointing this out, however, is far from sufficient. The main thrust of the argument is thus to show, concretely and formally, how we can develop social time referentials.

The Problem of Time Referentials

The clocks we use are *physical* ones. What other time can these clocks measure but physical time? Indeed, the clocks are built in such a way that they can only abide by the laws governing them. For example, a clock can be used to predict the position of a falling body, but this is symmetrical: the falling body can just as well be used as a clock to predict the physical state of the original clock. All we have here are two physical phenomena evolving in tandem through time. This, of course, begs the question: what reason is there to expect that all phenomena, especially social ones, should be in a certain sense parallel in duration

AUTHOR'S NOTE: Many people have provided me with constructive criticism on this topic, but for this paper I would like to thank Dina A. Zinnes, Claudio Cioffi-Revilla, Richard L. Merritt, Robert Muncaster, Steven T. Seitz, G. Robert Boynton, and Michael Nicholson for their very stimulating comments and Judith Jones for her editing, though I assume sole responsibility and wish to dissociate them from any wrong interpretations and weaknesses this paper may have. My thanks also go to Eileen Yoder for her efficient typing. The financial support from the George A. Miller Endowment through the Center for Advanced Study, University of Illinois at Urbana-Champaign, is gratefully acknowledged.

to the one determined by physical clocks? None — but for the fact that our notions of physical time are so deeply ingrained.

Our time referentials are directly borrowed from physics. Irregularities found in the evolution of various social processes are ascribed to irregularities in the processes themselves, to a misspecification of the analysis, or to changes in the general setting of these processes. Nobody seems to question the fact that we usually impose on our social processes the condition that they evolve in parallel to a process or concept taken from physics: physical or calendar time. Since our everyday behavior is governed by this physical concept, our reliance on it in studying social phenomena is understandable, but an uncritical application of physical time to social dynamics prevents us from thinking clearly about the latter. This situation is the more disturbing when we realize that, in their search for more elegant theories, physicists themselves have discarded some deeply ingrained notions of time and space.

Since the development of the Lorentz transformation equations relating two time frames and, especially, general relativity theory, modern physics has accepted the idea that changing frames of reference may account more elegantly for its phenomena. Newtonian space was "natural," following the postulates of Euclid. Einstein's world posits a different geometry, the Riemannian, to describe the harmony in the universe. Gravitational interactions happen in a "curved" space, where the distribution of masses and their motions account for its peculiarities. But most phenomena studied by the social, biological, and even the physical sciences are still pictured as unfolding against time as it was envisioned by the Greeks. It is stellar motion, later supplemented by mechanical and electronic clocks based on physical theories, that has provided mankind with its basic view of time.

The willingness of physicists to discard deeply ingrained notions of time and space should inspire those of us studying the social sciences. Why should we automatically continue to use calendar time, when physics itself is ready to reframe its standards of reference? Why should a *physical* clock be used to monitor the evolution of *social* phenomena? This chapter analyzes the meaning and implications of this question for the social sciences in general and for the study of international conflict in particular. It is an old question, raised many times by numerous scholars in different disciplines, but rarely addressed in such a way as to obtain answers specific enough to guide research. By 1937, for example, the sociologists Sorokin and Merton wrote:

> For facilitating and enriching research in the field of social dynamics, the concept of social time must be reintroduced as an auxiliary, if not

as a successor, of astronomical time . . . . What are the theoretical grounds, tacit or expressed, for expecting correlation between astronomical and social sequences? . . . . The fact is — and to the best of our knowledge its implications have been persistently overlooked — that *when social and astronomical ("time") phenomena are related, other social correlates of the same astronomical phenomena must be ascertained before these relations take on any scientific significance* [Sorokin and Merton, 1937: 628–629].

A quarter-century later, Moore (1963: 5) could still write that "the temporal ordering of social behavior has received only sporadic or intermittent attention by the sciences dealing with man." His statement is still valid today.

Before developing alternative conceptualizations of social time with different measures of duration from physical time, the question of a social time interpretation of physical clocks must be addressed. Accordingly, the next section discusses various attempts in this direction, mainly by historians. The following section then presents a formal method for developing social time referentials. It argues in particular that the intensity and magnitude of social processes can create varying social time durations. The final section examines and compares two concrete formulations of social time referentials: diplomatic time and event time.

Social Time Based on Physical Time Scales

The main problem in using calendar time to describe social processes is that it forces the researcher to use the duration units, and thus the rhythms prescribed by physical clocks, instead of focusing on the inter-relationships of social processes in time. It would be useful, in the beginning of our research at least, not to include those interrelationships automatically within the durational framework of calendar time, and to look instead at social sequences and covariations at different phase lags — where the phases are defined as theoretically relevant parts of the dynamic processes under consideration. Indeed, explaining processes by using, for example, various monthly or yearly lags (i.e., calendar time durations) may blur and sometimes completely mask the true relationships, which follow their own rhythms at a pace quite different and variable with respect to the duration of "regular" physical time. This pace may be highly irregular in terms of calendar time, but the social processes may nevertheless exhibit strong regularities in their interrelationships. Of course, the sequences themselves would be the same whether described in calendar or social time. There is only one time in this sense; or, more precisely put, there is only one ordinal time sequence for an observer. Calendar time is an invaluable tool for *dating* events. Since much of our social activity is constrained or even determined by the calendar, and our social data are collected in its framework, it makes no sense to discard it. What this chapter questions is only the uncritical acceptance of *the measure of the duration* with which calendar or physical time provides us.

Why abandon physical time when people and societies organize their activities within it? This obvious question must be answered before we venture to develop social time referentials. Biology has paid much attention to circadian rhythms, that is, rhythms having a regular cycle of approximately 24 hours (for an overview, see Whitrow, 1980: 142–159). An individual lives with the rhythm of day and night, as do societies. Elections are held every four years, and the calendar permits social coordination and regulation. Though parallel to physical time, these kinds of social time are not coincident. (Work, for example, is often rewarded in the form of monthly payments, whatever the number of working days in the month.) Social data are collected within calendar time, and our whole view of the world is strongly determined by this social frame of knowledge. But calendar time, as Sorokin and Merton reminded us, acquires significance because it is envisioned as a social construct. A satisfactory explanation of social phenomena in terms of physical time thus requires this physical time referential to be laden with a social meaning. Many historians, sociologists, and anthropologists have taken this approach.

The time problem[1] has been most pervasive in the field of history. In a famous article, the French historian Braudel (1958), addressing himself to social scientists, sought to make us aware of the plurality of social time. He distinguished among three "temporalities" or temporal perspectives (Braudel, 1966): the *longue durée*, a geographical–physical time which is quasi-immobile and concerns the individual in relation to his or her environment; *la conjoncture*, a more cyclical time, the social time of social groups; and, finally, *le temps événementiel*, a time relating not to mankind but to an event brought about by the individual. The use of different temporalities, common among French historians (see Vilar, 1974), is frequently metaphorical (Aron, 1971: 1350) and rarely denotes more than differing rates of change of various phenomena. This can go quite far. Braudel acknowledged that there may be scores of temporalities, each implying a particular history (Braudel, 1966, ii: 515). Such a view is in accordance with that of another influential historian, Collingwood; for him (cf. von Leyden, 1963), each natural or historical event requires a minimum or appropriate time to exist. This implies that, to "exist," that is, to be observed, a phenomenon must be looked at in its proper time frame. Thus, the observer will see different things according to the temporal dimension chosen. One might also say that everything needs a certain temporal quantum for its existence.

Historians have also insisted on the temporal succession of things as an essential explanatory factor. This has led them to three different views about evolution: cyclical, cataclysmic, and developmental (or progressive), each containing elements from the others (Eisenstein, 1966). Two basic approaches have been taken to explain evolution (Kracauer, 1966). First, some have explained it as "shaped time," that is, as intelligible sequences of events seen as successive "solutions" to a problem that concerns the whole series. Such a view implies that what counts is position in the particular series rather than the date, which is something constructed and universal. Second, others explain evolution in terms of chronological time common to all events. This perspective amounts to saying that the *Zeitgeist* is the main explanatory factor.

For the sociologist Durkheim (1912), time was not a Kantian a priori category but a social construct. Thus, the social scientist should study how the concept of time is related to other aspects of social life. Numerous sociologists and anthropologists have followed Durkheim's lead (cf. Goody, 1968). By assigning to physical time a social meaning, they no longer take physical time as given and hence analyze the *organization* of things in time. The time referential becomes part of this analysis — not a *deus ex machina*, an exogenous factor, or a simple scale against which change is measured. Physical time is put into perspective, and is not used before its social meanings are made explicit. It is envisioned from a distance, in the scholar's mind.

Nevertheless, in all the instances discussed here, the idea remains that calendar or physical time ultimately provides the measure of duration. There is no real break with physical time. We must thus move from physical time to a social time of different duration, a clear break in terms of time referentials.

Developing Social Time Referentials

There is only one time. By that I mean that there is only one succession of things in the stream of our consciousnesses. It is precisely because this order is the same for different individuals that communication is possible. Our everyday experience shows us that we all[2] envision the same succession of events or time order. For instance, questions are asked before answers are given. Thus, we can always relate physical time to whatever notion of social time we may develop since both are ultimately grounded in the streams of our consciousness. Modern physics has no other basis for time than its ultimate roots in the stream of consciousness (see references in Georgescu-Roegen, 1971: 132–134). Aristotle's *Physica* long ago made this point: "There is no awareness of time without a perceiving soul" (cf. Bochner, 1966: 148).

In what way, then, is social time (T) different from physical time (t)? Expressing this difference as

$$T \neq t$$

is not very enlightening, since one can simply be a transformation of the other, created, for example, by a shift in the origin or a proportional rescaling; that is, they are invariant up to an arbitrary linear relation. To change the frame of reference from a Christian calendar to the Iranian is therefore trivial in most cases of social analysis because both recognize the day as a unit of analysis. The same can be said for a time interval expressed in monthly instead of yearly terms. Just as there is no conceptual difference between a Celsius and a Fahrenheit scale for temperature, a linear transformation of a time scale will not further our understanding if it is a simple relabeling. A t-scale or a transformed one, $t' = at + c$, are equivalent in terms of time duration or time pace. But if this transformation has a social meaning (for example, a religious one), or implications for people's behavior, then the procedure makes sense and we are in the situation discussed in the preceding section.

Thus, a simple linear transformation of physical time does not provide us with a social time scale wherein time goes more slowly or more rapidly than in calendar time. A contraction or expansion of social time in terms of durations with respect to physical time requires a nonlinear — that is, nonproportional — transformation. Expressing the difference between time referentials through the use of a nonlinear function implies that the durations between events are not the same in the two time scales. This is not bothersome. Physics does not give us any proof whereby the intervals measured have the same duration. We accept this equivalency by convention. In any case, though, the acceptable functions must be monotonically strictly increasing ones so as to have only one succession of things in our streams of consciousness.

A time referential must preserve the same order between events as that which is perceived by individuals. Together with the notion that time does not stand still (in our consciousness), this implies that the referential must be described by a monotonically strictly increasing function. Let us define these terms. A function implies that, given a value of the argument, there is one and only one corresponding value of the function. For each state of the time referential, then, there is a unique time point associated with it. The qualifying term "monotonically strictly increasing" refers to a special class of functions: those that always increase. This requirement is needed for time irreversibility, in order to avoid a time referential going "backwards," toward the past. The function is always increasing; the past is always behind (below) and the future ahead (above). The term "strictly" implies that the function cannot keep a constant value: time never stands still. The question of whether or not the function is increasing is a matter of convention. A monotonically strictly decreasing function could also be used, but, since we envision time as going "to the right" and "up," this would be confusing and is therefore rejected.

Time is a flow and not a stock. Therefore I look at changes in the time scales I want to develop and label them, using differentials, as dT (social time flow) and dt (physical time flow). Were the two equal, I would write

$$dT = dt.$$

Since I want a different time frame with changing, nonproportional, durations, but also one related to physical time (to link it ultimately with this normal time referential), I write

$$dT = dt\, f(z). \tag{1}$$

As discussed above, this transformation function $f(z)$ will not be a constant term such as a, for instance, because we then would have

$$dT = a\, dt.$$

Integrating both sides yields

$$T = at + c,$$

where c is the constant of integration. This means that such a transformation function generates a social time referential which is simply a linear transformation of the physical. But we know that in most instances this is conceptually the same time frame in the sense that durations are the same, but for the constant factor a. Therefore, the transformation function in equation (1) should be of a kind different to a constant function.

Two different classes of transformation functions can be envisaged in this context. First, they could be functions of physical time itself, as for example

$$dT = a\, t\, dt.$$

Then our social time referential (*T*) would go faster and faster with respect to physical time (*t*), as can be demonstrated by integrating the above equation:

$$T = at^2/2 + c.$$

Such a formulation would make sense in two instances. First, a meaningful *definition* in social terms can be attached to the social time referential thus constructed. Second, this definition is meaningful in *theoretical* terms; that is, the model embodying such a time scale is simpler than a competing one or is the same or similar to models derived from other theories. In other words, the rescaling of time has allowed us to keep the model simpler, that is, valid under fewer restricting conditions, or social time has allowed us to preserve results obtained elsewhere.

The other class of transformation functions encompasses those that are independent of physical time. All kinds of functions can then be envisaged but, of course, the most meaningful ones will relate directly to the phenomena under study. Can we say something more specific about these functions? I believe we can, for a certain class of phenomena at least. A major phenomenon of interest to social scientists consists of rapid and important changes in the physical time of the events monitored. Of particular interest to political scientists are the rapid and wide-ranging changes, in terms of physical time, witnessed during a revolution, which comes after a long period of societal stability. Economists analyzing hyperinflations look at phenomena similar in this methodological sense. Scholars interested in the occurrence of international conflict also have problems in accounting for sudden outbreaks of violence after long peaceful periods. Other fields study similar phenomena at both the micro- and macro-social level.

For analyzing and modeling such cases, the time transformation function chosen could include variables associated with the intensity and magnitude of changes in the system under consideration. The social time referential would covary with the intensity and magnitude. In that way, the same system laws governing its evolution could be used for all periods, including those where little change is witnessed, by having the system evolve with respect to its own time referential. The social scientist would be following the historian in his traditional mode of analysis; he would thus extend crucial periods over social time and rapidly sweep across "stable" periods (where social time would almost stand still). The historian devotes whole chapters to "important" and intense periods witnessing great changes, and then rapidly treats longer "uneventful" or unimportant periods in a few words or paragraphs. But this importance stems directly from the number and intensity of events deemed to be in a relationship to one another and defining changes of interest to the historian. The social scientist would do the same, but in an explicit fashion based on a theory.

This approach may be contrasted with the prevailing one to highlight their differences. We often have difficulty in explaining why in some circumstances a social phenomenon takes perhaps four years while in other cases the same evolution occurs in one or two years. This means that the evolution of social processes is measured by physical durations. While this makes sense in many instances where the physical clock has social implications by regulating social activities, this can often be too stringent a requirement and can hamper our theoretical efforts.

How could we formulate this alternative procedure? Mathematically, let us denote this intensity of the phenomenon by i, and write

$$dT = dt\, f(i). \tag{2}$$

T as a function of i should be monotonically strictly increasing. So we need to have $f(i) > 0$. It could be fairly complex and would also have the following general characteristic:

$$\frac{df(i)}{di} > 0. \tag{3}$$

The greater the intensity, the faster the flow of social time; and, conversely, the less that is happening, the slower the flow of social time against which the social system is evolving. In the case where i is very small, we would have the whole system close to a "freezing" point with almost no movement. In mathematical terms, whenever $f(i) = 1$, then $dT = dt$. Both time scales move in parallel. When $f(i) > 1$, T moves faster than t, and when $f(i) < 1$, T is slower than t.

We can go a step further by dividing equation (2) on both sides by dt, which gives us the following differential equation:

$$\frac{dT}{dt} = f(i). \tag{4}$$

Note that we now have a *rate* of flow of social time with respect to calendar time, and not simple flows, as has been the case until now in our discussion. Now the system could for example be defined as a dynamic one obeying the following law:

$$\frac{d\mathbf{x}}{dT} = g(\mathbf{x}). \tag{5}$$

The *rate of change* of the social system represented by a vector or variables **x** with respect to *social* time T is given by a function vector $g(\mathbf{x})$. **x** might be equivalent to i but in most cases i will be a small subset of **x**: only a few variables will be used to develop the social time referential, mainly those related to the intensity and magnitude of the phenomenon.

We can rewrite the whole system formed by (4) and (5) in a simpler form by multiplying (4) and (5):

$$\frac{dT}{dt} \cdot \frac{d\mathbf{x}}{dT} = g(\mathbf{x})f(i).$$

Using the chain rule, we can write:[3]

$$\frac{d\mathbf{x}}{dt} = g(\mathbf{x})f(i). \tag{6}$$

In this equation, social time T is implicit (through the social time functions $f(i)$). The empirical version of a theory could use formulation (6), more useful than (4) and (5), which require an empirical measure of social time T (which in turn would in most cases be difficult to provide). The ultimate independent variable in (6) is physical time t. But the physical time scale in (6) has a social meaning, or at least a theoretical meaning, by allowing the dynamic system laws $g(x)$ to be simpler or to be applicable to a wider range of phenomena.

Before discussing some examples, I would like to point out a few (unintended) similarities between Einstein's theory of physical time based on the Lorentz equations (see Lucas, 1973: 228–235; Whitrow, 1980: 253–259) and equations (2) and (3) above. Einstein argued that the velocity of light is the same with respect to all frames of references in uniform relative motion. This hypothesis was not rejected experimentally, thus prompting theoretical interpretations according to which motion produces an actual physical contraction, in length for instance. Rejecting these ideas, Einstein's theory of physical time posits only apparent changes and not structural ones. A time dilation occurs in the theory of relativity in the *measurement* of time durations, which is a function of the relative motion of the observers. If we define δt as the duration recorded by observer B and δT as the evaluation of this duration by observer A, then we have the following form of the Lorentz equations:

$$\delta T = \delta t \; \frac{1}{\sqrt{1 - (v^2/c^2)}} \tag{7}$$

with v being the velocity of their relative motion, and c the constant speed of light. We thus have an identity in time measurements only when the two observers are not moving with respect to each other, that is, when $v = 0$. Whenever they start moving, $\delta T > \delta t$ because the last term on the right-hand side of equation (7) is always positive. Mathematically, we can define

$$\frac{1}{\sqrt{1 - (v^2/c^2)}} = f(v).$$

We then have

$$\delta T = \delta t\, f(v) \tag{8}$$

with

$$\frac{df(v)}{dv} > 0. \tag{9}$$

There is great formal similarity between equations (2) and (3) above and equations (8) and (9). The former relate social time flow (dT) to physical time flow (dt) as a positive function of the intensity ($f(i)$) of a social phenomenon:

$$dT = dt\, f(i) \tag{2}$$

with

$$\frac{df(i)}{di} > 0. \tag{3}$$

Thus, in the Lorentz equations v plays the role assigned to i in equation (2). In the relativistic frame of reference, velocity is absolute and time only relative. In the social frame of reference, intensity is absolute and time only relative. This also appears to hold psychogenetically. The psychologist Piaget (1946), in studying the notion of time as children perceived it, showed that the cognitive apprehension of time was a construction based on a coordination of velocities. Psychologically, then, velocities are absolute whereas time is a relative concept.

We shall now see how similar notions — intensity of conflict, conflictual escalation, or velocity of international hostility — have been studied and formally analyzed using different conceptions of time. We shall compare in particular two concrete examples of a formulation of social time.

Time and the Study of International Conflict

In the social sciences, *formal* developments of alternative notions to physical time are very rare. The economist Allais (1965, 1972) defined a psychological time for economic agents, for which there is a constant rate of forgetting per time-unit. He uses this notion to develop a model of money demand that works extremely well in cases of both inflation and hyperinflation. Samuelson (1976) proposed a model using a subjective time scale to account for the "speeding up of time with age in recognition of life as fleeting." Psychologists studying subjective durations (e.g. Eisler, 1976) have performed numerous experiments, but their emphasis clearly is on the relationship between subjective and physical time — and this usually for very short time periods not exceeding several minutes — rather than on the construction of alternative time scales within theories.

Instead of examining these various approaches, I shall concentrate on a particular field, international relations, which is special in that there have been several attempts to develop alternative notions to physical time. The first one to my knowledge was by Isard (1971) who, inspired by relativity theory and gravity models, suggested relativistic perceptions of both time and space. Rummel (1972) used social field theory to describe nations progressing at different speeds in certain social dimensions. He presented the idea whereby the concept of a social distance generated in this way could be related directly to a social time. One nation could thus be ahead in terms of, let us say, its economic development, while trailing in terms of military power. This view is analogous to Organski's power transition theory (see Organski and Kugler, 1979), which explained major wars as resulting from a transition in power terms among major actors in the international system. However, while this theory says something concrete about what will happen in specific instances, Rummel's view is descriptive in the same vein as that of historians arguing for a plurality of temporal perspectives (meaning little more than varying rates of change). The contributions of both Isard (1971; see also Isard and Liossatos, 1979) and Rummel (1972) are important in arguing for theoretical approaches in which time and its related theorized phenomena are relative and not absolute in the everyday sense of the term, where physical time governs alone. But none of these attempts gives us a concrete formalization of a social time referential within a model. Two such attempts will now be presented, starting with the concept of "diplomatic time" and then looking at "event time."

Using some of the concepts discussed above, I have developed a theory explaining international conflicts as they unfold in physical and diplomatic time. The model belongs to the family of models presented above (equations (4) and (5)). I shall not go into the details of my conception because they can be found elsewhere (Allan, 1980, 1983).

Rather, I shall show the social meaning that can be attached to such a social time concept as my diplomatic time. This will provide the reader with a specific illustration of the development of an alternative time referential and will go beyond the discussion in terms of the system of equations (4) and (5) where the social time scale was stated simply in terms of the intensity or magnitude of changes occurring.

In periods of international crisis, characterized by escalation and high conflict levels, time as perceived by decision-makers goes much faster. The decision-makers are under stress, live "around the clock," and fear a loss of control over the situation. Reaction time shortens. Threats imply a time limit, and the more intense the threat, the shorter will seem the time available for responding. Research in psychology shows that the sheer number, intensity, and non-redundancy or complexity of information signals lead people to experience time as flowing at a faster pace.

All these various factors relate to a hostility scale. The more intense the conflict, the faster diplomatic time will flow with respect to physical time:

$$\frac{dT}{dt} = \mu \ln (x + y + 1),$$

where $x, y > 0$, $\mu > 0$, x is conflict directed by nation A toward nation B, and y is B's conflict directed toward A. The specific functional form used here — a natural logarithm of a number $(x + y + 1) > 0$ — will satisfy condition (3). A decision-making model describing a nation's actions in terms of a change in its conflict level directed toward another nation was developed on two bases: rational considerations as embodied in game theory and based on bargaining power, and a consideration of the past as it influences decision-makers. The model is of the following form:

$$\frac{dx}{dT} = g_1 (x, y, \ldots),$$

$$\frac{dy}{dT} = g_2 (x, y, \ldots).$$

Policy-makers thus make decisions within their own (diplomatic) time frame T. Decisions are explained by the same model, whether the situation is one of crisis or a more peaceful one. It is through diplomatic time that policy-makers' responses vary, according to the dynamics of the complete model. The model (equations g_1 and g_2) is thus simpler than if it had to account for the differences between crisis decision-making and normal decision-making.

Recently, Zinnes (1982, 1983), in her analysis of evolving hostility in a given international system, developed another way of looking at time. Instead of having

$$dT = dt\, f(i), \qquad (2)$$

it is the other way around. Physical or calendar time, d_t, is the explained variable, and it is the phenomenon itself that determines the duration between events — in physical time. What we have, in effect, is a model in which the succession in time is determined and driven by the phenomenon itself, which is why it is called an "event model." The specific formulation is

$$d(j+1) - d(j) = -a_1 d(j) - a_2 h(j),$$

where $d(j)$ is the (physical) time that elapses between event j and event $(j + 1)$, and $d(j + 1)$ is the (physical) time duration that elapses between event $(j + 1)$ and event $(j + 2)$. The left-hand side of the equation — the dependent variable — represents the change in the durations between sequential events. For example, if

$$d(j + 1) - d(j) < 0,$$

then $d(j + 1) < d(j)$; that is, the events are getting closer to each other in time. In other words, there is an escalation. This time duration dt (in physical time) is driven by event time (a social time referential), which moves forward exactly one unit of social time in every instance of a new event, following the sequential order of the index of the events:

$$1, 2, \ldots, j, j + 1, \ldots, n.$$

The independent variables are the physical time duration $d(j)$ and the hostile intensity $h(j)$ of event j. Parameters a_1 and a_2 are positive. There is a tendency for time intervals to decrease in length: the greater the intensity in hostility, the larger this decrease. This is how an escalation, given hostile intensity (h), can feed upon itself (d).

Another equation expresses change in hostile intensity $h(j)$ as a positive function of the hostile intensity and a negative one of duration. The longer the duration, the less intense the next event. There is a "cooling-down" phenomenon ($b_1, b_2 > 0$):

$$h(j + 1) - h(j) = -b_1 d(j) + b_2 h(j).$$

These two equations are then applied to several pre-crisis periods.

Zinnes's (1983: 2–6) rationale is that the historical sequence of events is lost when looking at conflict interactions between two nations: the whole sequence needs to be preserved. This can be done by looking at the conflict events within the whole dyadic system formed by the two actors. The independent variable then becomes the event, not in such characteristics as hostility or the time duration associated with it, but only in the sense of a defined sequence in time.

Event time is discrete time in the sense that no event happens between any two original events defining the time event sequence.[4] But this is a matter of measurement. The currently most precise physical clocks such as atomic clocks are also based on discrete physical events. Nevertheless, we may still think conceptually in terms of the duration between each pair of atomic "beats," and this duration will eventually be measured with another clock "beating" at a faster rate than the current ones.

One can rewrite Zinnes's (1983) model in the following way, using the symbol Δ for expressing discrete changes in a variable between j and $j + 1$:

$$\Delta(\Delta t) = (-a_1\Delta t - a_2 h)\, \Delta e,$$
$$\Delta h = (-b_1\Delta t + b_2 h)\, \Delta e,$$

where e is moving one event time step forward with each new event; that is,

$$\Delta e = 1.$$

One can also express this the following way:

$$\Delta e = (j + 1) - j = 1,$$

where j is the event index used above.

Zinnes's (1982, 1983) perspective is the explanation of hostility and duration, with each explaining the other, and with the ultimate explanatory or independent variable being event time, a *given sequence* of events. Conceptually, this can be expressed as in Figure 5.1.

It is event time that is "driving" the dynamics of the whole process. This perspective can be contrasted in a conceptual way to my own approach (Allan, 1980, 1983) to modeling international conflict:

dx	$=$	$g(x)$	$\cdot$	$f(i)$	$\cdot$	dt
change in variables of interest (e.g. conflict/ hostility of A toward B)		decision- making model		diplomatic time function		physical time (the ultimate independent variable)

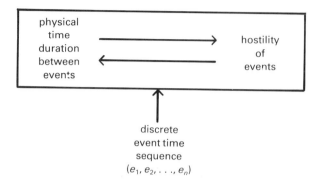

Figure 5.1 Hostility and Physical Time Duration, With Event Time as Independent Variable

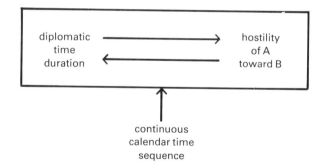

Figure 5.2 Hostility and Diplomatic Time Duration, With Physical Time as Independent Variable

where

$$f(i)\,dt = \quad dT$$

> diplomatic
> time
> duration.

Here it is t, moving continuously forward with a constant speed, that is the ultimate independent variable driving the dynamics of the whole process. Figure 5.2, contrasted with Figure 5.1, shows the major conceptual similarities and differences in terms of the time perspective between these two approaches to modeling international conflict.

Toward Building Social Clocks

Theorizing in the social sciences could benefit from the development of time referentials proper to them. This chapter has proposed ways to construct such referentials. It emphasized two alternative conceptions. The first looks at social phenomena measured in calendar or physical time and proposes ways to model social dynamics by using a social time referential. While physical time is then the ultimate independent variable, the duration of the social processes is expressed within a social time referential. The other conception uses a sequence of social events as defining time. The duration between pairs of events is measured by physical time units. Physical time then becomes a dependent variable.

Both attempts demonstrate the importance and also the pervasiveness of physical time, which has provided man with a calendar within which to position social events and measure their duration. The social scientist "naturally" feels constrained by this fact. But this need not be so: dynamic theories could be developed without any reference whatever to physical time. Their predictions would be examined only with respect to the time sequence of certain social phenomena. In this perspective, the (physical) duration between social events (i.e., the time "markers") would be of no concern to the theoretician.

But would that not constitute a step backward in terms of social science theorizing? No, because social researchers would focus on sequences rather than attempting to derive from their dynamic theories predictions with respect to physical time which force them to satisfy the strong requirement of equal physical time durations. But would not such a research strategy preclude the possibility of any precise predictions in time? This would not be the case, because we can develop theories that hold invariant owing to a proper choice of the (social) time referential against which the analyzed phenomena evolve.

Once we discover an invariancy between the time sequence evolution of two social phenomena, we can use either one of them as a clock to monitor the other. We shall then have a parallelism in time between two social processes and can hope to develop a rigorous theory of social processes. It will be a closed one, including its own clock, which will establish both the time sequence and the dynamic social laws. In other words, social time could become a frame of reference, a *normal* time, the time within which we envision social reality in some of its parts. So let us think about social time, build social clocks, and develop a sociochronology!

NOTES

1. A good introduction to the literature on time is Whitrow (1980). Lucas (1973) presents an analytically dense but highly interesting philosophical discussion. There is a useful bibliography by Kindy et al. (1976). Heirich (1964) reviews the use of the concept of time by some major sociologists.

2. Those who do not are labeled "mentally ill," "senile," etc. Indeed, these do have alternative time conceptions, but they lack sufficient intersubjective reliability to be useful for our purposes.

3. This can be done in most cases.

4. In fact, it is event *sets* that are defined rather than individual events, owing to the imprecise measurements made whereby events are defined only by their occurrence within a specific day and not at a precise hour, minute, second, etc. But in my discussion, I follow the conceptual definition.

REFERENCES

ALLAIS, M. (1965) "Reformulation de la théorie quantitative de la monnaie." Bulletin SEDEIS, No. 928 (10 September), Supplément.

———— (1972) "Forgetfulness and interest." Journal of Money, Credit and Banking 4 (February): 40–73.

ALLAN, P. (1980) "Diplomatic time and climate: a formal model." Journal of Peace Science 4 (Spring): 133–150.

———— (1983) Crisis Bargaining and the Arms Race: A Theoretical Model. Cambridge, Mass.: Ballinger.

ARON, R. (1971) "Comment l'historien écrit l'épistémologie: a propos du livre de Paul Veyne." Annales: Économies, Sociétés, Civilisations 26 (November–December): 1319–1354.

BOCHNER, S. (1966) The Role of Mathematics in the Rise of Science. Princeton, NJ: Princeton University Press.

BRAUDEL, F. (1958) "Histoire et sciences sociales: la longue durée." Annales: Économies, Société, Civilisations 13 (October–December): 725–753.

———— (1966) La Méditerranée et le monde méditerranéen à l'époque de Phillippe II, 2d ed. Paris: Armand Colin.

DURKHEIM, E. (1912) Les formes élémentaires de la vie religieuse. Paris: Alcan.

EISENSTEIN, E. L. (1966) "Clio and Chronos: an essay on the making and breaking of history-book time." History and Theory, Beiheft 6: 36–64.

EISLER, H. (1976) "Experiments on subjective duration, 1868–1975: a collection of power function exponents." Psychological Bulletin 83 (November): 1154–1171.

GEORGESCU-ROEGEN, N. (1971) The Entropy Law and the Economic Process. Cambridge, Mass.: Harvard University Press.

GOODY, J. (1968) "Time: social organization," pp. 30–42 in D. L. Sills (ed.), International Encyclopedia of the Social Sciences, vol. 16. New York: Macmillan and Free Press.

HEIRICH, M. (1964) "The use of time in the study of social change." American Sociological Review 29 (June): 386–397.

ISARD, W. (1971) "Preliminary notes on relativistic concepts and the dynamics of multination interaction." Peace Research Society (International), Papers 17: 1–6.

——— and P. LIOSSATOS (1979) Spatial Dynamics and Optimal Space-Time Development. New York: North-Holland.

KINDY, E. S. et al. (1976) Time: A Bibliography. Washington, DC: Information Retrieval.

KRACAUER, S. (1966) "Time and history." History and Theory, Beiheft 6: 65–78.

LUCAS, J. R. (1973) A Treatise on Time and Space. London: Methuen.

MOORE, W. E. (1963) Man, Time, and Society. New York: John Wiley.

ORGANSKI, A. F. K. and J. KUGLER (1979) The War Ledger. New York: Alfred A. Knopf.

PIAGET, J. (1946) Le développement de la notion de temps chez l'enfant. Paris: Presses Universitaires de France.

RUMMEL, R. J. (1972) "Social time and international relations." General Systems 17: 145–158.

SAMUELSON, P. A. (1976) "Speeding up of time with age in recognition of life as fleeting," pp. 153–168 in A. M. Tang, F. M. Westfield, and J. S. Worley (eds), Evolution, Welfare, and Time in Economics: Essays in Honor of Nicholas Georgescu-Roegen. Lexington, Mass: D. C. Heath and Company, Lexington Books.

SOROKIN, P. A. and R. K. MERTON (1937) "Social time: a methodological and functional analysis." American Journal of Sociology 42 (March): 615–629.

VILAR, P. (1974) "Histoire marxiste, histoire en construction," pp. 169–209 in J. Le Goff and P. Nora (eds), Faire de l'histoire, Nouveaux Problèmes. Paris: Gallimard.

VON LEYDEN, W. (1963) "History and the concept of relative time." History and Theory 2, 3: 263–285.

WHITROW, G. J. (1980) The Natural Philosophy of Time. Oxford: Clarendon Press.

ZINNES, D. A. (1982) "A hostile/cooperative event model of conflict dynamics." Paper presented at the Merriam Seminar and meeting of the Institute for the Study of Conflict Theory and International Security, University of Illinois, Urbana, September 24–25.

——— (1983) "An event model of conflict interaction," pp. 119–148 in D. A. Zinnes (ed.), Conflict Processes and the Breakdown of International Systems. Merriam Seminar Series on Research Frontiers. Denver, Colo.: University of Denver, Graduate School of International Studies, Monograph Series in World Affairs, 20:2.

PART II

Information and Bargaining

CHAPTER 6

MISPERCEPTION AND SATISFICING IN INTERNATIONAL CONFLICT

MICHAEL NICHOLSON

National decision-makers frequently experience surprises in the course of international conflicts. The actions of an opponent can be totally unexpected. Standard analyses of interactive decision-making, such as game theory, assume that, with full or at least reasonably good information, surprises will not often occur, and they normally attribute those that do to faulty decision-making. However, this conclusion is not useful for understanding international decision-making. It is therefore suggested that the typical interactive decision-making frameworks need to be modified.

This chapter explores how surprise can occur as a consequence of modifying the assumption about full information. While information may be good, the complexity of the system often does not permit even the most sophisticated decision-makers fully to comprehend it. In addition, information, particularly about intentions, is probabilistic in nature. These points suggest that assumptions about information in interactive decision-making models need to be modified for application to international conflict situations. The chapter discusses such modifications, drawing illustrations from the Falklands war of 1982, in which both parties were very surprised at one time or another.

Conflict and Games

A *conflict* is a situation in which the interests of the parties are at least partly inconsistent; that is, not all parties can be at once simultaneously and completely satisfied. A zero-sum conflict is the limiting case. Both parties totally oppose each other, so that a gain for one is a corresponding loss for the other. Since zero-sum games are rare in social life (apart from such designed games as poker), we shall not deal with them here.

A *game* is a formalized representation of a conflict (see Savage, 1977; Brams, 1975). Working within the tradition of game theory, bargaining theory, decision theory, and the like, this chapter pursues a twofold goal: (1) to modify these models to make them sufficiently flexible to be applicable to international conflict situations, while (2) retaining the analytic rigor inherent in the models.

DEFINITIONS AND FRAMEWORK

The components of the model, restricted for simplicity's sake to two-party games, are the *actors*, A and B. Each actor has a set of *strategies* or *acts*: $A = A_1, A_2, \ldots A_m$; and $B = B_1, B_2, \ldots B_n$. A *decision* by A or B, respectively, is the choice of one of these acts, as illustrated in Figure 6.1.

The conjunction of a decision by A, say A_i, and a decision by B, say B_j, yields a *consequence,* C_{ij}, which is an event or set of events in the world. This is expressed as $F(A_i, B_j) = C_{ij}$; that is, there is a function F which maps acts onto states of the world. In a game of cards a consequence might be simply the distribution of a set of monetary pay-offs. In more complex international situations, it might be a mineral rights agreement with its many ramifications.

Each actor has a *utility function,* $U_a(C_{ij})$ and $U_b(C_{ij})$, with the usual properties (e.g., complete transitive ordering over the set of consequences). The utility function is defined such that the actor maximizes the mathematical expectation of the function under situations of risk (mathematical expectation being defined, following convention, as the sum, over all the outcomes of an act, of the utility of each outcome times the probability of its occurrence). The utility function is known not only to A but also to A's rival, B. Thus we have a situation in which (1) both pay-off matrices are expressed in utility terms, (2) both matrices are known to both actors, and (3) the conflict or game can be solved.

A *solution* is a consequence from which neither side can move and gain unilateral advantage (although in certain sorts of bargaining problems there may also be appeals to concepts such as "fairness"). In highly stylized games, we commonly speak of a solution, though not necessarily a unique one, known to the players.

1. There exists a function F that maps every pair (A_i, B_j) onto a point C_{ij}. Formally, $F(A_i, B_j) \rightarrow C_{ij}$, for all $A_i \epsilon A$, $B_j \epsilon B$.

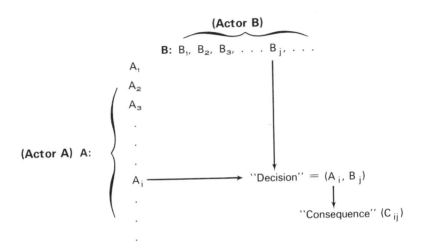

2. There exist utility functions $U_a(C_{ij})$, $U_b(C_{ij})$ known to *both* A and B and having the usual properties. Thus the general functional framework is:

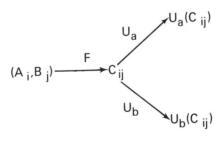

Figure 6.1   Basic Framework for Analyzing Surprise in Two-Actor Game

These definitions represent the conventional statement of a game with full information. They will be used to examine misjudgment and misperception. Surprise results when (1) an event with low probability in fact occurs or (2) an event that was not considered occurs. It is only in the second instance that one can speak of misperception or misjudgment. Our focus will therefore be on this second situation. We shall return later to the problematic case of an event that was considered but excluded from consideration because of its low probability of occurrence.[1]

SOURCES AND TYPES OF ERROR

There are at least three types of misperception/misjudgment (or error), any of which can produce surprise:

(1) One or both of the parties to the conflict may incorrectly predict the consequences of the act; that is, the expected C_{ij} differs from the one that actually occurs. Formally, this means that the function F that maps the sets of acts onto the sets of consequences is incorrectly specified.

(2) A may have an incorrect view of B's utility function (and/or vice versa).

(3) A may not realize the full range of B's alternatives (or strategy set); that is, B may have done something that A has not considered at all.

Standard game theory assumes that the players know the structure of the game, but A may not know which strategy B will select (although in a world in which all games were solved A would know this, at least in the sense of a mixed strategy). Thus, from the perspective of formal game theory, the above cases are situations in which the players do not agree on the game being played.

By slightly extending Bennett's (1977) definition, we may call a game played where any or all the above three conditions hold a *hypergame*. In effect, these are games where one player perceives itself to be playing one game, while its rival perceives itself to be playing another. In a two-person situation we are thus positing a hypergame consisting of two "ordinary" games: the game according to A, and the game according to B. The hypergame may be represented by a *pair* of matrices, not just the single matrix that usually represents an ordinary game, such as that in Figure 6.1. Clearly, we may extend this without difficulty to say that, in the *n*-person hypergame, there are *n* pay-off matrices (some of which may be identical), with each matrix representing the game as perceived by each of the *n* players. Ordinary game theory, then, is the limiting case in which the *n* matrices are identical and there is no misperception.

There is a qualification concerning the first of these. *F* was defined as giving a unique mapping from a pair of strategies to a single outcome. It could be construed as giving a set of outcomes $C_{ij}^{(1)}$, $C_{ij}^{(2)}$, . . ., $C_{ij}^{(n)}$, each with probabilities $p_{ij}^{(1)}$, $p_{ij}^{(2)}$, . . . , $p_{ij}^{(n)}$ of occurring. In these cases a single number in the matrix of a game would represent the sum of the expected utilities of these outcomes; that is,

$$\sum_{k=1}^{n} P_{ij}^{(k)} u(C_{ij}^{(k)}).$$

This raises the problem that, if a low probability outcome turns out, after the fact, to be the case, then we cannot refer to the choice resulting in this as a "mistake," but must merely say that the decision-maker was unlucky (or lucky). As in singular events, the one observation tells us nothing about the prior probability distribution (other than that the event has a nonzero probability); we may never speak of mistakes from post hoc observations alone. This is obviously a conceptual point. We are, however, entitled to take into account evidence about how, prior to the event, the decision-makers evaluated their options, and can refer to something as a "mistake" if the evidence suggests that they did not seriously consider an option — that is, that they gave it a (subjective) probability of zero.

A similar point could be made about item (3), where A might think that with some probability an element is within B's strategy set. I shall nevertheless follow the general form of Bennett's analysis and consider strategies as falling into the dichotomy of "considered" or "not considered." The increase in explanatory power, at least for the cases we consider, of using probabilistic expectations is small, but the increase in complexity is great.

ANALYSIS AND EXAMPLES

The earlier definitions used the word "consequence" for C_{ij}, the result of A_i and B_j. This was a deliberate though by no means original deviation from the common practice of referring to these consequences as "pay-offs." In formulating a game, it is common to represent the consequences as a pair of numbers (a_{ij}, b_{ij}) which are the pay-offs to the two players. In games in the everyday sense these pay-offs are literally payments to the two participants. I wish to emphasize, however, that in the issues of interest here we have a single consequence, C_{ij}, and the ordered pair of pay-offs is $[u_a(C_{ij}), u_b(C_{ij})]$, where the utilities are the different valuations of the state of affairs, C_{ij}, which both participants expect as the consequence of their joint act.

Strictly speaking, this distinction between consequences and pay-offs is only terminological. It does emphasize, however, that a consequence is a common property of the game. In the sort of problems under discussion the properties are complex, and in part the complexities lead to some of the difficulties — both in the sense of actually working out the large range of consequences that is involved and in then getting for the players even an ordinal preference estimate of these consequences.

We may now return to discuss in greater detail, with examples, the different forms of error. At the time of the Suez war (1956), the British confidently believed that the nationalization of the Suez Canal and its operation by Egyptian pilots would be a prescription for disaster, since they assumed that the Egyptian pilots would not be competent. This turned out to be incorrect: the Egyptian pilots proved to be perfectly able to do the job (see Thomas, 1967). This case is relatively straightforward in the sense that a player misjudged the consequences of an act in a fairly precisely defined (or definable) way. It was thus a mistake about the function F.

With regard to the earlier point about mistakes in probabilistic situations, this assertion implies that the possibility that the Egyptian pilots were competent was given a probability of zero and not merely a low probability. The evidence on this point — voluminous, ambiguous, and often self-justifying — suggests that British decision-makers, or at least Prime Minister Anthony Eden, did in fact exclude the possibility. Describing Eden's choice as a mistake is thus legitimate. Although it is less likely that decision-making members of the Foreign Office were similarly deluded, it remains true that in this situation Eden took great care to distance himself from uncongenial advice.

It is just as easy — we might almost say that there is a predilection — to misjudge the effects of an act on the morale of a state in warfare. A classic example was the Allied program during World War II of strategic bombing aimed at Germany, which was expected to affect both morale and production far in excess of what actually occurred (Paskins and Dockrill, 1979). Again, it was not just a matter of a low-probability event in fact occurring, but rather a failure to consider as a possibility what actually happened and hence assigning it a probability of zero. As with the Suez case, contrary advice was dismissed (notably, in the case of Britain, by Churchill, his scientific adviser Lindemann, and the responsible military commander, Harris). It is not surprising that, in a complex world, our fairly primitive tools of social science make faulty predictions of the consequences of acts. Any analysis of social conflict using game theory or its derivatives, however, should be aware of that fact.

The second form of error is A's possible misperception of B's utility function (and vice versa). For the sake of simplicity, we shall assume that both parties correctly predict the literal consequences of act C_{ij}. They thus correctly perceive the function F but not necessarily its desirability for the opponent. In accordance with the Schlieffen plan, with which it opened World War I, Germany invaded France by going through Belgium. The Germans had no doubt that Britain would disapprove of this act. They did not, however, realize just how seriously Britain viewed the Schlieffen plan — despite the fact that it had been in existence for many years and the Germans had had ample opportunity to consider the problem (see Taylor, 1965). The point is that an external observer as well as a participant may in some instances have substantial difficulty knowing how positively or negatively another participant values some attribute. This is especially true when war or some other form of violence is at stake. Attitudes to war are not simple but ambivalent, a concept not easily brought into conventional decision theory.

The final area in which A might err about its opponent is in the set of alternative acts available to B. A may not know all of B's options. In the case of Iran, the US government never considered large-scale hostage-taking as a member of the possible set of acts which the Iranian government might pursue.

Other examples abound in history. The Argentine invasion of the Falkland Islands posed a somewhat different situation.[2] The British government thought that the dispute over the Falklands, which had gone on for nearly 150 years, was dormant. It was accordingly surprised when the Argentines decided to activate the conflict. Had the British contemplated the possibility that the Argentines would do this, then perhaps an invasion would have come as no great surprise. Similarly, in 1940 the French did not realize that German tanks could enter France through the Ardennes (Bennett and Dando, 1979). Hence, they took no steps to combat such a possibility — with disastrous results. In this case the Germans did what any military commander tries to do: use as a strategy not one that the other side has dismissed but, better yet, one of which it has never thought.

The Activation of Dormant Conflict

Game theory models and their derivatives are optimizing models. The underlying assumption of an optimizing model is that each actor has a preference ordering over all conceivable alternatives, and that all alternatives are always available. If the actor can improve its position through unilateral action (allowing for others' responses to such action), then it will do so. Moreover, it will continue to do so until there are no acts available likely to produce more positive outcomes for the actor. When both actors have reached this stage they are said to be "in equilibrium."

We shall assume that actors in a social system are in equilibrium, that is, that there are no additional available acts that enhance their expected utility. (In this way microeconomics conceives of a firm or consumer being in equilibrium — a construct that, however useful, should not be confused with the situation common in reality.) What then produces disequilibrium? Disequilibrium could result from any of the three sources of misperception discussed above:

(1) A might perceive that the function F that maps acts onto consequences has changed.

(2) A's utility function U_a over the set of consequences might change, or it might perceive (rightly or wrongly) that B's utility function U_b had changed.

(3) A might perceive that the set of acts A available to it had changed, owing possibly to some technical development; likewise, it might perceive that B's set of acts B had changed.

One issue is particularly important here. If B's strategy set changes but this is not perceived by A, then, of course, A will do nothing about it: A mistakenly believes that it is optimizing. This possibility brings us back to the analysis of hypergames. By extension, if a conflict changes its form so that an actor has a positive expected value in utility terms from initiating the conflict, then it will do so.

Thus, a conflict may begin because of a perceived change in the state of the world. A formerly non-advantageous conflict becomes advantageous. For example, in the Falklands conflict the Argentines believed that the game had changed: what they had seen a year earlier as a set of acts with a negative expected utility now came to have a positive expected utility. In principle, this could have come about either because they had revised their estimates of the probability of a quick success, or because they had altered the utility functions by increasing the utility of war (owing to their expectation that it would increase internal cohesion, enhance governmental popularity, and so forth). On the basis of still incomplete evidence, the most plausible interpretation is that *both* moved in the direction of increasing the value of the expected utility.

Game-theoretic models are normally understood to be optimizing models. All possible alternatives are considered and the "best" according to some criterion is selected. However, we can modify the general approach by introducing the concept of *satisficing*. In contrast to optimizing, satisficing does *not* assume that decision-makers continuously consider the whole range of possible actions and their consequences. Instead, it assumes that a set of acts, with positive expected utility, may exist but is not acted on because the decision-makers do not examine it. (Rephrased in optimizing terms, the idea is that, if the search for and continuous review of all possible situations is costly, the gains from the "lost" opportunities may well be less than the cost of the search.) States keep some relationships at the forefront of their attention. This was certainly true for Britain and Argentina with respect to their ties to the United States. Other relationships, such as that between Britain and Argentina before 1982, come into view only intermittently. "Political attention" as a resource is only occasionally turned toward still other actors in the system.

The question then arises, when does a dormant relationship between two countries become active? In particular, when does a dormant conflict become active? A dormant conflict is one in which there is a positive expected utility for at least one of the parties, let us say A, but its decision-makers have not discovered it in any search procedure. Thus a dormant conflict becomes active when goal achievement falls below an acceptable level so that utility gains resulting from some act increase. Decision-makers may overlook small failures to optimize, but large failures intrude on their attention. This comes about for any of the following reasons:

(1) The environment or the reactions of third parties has altered so that the consequence of any pair of acts is different; that is, the function F changes.

(2) The utilities of the decision-making group change either because of altered preferences, because new decision-makers have replaced the old ones, or because of new pressures on the decision-makers; that is, because U_a changes.

(3) Performance in other decision-making areas has fallen below expectation or need, and success in another area such as a conflict becomes important.

(4) The perceived probability functions P_a and P_b, defined over the set C of consequences, may be revised, thereby increasing the expected utility of activating the previously dormant conflict.

In the third situation, initiating a conflict (which one hopes will be successful) seeks to make up for failure in another area perhaps totally unrelated to the conflict itself. This implies, not implausibly, that decision-makers seek overall goal achievement with respect to a large number of areas.

For these reasons, the Falklands issue became salient for Argentina during 1981, and the need felt by Argentine decision-makers for some sort of initiative becomes comprehensible (although not necessarily predictable). To place the Falklands conflict into the satisficing framework and apply the matrix form of representation requires some elaboration of the conventional representation of a game.

Devices of Representation

Continual tension in the representation of "reality" in formal terms exists between making the formulation rich enough to add something to our interpretation of real-world events and defining it strictly enough to enable us to get beyond simple description. Analyzing the Falklands war poses two problems, neither of them specific to that conflict as such but common to many decision-making situations. First, governments are not unitary decision-makers but, rather, groups of individuals and sub-organizations that in a given conflict often have different utility functions over the relevant alternatives. This presents us with the task, both conceptual and practical, of amalgamating the different preferences to provide an overall utility function that can be regarded as that of the group as a whole. I shall offer a shorthand device for responding to this task rather than a solution. Second, while we can neatly define games in the formal sense, conflicts in real life are often messy affairs, and it is not always clear just where they begin and where they end. Some conflicts are in fact most easily represented not as a single game but as a sequence of games in which the pay-off in one game determines either the starting point of a second game or which of a set of alternative games will be played. (Thus, the discussion below represents the Falklands conflict as a sequence of two conflicts.) I shall deal with these two problems in reverse order.

Various studies relying on utility theory have used the conceptual device of a gamble, where the prize is a lottery ticket for another gamble. This procedure could be used for as many sequences as desired, although presumably, to make the game of interest, there must be a final lottery in which there is an actual pay-off. A similar device may be used in games, as the following example (which has no bearing whatever on the Falklands conflict) shows.

Consider an initial game G in which two players each have a pair of strategies, A_1, A_2 and B_1, B_2, respectively. The interaction of these strategies in the initial game produces a set of four further games:

	B_1	B_2
A_1	G_1	G_2
A_2	G_3	G_4

These four games are each a prisoner's dilemma game, as follows:

$$G_1 = \begin{bmatrix} (12,12) & (4,16) \\ (16,4) & (8,8) \end{bmatrix}$$

$$G_2 = \begin{bmatrix} (6,6) & (2,8) \\ (8,2) & (4,4) \end{bmatrix}$$

$$G_3 = \begin{bmatrix} (9,9) & (3,12) \\ (12,3) & (6,6) \end{bmatrix}$$

$$G_4 = \begin{bmatrix} (3,3) & (1,4) \\ (4,1) & (2,2) \end{bmatrix}$$

Solving such a structure of games requires us to move in reverse order, that is, to solve the secondary set of games as a prior step to solving the initial game. First, on the assumption that the players know the structure of games $G_1, \ldots, G_4$, we obtain what we may call the "anticipated value" of each. We use this more informal concept, "anticipated value," which refers to what the players *anticipate* will be the outcome, rather than "expected value," because the solution and hence value of a prisoner's dilemma game are unclear and can depend on social factors external to the game. In this case I shall make the normal assumption that they play the "defect" strategy in each of the above four games. Next, we put these anticipated values into the original game:

	B_1	B_2
A_1	(8,8)	(4,4)
A_2	(6,6)	(2,2)

An initial game containing these anticipated values — itself *not* a prisoner's dilemma game, it should be noted — would commonly be supposed to have a solution of A_1, B_1 and a value of (8,8).

There are many conceivable variations of this structure of games. One would be a basic game with three cells that are direct pay-offs and just one cell that is a game, another would have cells that have direct pay-offs plus a game, and so forth. In our analysis of the Falklands conflict we shall use the first of these variations, namely, a basic game in which only one cell is a further game. Such two-stage games in which the subgames are simple pose little difficulty, but the difficulty of the games mounts with the number of sequences they contain. (This is especially so if we assume that the reliability of information decreases the further we go into the future — but we may ignore this issue here.)

The second problem results from the fact that governments are non-unitary, with various parties to a decision often having quite different attitudes about its outcome. Of the many facets of this problem, one is of particular importance here: What can party A do if it perceives within B disagreements about preference orderings of some outcomes that will affect B's behavior in the game? The information on which A is basing its perception of the disagreement and its extent may well be incomplete and ambiguous. Moreover, A knows that it must resist wishful thinking: it must not adopt as the definitive preference ordering the preferences of the group most favorable to a course of action desired by A. It must resist this temptation because it does not know which of the subgroups in B will be successful in establishing its preference ordering, or whether some compromise will be reached. (In examining the Falklands conflict, in which such a diffusion of preference orderings actually existed, I resolved this problem by inserting as one entry in the matrix a pair of numbers intended to be A's perception of the utility of two contending groups within B.)

The Falklands War: An Example of Surprises

The Falklands war illustrates a number of the issues raised in this paper. The relevant events are as follows.[3]

Since 1833 the British have occupied the Falklands while Argentina has claimed rightful ownership of them. The islands' legal status remains unclear. Intermittent negotiations since 1919 have failed to solve the question of sovereignty. On April 2, 1982, Argentina invaded and seized the Falklands. The Argentine government, well aware that such an act would be popular, may well have acted more to gain much needed domestic support than from any feeling that the time had come to force the issue. It may have been encouraged in this move, however, by British actions — most notably, Britain's withdrawal of a Royal Navy supply ship that doubled as a defense force. The invasion caught the British government totally by surprise. Indeed, the British government was unaware of any danger until two days before the invasion occurred. The British response was to assemble a naval task force and invade the islands in its turn. This move took the Argentine government by surprise. The war was relatively brief and ended on June 14 when the Argentine troops withdrew. But it was a situation where each party did something that was very unexpected by the other, and by most third-party observers.

The Falklands war may be analyzed as a "game within a game" in the sense described above, where a basic game has as some of its pay-offs another game. The basic game was a "negotiation game" in which some of the strategies were negotiation strategies. It was a hypergame in the sense that B (in this case, Britain) regarded it as entirely a negotiation game while A (or Argentina), conceiving of the military option, saw the situation structured differently. There was just one subsidiary game, a "war game."

Again, we must be careful about specifying which party saw what and when. A presumably saw the possibilities of such a game during 1981 as domestic circumstances increased the utilities of such an action. B realized the existence (or at least relevance) of the war game only just before it started. However, having realized its existence, B perceived a broader range of strategies open to it than A had done, thereby making it in its turn a hypergame. In simplified form, the various strategies were as follows.

—B's strategies in the negotiation game:

BN_1 Status quo strategy: continue negotiating in a rather desultory way, particularly on the sovereignty issue.

BN_2 Increase seriousness of negotiation.

BN_3 Build up sufficient military force in the Falklands to make military attack difficult or costly.

—A's strategies in the negotiation game:

AN_1 Status quo strategy: continue negotiating with the diffident British, while recognizing that, although a settlement might occur eventually, it would be a long time in coming.

AN_2 Force the salience of the issue (e.g. at the United Nations, with the United States, with Third World countries).

AN_3 Launch a military attack.

As pointed out earlier, B did not think that A was even considering strategy AN_3.

—A's strategies in the war game:

AW_1 Do nothing.

AW_2 Invade the Falklands.

—B's strategies in the war game:

BW_1 Do nothing.

BW_2 Undertake economic and diplomatic sanctions.

BW_3 Counterinvade.

TABLE 6.1 The Negotiation Game as Seen by A (Argentina)

A's Strategies	B's Strategies		
	Do nothing	Increase seriousness of negotiation	Build up deterrent force
Do nothing	0, 0	$+2, \begin{cases} +2 \\ -2 \end{cases}$	$-2, -1$
Force saliency	$+1, -1$	$+3, \begin{cases} +2 \\ -2 \end{cases}$	$+1,\ \ 0$
Launch military attack	$+4, -2$	$+4,\ \ -2$	$-5, +2$

Again, BW_3, of which A was unaware or which it had dismissed, introduced the hypergame element.

These strategies are illustrated in a set of four matrices: the negotiation game as perceived by A (Table 6.1), the negotiation game as perceived by B (Table 6.2), the war game as perceived by A (Table 6.3), and the war game as perceived by B (Table 6.4). The pay-offs in the matrices, although doubtless something more than ordering relationships, do not have any specific empirical import. I have rated utilities from +5 (= very advantageous outcome) to –5 (= very disadvantageous outcome). I shall assume that the perceived consequence of any pair of acts is shared by the two parties, or, using the earlier terminology, that both agree on $F(A_iB_j)$. There is, however, some degree of misperception of the other's utility function. The analysis itself deals directly with the two utilities as represented by a pair of numbers.

B's Perception of the Negotiation Game

On what basis can we assign numbers to the individual cells of the matrices? Let us first look at Table 6.2, the matrix showing B's perception of the negotiation game. Our "base utility" is the status quo

TABLE 6.2 The Negotiation Game as Seen by B (Britain)

A's Strategies	B's Strategies		
	Do nothing	Increase seriousness of negotiation	Build up deterrent force
Do nothing	0, 0	$+1, -1$	$-1, -1$
Force saliency	$+1, -1$	$+2, -1$	$+1, 0$

point, at which both parties continue doing what they were doing before. Accordingly, we assign to the first cell in the matrix the score of (0,0). Consider now the other boxes in the top row of the matrix. B would perceive the consequences of any decision on its part to increase the speed of negotiation (where "do nothing" for A means "respond" rather than literally doing nothing) as being clearly to A's advantage, since A would gain something and lose nothing.

It seems, however, that B's decision-makers did not generally realize that the issue was of any real significance to A, apart from A's interest in improving its negotiating position with respect to Antarctic mineral rights. B simply did not understand the very great symbolic significance that A attached to the Falklands. For B to build up a deterrent force would be worse, because more expensive, than the overall status quo. (Such a deterrent force would doubtless have been much less expensive than maintaining the current British military presence in the Falklands.) Thus, the existence of a deterrent force would also be seen as slightly harmful to A, since it might wound A's pride and create in A a sense of mistrust.

Consider now the second row in the matrix. B would perceive any failure to respond as giving A some advantage while suffering some disadvantage itself in the form of mild international embarrassment. More problematic is the pay-off should B decide to respond by increasing the speed of negotiations. (In the next section I shall argue that this situation is not peculiar to the Falklands war as such but raises some genuine issues of principle with respect to the application of game theory models to real-world situations; here, however, I argue practicalities.)

Explaining our scoring of the latter cell requires a brief outline of some concrete aspects of the Falklands situation. It appears that the British Foreign Office in fact had long wanted to come to some arrangement with Argentina. What kept it from doing so was its concern with the status of territories in a similar situation, notably Gibraltar, which another state claimed with some legal justification although the population wished to remain under British administration. The difference between the two was that, whereas Gibraltar played a great part in British myth, until the outbreak of the Falklands war few people in Britain knew or cared where the islands were. A small but vociferous Falklands lobby had nonetheless always existed in Britain. In the poorly attended debates on the issue in the House of Commons, this lobby could ensure the continuation of a policy of no change. Hence, any announced governmental intention to increase the speed of negotiation would have aroused internal wrangling — a negative utility, albeit small, from the overall British perspective. (In the corresponding box for A's perception of the negotiation game, Table 6.2, I have placed a pair of numbers to indicate that A, aware of this division of opinion, was in doubt about what B's utilities were.)

The outcome of A's decision to force saliency and B's decision to build up its deterrent force also requires comment. The latter decision, of course, would not be one that B could adopt as an immediate response to A's action, since developing a deterrent force takes time. It would have to have been a response carried out earlier. Either way, there would be a cost in financial terms and hence a negative utility for B. Should A force saliency, then, as suggested earlier, the negative utility might approach zero as B uses the threat of a deterrent force as a bargaining counter. It must be stressed again that this strategy becomes relevant only if B, contrary to fact, had actually regarded the military attack strategy as a possibility, however low its probability of occurrence. It also makes sense if we argue that B never excluded the possibility that A would attack, but simply did not consider it just prior to A's actual attack. We shall return to this point in the next section.

Assuming that the assigned pay-offs are realistic — and, it should be noted, ordinal measures should suffice — then B would have expected A to play strategy AN_2, to which it would have responded with strategy BN_3. This did not happen, for reasons to be discussed in the next section.

A's Perception of the Negotiation Game

Apart from slightly altered intensities and, as indicated, noting the ambiguous case of AN_1BN_2, the utilities in the negotiation game as perceived by A (Table 6.1) are similar to those perceived by B. What is added in A's version of the game is its attack option. The entries in the first two columns for the attack strategy are derived from the war game below. Had B adopted BN_3, then A would have found AN_3 costly to implement and AN_2, the strategy forcing the saliency of the issue, would be the best one to adopt. Since B did not adopt strategy BN_3 (which, had it realized the nature of the game, it surely would have done), the military attack strategy becomes the dominant one for A in a game consisting of the first two columns only. This is the game A evidently perceived itself to be playing; and, from the point of view of strategies available (if not outcomes), the attack strategy was entirely correct.

Perception of the War Games

The pay-offs in the war games (Tables 6.3 and 6.4) are fairly self-explanatory. I have assumed that A underestimated its own negative

TABLE 6.3 The War Game as Seen by A (Argentina)

	B's Strategies	
A's Strategies	*Do nothing*	*Apply economic and diplomatic pressure*
Do not attack	0, 0	x
Attack	+5, −3	+4, −2

TABLE 6.4 The War Game as Seen by B (Britain)

	B's Strategies		
A's Strategies	*Do nothing*	*Apply economic and diplomatic pressure*	*Counterattack*
Do not attack	0, 0	x	x
Attack	+5, −5	+3, −4	−3, +5

utility in the event of an unresisted invasion. Had A envisioned the counterattack strategy, it would have restricted itself to the negotiation game. In making the decision to attack, however, A saw only the situation in Table 6.3: that is, the likelihood of economic and diplomatic pressure, but no more. It was thus this entry (+4, −2) that went into the appropriate cell in the matrix for the negotiation game (Table 6.1).

Given this interpretation, the Falklands episode occurred because both sides failed to perceive the alternatives (namely, major military action) that the other side was prepared to consider. This perceptual failure is the major issue in the problem.

Game-Theoretic Lessons of the Falklands War

There is a further issue. If the matrices in Tables 6.1 and 6.2 are correct, then, according to this analysis, the Falklands war would not have occurred. We are thus led to question the discrepancy between the results of our analysis and the historical outcome. Several possible explanations can be offered. One class of arguments is that the analysis itself is wrong. Many international theorists argue that this form of analysis is inherently flawed, that it succeeds only by knowing the answer before it begins. Accordingly, it misses what international or, indeed, any other form of conflict behavior is really about. I shall not dispute this point here, although I have done so elsewhere (Nicholson, 1983).

A more mundane point is that the utilities attributed to the participants are incorrect. Since the weights of these numbers are no more than what I think is plausible on the basis of my understanding of the Falklands conflict, they clearly have little scientific significance. However, whether the attribution of specific utilities is right or wrong, it is reasonable to contend that they are correct in terms of rank orders.

Other answers are more interesting theoretically. A third one is that the Falklands war was the result of irrational decision-making; that is, the parties did not use the usual strategies of optimization or satisficing. A fourth answer is that the parties dismissed acts perceived as having a low probability of occurrence. These possibilities suggest that we turn to two related issues: (1) preferences and utilities, and (2) satisficing and bounded rationality (Simon, 1957, 1972).

PREFERENCES AND UTILITIES

Game theorists commonly use the term "utility" in the manner defined by Von Neumann and Morgenstern (1944): a function defined in the context of a hypothetical risk-taking situation. We can broaden this definition by defining utility as a preference ordering or the degree of attractiveness of an outcome. This is the approach taken here. There are nevertheless some problematic issues concerning the concept of utility as applied to groups, as illustrated in pre-crisis British attitudes toward the Falklands question, particularly the issue of sovereignty.

Attributing to a group concepts of utility and preference similar to those of individuals raises some problems. If a voting system is adopted for selecting among individual preferences of the members of a group, then transitivity is not guaranteed (Arrow's theorem). Even more problematic in many real-world problems is the issue of the ambiguity of B's utilities. This is particularly true in the Falklands case before the war. Most people in Britain were ignorant of, or at best indifferent to, the problems of the Falklands: they had no preference ordering. The few interested parties with clear preference orderings had sharply differing ones. The Falklands lobby wished to preserve the existing situation, while the Foreign Office thought that in the long run there would have to be some change in that status. Given these contrary preferences, the absence of any stimulus from A meant that the safest option for B was to do as little as possible. It was also unclear how B would respond to such a stimulus from A. In a sense, too, A's overall utility was indeterminate within a certain range. It was not known, perhaps even to those actually involved in the decision process, just what sort of choice A would make in any given situation.

This was the worst of both worlds. A settlement before A's utilities had reached the point at which war was the best alternative (given A's misperceptions of B's strategy set) would have aborted such a policy, while B's build-up of a deterrent force would have made it unprofitable. The absence of any clear preference ordering, then, made conflict more probable.

It should be emphasized that such group indecision is not really the same as indifference in conventional utility theory. It is more akin to a probabilistic preference ordering (Luce, 1959). In a probabilistic preference ordering, neither the opponent nor indeed an individual member of the group knows what will happen in a situation in which a decision is forced and preferences are relevant.

SATISFICING AND BOUNDED RATIONALITY

In the satisficing world discussed earlier, an actor can only accidentally play optimal strategies vis-à-vis a non-salient issue. This seems to be a perfectly plausible description of reality and, in particular, the Falklands case.

Two concerns are relevant here. One is that game theory is normally presented as an optimizing model. We tacitly assume it to be a global optimizing model in the sense that, if a game exists with positive expected values (or, to use our earlier term, anticipated values), then a player will enter that game. Yet this is quite inconsistent with the assumption of bounded rationality. The idea of bounded rationality permits actors to optimize in one game, once it becomes salient, while ignoring other games with positive expected values. This was, in a manner of speaking, the British attitude toward the situation in the Falklands. Britain did not initially take the Falklands question seriously and hence failed to take appropriate actions. (Again, we must note the alternative explanation that the Argentine attack was a low-probability event outside the boundary of attention that in fact occurred.) Whether or not, according to some criterion, B should have drawn the boundary of attention more broadly is, of course, arguable.

This brings us to a curious proposition. There may exist some "latent" utility or preference ordering, one that would have pertained had the decision-makers thought of it. Once drawn to their attention, such a preference ordering is no longer latent but actualized. The whole notion of latent games and latent utilities introduces a complexity into the analysis that must be addressed if utility theory and game theory are to be of help in analyzing international situations.

Another concern derives from the fact that some preferences have a deeper and more complex significance than others. Utility theory can in principle deal with this concern, but its formal statements do not make it obvious that it has done so. The point is that some acts and consequences involve fundamental values whereas others involve simply preference orderings over consequences. Thus we may argue that B's reaction to A's invasion of the Falklands was not due to any estimate of probable costs and benefits but rather to the view of B's decision-makers (especially the prime minister) that the issue was one of moral absolutes. (Note that this conception of the issue is rather different from the earlier points that attitudes to violence are very complex and ambiguous, and that it is by no means clear that decision-makers always regard war as a cost.)

How do we deal with distinctions between fundamental and more superficial preferences? One way is to cast the problem into utility terms by representing moral absolutes with very large utility numbers ("very large" rather than "infinite," since "absolutes" are usually only "fairly absolute"). While this might serve as an interim solution, however, it is hardly satisfactory as a general solution to the issue. Game theory, if it is to be used in analyzing such emotionally entangled issues as war and peace, must recognize that preferences entail rather more complex psychological processes than the choice between coffee and tea. The irony is that decision-makers often view their opponents as considering options in a relatively cool, cost–benefit manner, while they themselves are thinking in absolute terms. It does not appear that either side in the Falklands case perceived the other as actually valuing the military virtues it valued highly itself.

The final question to be posed is whether or not it is appropriate to regard a hypergame as something distinct from an "ordinary" game, especially an ordinary game in which a particular strategy choice by an opponent is given a low probability. In the Falklands case, it cannot be denied that elements in Britain had from time to time, albeit at a low level, drawn attention to the possibility of an Argentine invasion. But decision-makers, if they had continuously to consider all low-probability acts on the part of potential opponents, would find life unbearably complex. It would be rational for these decision-makers to exclude such options and anticipate that a certain number of surprises will occur from time to time. (For, with a large enough number of low-probability events, there is a high probability that one or another of them will take place.) Britain's failure to take action before the Argentine invasion was thus not a mistake. It was merely the consequence of a justifiable decision rule.

Likewise, the Argentine government must have considered the possibility that Britain would react militarily, but dismissed the option as either highly unlikely or so costly that Britain would avoid it. Thus, a mistaken perception of British utilities and a failure to understand that key British decision-makers considered these utilities to be of fundamental importance led Argentina to assign a counterattack strategy by Britain a probability near zero. Again, the error is understandable. It could be argued that, apart from Churchill, no postwar British prime minister in similar circumstances would have adopted such a course. It was nevertheless a misjudgment with serious consequences for the Argentines.

This is the case with many situations that might lend themselves to hypergame analysis. The strategies that an opponent incorrectly omits from the rival's strategy set are not strategies ignored but rather are those considered and assigned an extremely low probability. Individuals do this through a perfectly rational technique of simplification. The same thing occurs in groups. Indeed, for the latter there is an even greater justification. Getting a group to determine its preference ordering over a number of possible situations is administratively costly. If acts that are unlikely to occur occasion a cost in terms of group decision-making, then it quickly becomes obvious that it is irrational to consider them.

The argument of this chapter has been that optimizing actors with a proper appreciation of the nature of the game "ought" not to have fought the Falklands war. The British and Argentine failures to optimize resulted not from folly but rather from their use of bounded rationality. (I am deliberately excluding moral objections to either side's resort to war.) This nevertheless raises the question of whether or not the governments should have extended the bounds within which their bounded rationality lies. With the wisdom of hindsight, it seems obvious that, if the British government had analyzed the situation (explicitly or de facto) in terms of expected utilities, it would have kept a larger permanent force in the Falklands on the grounds that its cost would have been very small compared with significant military action. The standard objection to such deterrent strategies — that they provoke hostility among those they are intended to deter and initiate a cycle of hostile acts — is less significant in this case than in many others. At most, their negative effects would have been minor. All parties regarded (and still regard) as totally unfeasible a British military attack on the Argentine mainland. Hence, even a very low probability of an Argentine invasion would still have accorded positive expected utilities to the strategy of maintaining a deterrent force.

That the British did not institute such a force must therefore be explained as an instance of either irrationality (in the sense of inconsistency) or bounded rationality in which the events lay outside the bounds. Since the Falklands case was no odder than many international situations, it prompts the reflection that the governments of at least the larger states might well find it worthwhile to devote more resources to the observation of low-probability events. The cost of such a search is trivial compared with the potential cost of otherwise unforeseen consequences of unforeseen acts.

NOTES

1. A measure of uncertainty called "potential surprise," which highlights precisely these points, was developed by Shackle (1952) as a psychologically more compelling measure than subjective probability. I am not aware, however, of any analysis using the concept that could not be translated into subjective probability terms. Perhaps it is for this reason that its use has not been widespread. Other aspects of uncertainty, particularly within the context of diplomatic or political communication, are reviewed in Cioffi-Revilla (1979).

2. Since the Argentines call these islands the Malvinas, many commentators tactfully write "Falklands/Malvinas." My use of the descriptor "Falklands" should not be taken as implying any view on the issue of sovereignty.

3. Much remains controversial today. The background discussion by the *Sunday Times* "Insight" team (Eddy and Linklater et al., 1982) gives a fairly balanced account.

REFERENCES

BENNETT, P. G. (1977) "Toward a theory of hypergames." Omega: The Journal of Management Science 5, 6: 749–751.

——— and M. R. DANDO (1979) "Complex strategic analysis: a hypergame study of the fall of France." OR: The Journal of Operational Research 30 (January): 23–32.

BRAMS, S. J. (1975) Game Theory and Politics. New York: Free Press.

CIOFFI-REVILLA, C. (1979) "Diplomatic communication theory: signals, channels, networks." International Interactions 6, 3 (Fall): 209–265.

EDDY, P. and M. LINKLATER et al. (1982) The Falklands War. London: André Deutsch.

LUCE, R. D. (1959) Individual Choice Behavior: A Theoretical Analysis. New York: John Wiley.

NICHOLSON, M. (1983) The Scientific Analysis of Social Behaviour: A Defence of Empiricism in Social Science. London: Frances Pinter.

PASKINS, B. A. and M. DOCKRILL (1979) The Ethics of War. London: Gerald Duckworth.

SAVAGE, L. J. (1977) The Foundations of Statistics (2d ed.). New York: Dover Publications.

SHACKLE, G. L. S. (1952) Expectation in Economics (2d ed.). Cambridge: Cambridge University Press.

SIMON, H. A. (1957) "A behavioral model of rational choice," pp. 241–260 in H. A. Simon, Models of Man: Social and Rational. New York: John Wiley.

——— (1972) "Theories of bounded rationality," pp. 161–176 in C. B. McGuire and R. Radner (eds), Decision and Organization: A Volume in Honor of Jacob Marschak. Amsterdam: North-Holland.

TAYLOR, A. J. P. (1965) English History, 1914–1945. Oxford: Clarendon Press.

THOMAS, H. (1967) Suez. New York and London: Harper & Row.

VON NEUMANN, J. and O. MORGENSTERN (1944) Theory of Games and Economic Behavior. Princeton, NJ: Princeton University Press.

CHAPTER 7

THE VERIFICATION PROBLEM IN ARMS CONTROL: A GAME-THEORETIC ANALYSIS

STEVEN J. BRAMS
MORTON D. DAVIS

Verification: The Critical Element in Arms Control, the title of a US Arms Control and Disarmament Agency (1976) publication, clearly underscores the overriding significance that each superpower attaches to its ability to verify that the provisions of an arms control agreement are adhered to by the other superpower. Indeed, the two superpowers spend billions of dollars annually to conduct reconnaissance and otherwise monitor the communications and physical moves of each other. These expenditures indicate the paramount importance for each of ascertaining what the other side is doing, and checking this observed behavior against statements on the other side about its actions.

The so-called verification problem in arms control concerns the impediments that may undermine one's ability to determine compliance with arms control treaty provisions (Meyer, 1984), and the correspondence between statements and observed actions of the other side. Its solution lies in formulating strategies that enable each side to ensure that it makes optimal use of its monitoring capabilities in the face of these impediments. There is a large literature, mostly descrip-

AUTHORS' NOTE: This chapter is based on a paper delivered by Steven J. Brams at the round table, "Global Communications: Policy and Process," of the Study Group on Global Communications of the International Political Science Association, University of Illinois at Urbana-Champaign, September 6–8, 1983, who expanded it for publication in Brams (1985: Ch. 4). The permission of Yale University Press to reprint parts of this chapter is gratefully acknowledged. The present version omits a mathematical appendix given in Brams (1985), which generalizes some of the analysis of the Truth Game developed herein.

tive, on obstacles that may arise, but little rigorous analysis has been devoted to possible solutions, other than to calculate certain physical effects (e.g., of cloud cover) on one's ability to detect certain kinds of military-related activities of the other side.

By "solution" we do not mean the specific safeguards that one might take against being deceived, which are well described with respect to different weapon systems and the military–strategic doctrines of the two superpowers by the several articles in a volume edited by Potter (1980), among other places. Rather, we mean general principles for dealing with problems of detecting the truth, based on an analysis of optimal strategies in games wherein the truth may be fugitive.

To try to elucidate these principles and highlight the theoretical issues they raise, we shall model the verification problem by a simple two-person, nonconstant-sum game of imperfect information played between a "signaler" and a "detector." The signaler can either tell the truth or lie, and the detector can ascertain, with a specified probability, the strategy choice of the signaler and, on this basis, choose to believe or not believe the choice he detects.

If the signaler wants to hide the truth and the detector wants to discover it, sometimes, paradoxically, *both* the detector and the signaler can do better when the detector completely ignores, rather than relies on, his detection equipment. In general, however, the detector should pay *selective attention* to the signal he detects in order to maximize his expected pay-off by (1) inducing the signaler to be truthful, or (2) guaranteeing himself an expected pay-off whatever the signaler does (tells the truth or lies).

Whether the detector chooses an optimal "inducement" or "guarantee" strategy, it will always be mixed (randomized) if his detection equipment is not perfect. Similarly, the signaler has his choice of these two qualitatively different strategies to (1) induce the detector to believe his signal, or (2) guarantee himself an expected pay-off whatever the detector does (believes or doesn't believe).

The fact that, in *all* circumstances, the optimal inducement and guarantee strategies of both the signaler and the detector are mixed when the detector's detection equipment is not perfect might appear surprising for two reasons, one theoretical and one substantive: (1) theoretically, in two-person, nonconstant-sum games — at least without detection probabilities — wherein the two players cannot ensure a (common) value (as in constant-sum games), mixed strategies have not been considered optimal; (2) substantively, the idea of ignoring one's detection equipment, even when its reliability is high, seems to violate common sense.

But perhaps, on this second point, this argument is really no more than an elaboration and formalization of the well-known strategic principle that one should keep one's opponent guessing, making him uncertain of what one's choice may be in a possible conflict by "leaving something to chance" (Schelling, 1960) or creating "strategic uncertainty" (Snow, 1983). What our formalization provides in addition, we believe, is a rigorous demonstration that this confusion principle is sound, even when there is rather reliable detection equipment that enables both players to calculate the expected risks to themselves.

That these calculations, and the resulting maximization strategies they imply, may lead to mutual benefits to the players in the non-constant-sum game posited — or at least may provide guarantees of the expected pay-offs they can ensure for themselves — offers, we think, a compelling justification that these mixed strategies are indeed "optimal." It needs to be emphasized, however, that we are not arguing that mixed strategies are generally optimal in two-person, nonconstant-sum games without detection, but, rather, that the introduction of detection probabilities in such games may render mixed strategies appropriate within an expected pay-off game-theoretic framework.

We shall proceed first by defining a generic 2 × 2 game we call the "Truth Game," based on strict ordinal rankings of the outcomes by the two players that satisfy specified primary and secondary goals. Then, assuming particular cardinal utilities/pay-offs consistent with these rankings, we shall illustrate a number of propositions about optimal mixed inducement and guarantee strategies on the part of each player which hold for the Truth Game generally. We shall conclude with some remarks on the relevance of these propositions to current strategic doctrine, and the ethical issues raised about acting arbitrarily.

The Truth Game

In the Truth Game, assume that a *signaler* (S) must choose between telling the truth and lying, and that, having made this choice, a *detector* (D) must then decide to believe him or not. Their choices, therefore, are not simultaneous. Yet, though S is assumed to choose prior to D, this game cannot be modeled as one of sequential play with perfect information.

This is because we assume that D cannot tell for certain whether S was truthful or not and thus cannot respond to S's strategy by always choosing his better strategy (believe or not believe) associated with S's prior strategy choice (be truthful or lie). Since D is unsure which strategy S chooses (later we shall assume that he can make predictions by consulting his detection equipment), this is technically a *game of imperfect information*, though both players are assumed to have complete information about the pay-offs shown in Figure 7.1.

Assume that these pay-offs are cardinal utilities, where a_4 and b_4 are the best outcomes for S and D, respectively, and a_1 and b_1 the worst. Thus, as before, the higher the subscripts, the better the pay-offs for the players, though the subscripts indicate only the rankings of these pay-offs by the players and not the utilities (a_i, b_j) that they associate with each outcome. Optimality calculations, with numerical values for the pay-offs, will be illustrated later.

Implicit in the rankings of the outcomes by S and D are the following goals:

S: (1) Primary goal: wants to hide the truth or lack thereof (two best outcomes off main diagonal)
   (2) Secondary goal: prefers to be believed
D: (1) Primary goal: wants to discover the truth or lack thereof (two best outcomes on main diagonal)
   (2) Secondary goal: prefers S to be truthful

The primary and secondary goals of each player *completely* specify their ordering of outcomes from best to worst: yes/no answers for each player and each goal automatically rank the four cells of a 2 × 2 game (a

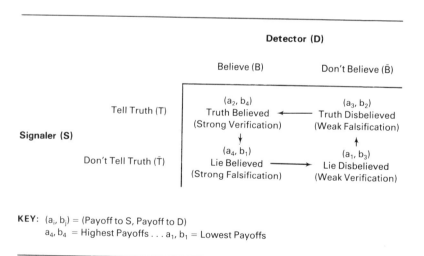

KEY: (a_i, b_j) = (Payoff to S, Payoff to D)
     a_4, b_4 = Highest Payoffs . . . a_1, b_1 = Lowest Payoffs

Figure 7.1 The Truth Game: Ordinal Rankings by the Players

tertiary goal would rank the eight cells of a $2 \times 2 \times 2$ game). This is an example of a lexicographic decision rule, whereby outcomes are ordered first on the basis of a most important criterion (primary goal), then on the basis of a next most important criterion (secondary goal), and so on (Fishburn, 1974).

In S's case, the primary goal establishes that he prefers outcomes off the main diagonal, where he lies and is believed (a_4), or tells the truth and is not believed (a_3). In either case, S succeeds in hiding the truth, whereas on the main diagonal the truth is discovered, either because S tells the truth and is believed (a_2), or because he lies and is not believed (a_1). The secondary goal establishes that, between the outcomes on and off the main diagonal, S prefers those associated with D's believing (first column) over not believing (second column).

In D's case, the primary goal says that he prefers outcomes on the main diagonal (b_4 and b_3), where he succeeds in discovering the truth, to those off the diagonal (b_2 and b_1), where he is foiled in his attempt to uncover the truth. The secondary goal says that, between the outcomes on and off the main diagonal, D prefers those associated with S's being truthful (first row) over S's lying (second row).

In the superpower arms race, these seem reasonable goals to impute to the two sides insofar as each desires to gain an edge over the other, or simply to maintain parity if it thinks the other side may be cheating. This may be a cynical view of the motives of each superpower in the nuclear arms race, and from a normative perspective undesirable. Nevertheless, the suspicions of each side probably drive each to try to cover up what exactly it is doing in certain areas, which gives rise to a natural counterdesire on the part of the other side to unmask the possible cover-up.

Each side, of course, knows that certain activities it wants to hide may be detected, so it cannot be certain that its cover-up will succeed. Yet, this fact does not invalidate its having the goals attributed to it, though, as we shall show, its optimal strategy choices will be affected by its realization that, as S, it can be detected with a specific probability by D; and, as D, this probability governs its success in realizing its goals in responding to S.[1]

We shall say more later about how well optimal strategies in the Truth Game seem to model the verification problem in the superpower arms race. But we are not so wedded to this particular game as to presume that there are no other candidates that might be descriptive of the clash of goals over verification. For example, the same methodology that we shall describe could be applied to a game in which a_2 and a_3 are interchanged in the Truth Game, making belief in the truth preferable to disbelief for S as well as D and thereby downgrading the importance for S of deceiving D.

It is worth noting that as a hide/discover-the-truth game, with a secondary emphasis on S's desire to be believed and D's desire that S be truthful, the Truth Game enables one not only to distinguish "verification" (main-diagonal outcomes) from "falsification" (off-diagonal outcomes); in addition, it suggests a "strong" and "weak" distinction in each of these main categories (see Figure 7.1). Thus, we consider verification stronger when one believes the truth than when one disbelieves a lie, because "the truth" is still elusive in the latter case — one may still not know what to believe, indicating non-falsification more than verification. Similarly, falsification seems stronger when a lie is believed than when the truth is disbelieved, because disbelief in the truth case says that one has missed the truth but not necessarily that one has been hoodwinked into believing a falsehood.

Note also that, despite the fact that the primary goals of the two players are diametrically opposed in the Truth Game, it is not one of total conflict: *both* players do better at (a_2, b_4) than at (a_1, b_3), so what one player "wins" the other does not necessarily "lose." Because the pay-offs to the two players, and necessarily their sum, are greater at (a_2, b_4) than at (a_1, b_3) — whatever the cardinal utilities one associates with the ordinal rankings of the four outcomes — the Truth Game is not constant-sum but variable-sum, and therefore, a game of *partial conflict*. In addition, the fact that (a_2, b_4) is better for both players than (a_1, b_3), and that there is not another outcome better for at least one player and not worse for the other than (a_2, b_4), means that (a_2, b_4) is *Pareto-superior*, whereas (a_1, b_3) is *Pareto-inferior*.

There is no stability in the Truth Game, as the arrows indicating cyclical preferences over the four outcomes in Figure 7.1 make evident. S can do immediately better by departing, in the directions shown by the vertical arrows, from (a_2, b_4) and (a_1, b_3), and D can do immediately better by departing, in the directions shown by the horizontal arrows, from (a_4, b_1), and (a_3, b_2). Because one player always has an incentive to depart from every outcome, no outcome is a *Nash equilibrium* (Nash, 1951), from which neither player would have an incentive to depart unilaterally. Neither does this game have a non-myopic equilibrium (Brams and Wittman, 1981), though (a_2, b_4) is an absorbing outcome (Brams and Hessel, 1982). On the other hand, if D could predict S's strategy choice with certainty, and if S knew this, the game would have an equilibrium if it were played sequentially: S would choose T (tell the truth), and D would respond with B (believe S); each would do worse by departing from these strategies.

S can induce his next-best outcome (a_3), and D his best outcome (b_4), with moving power (Brams, 1982) or staying power (Brams and Hessel, 1983), but neither player has threat power in this game (Brams and Hessel, 1982). The power-induced outcomes, however, do not seem particularly meaningful in games of imperfect information such as the Truth Game, for they presuppose that each player can respond to the other player's strategy choice according to the theory of moves. Yet, the initial strategy choice of S is, by assumption, not known with certainty by D, making the application of this theory problematic.

To illustrate the first proposition, and demonstrate the possibly paradoxical effects of D's detection capability in the Truth Game, assume that the pay-offs to the two players are as shown in Figure 7.2. These particular pay-offs were chosen to illustrate certain points that follow from the calculations to be described shortly; other assignments of cardinal utility values, consistent with the ordinal rankings of Figure 7.1, could be chosen. Observe that the best and worst pay-offs of each player are 10 and 0, respectively, whereas the intermediate pay-offs for S are 2 and 3 (S associates relatively low value with telling the truth), and for D, 7 and 8 (D associates relatively high value with being skeptical by not believing—see Figure 7.2).

Assume

p = the conditional probability that D's signal of S's strategy choice is correct (i.e. that D detects T when S chooses T and detects $\overline{T}$ when S chooses $\overline{T}$).[2]

One could distinguish between D's ability to detect T or $\overline{T}$, with possibly different probabilities; but in the calculation that follows, one need not make this distinction to establish the suboptimal consequences for D (as well as S) when D follows a *tit-for-tat policy* of B/$\overline{B}$ — believes if he detects T, doesn't believe if he detects $\overline{T}$.[3]

		Detector (D)	
		Believe (B)	Don't Believe (B̄)
	Tell Truth (T)	(2,10)	(3,7)
Signaler (S)	Don't Tell Truth (T̄)	(10,0)	(0,8)

KEY: (a_i,b_j) = (Pay-off to S, Pay-off to D)

Figure 7.2 The Truth Game: An Example

Assume that S and D know p, and also that D will respond to *his detection* of S's choice of T or $\overline{T}$ with tit-for-tat. Then, based on the Figure 7.2 pay-offs, S's expected pay-off, E_S, associated with each of his strategies, is

$$E_S(T) = 2p + 3(1 - p) = 3 - p$$
$$E_S(\overline{T}) = 10(1 - p) + 0p = 10 - 10p.$$

Lying is rational if $E(T) < E(\overline{T})$, or if

$$10 - 10p > 3 - p$$
$$p < 7/9 = 0.78.$$

For purposes of illustration, assume that $p = 3/4 = 0.75$. Then it is rational for S to lie, yielding

$$E_S(\overline{T}) = (10)(1/4) + (0)(3/4) = 10/4 = 2.50,$$

which compares with

$$E_S(T) = (2)(3/4) + (3)(1/4) = 2.25.$$

Now when S lies, D, using his detection equipment, will correctly detect $\overline{T}$ three-fourths of the time and incorrectly detect T one-fourth of the time; so his tit-for-tat policy will yield him

$$E_D(\text{tit-for-tat}) = (8)(3/4) + (0)(1/4) = 24/4 = 6.00.$$

Hence, S does worse than his next-*best* pay-off of 3, and D does worse than his next-*worst* pay-off of 7. Comparatively speaking, then, D ranks his expected pay-off lower than S does, but quantitatively D does much better than S (assuming that their utilities are measured on the same scale and can be compared).

Based on the pay-offs in the Figure 7.2 games, we shall next illustrate the following proposition:

Proposition 1: There may be a mixed strategy that D can adopt, independent of his detection probability $p = 0.75$, such that, if S responds optimally to it, both players will benefit over what they would obtain when D chooses tit-for-tat and S responds optimally to this policy.

We have already calculated the expected pay-offs of D's tit-for-tat policy when $p = 3/4$. Now assume that D follows a *mixed strategy* $(m, 1 - m)$, where

$$m = \text{probability that D chooses "believe" (B)},$$
$$1 - m = \text{probability that D chooses "don't believe" } (\overline{B}).$$

Note that $(m, 1 - m)$ are *unconditional probabilities*: they take no account of p; in effect, D ignores his detection equipment.

The difference Δ between the expected pay-off to S of telling the truth and lying is

$$\Delta = E_S(T) - E_S(\overline{T}).$$

For a given m and the Figure 7.2 pay-offs,

$$\Delta = \{2m + 3(1 - m)\} - \{10m + 0(1 - m)\}$$
$$= (3 - m) - 10m = 3 - 11m.$$

Thus, $\Delta > 0$ iff (if and only if) $m < 3/11$. If $m = 3/11^-$, where "$-$" indicates that m is slightly less than 3/11, it is rational for S to choose T, yielding

$$E_S(T) = 3 - (3/11)^- = 30/11^+ = 2.73^+,$$

where "$+$" indicates that $E_S(T)$ is slightly greater than 2.73. Observe that this value for $E_S(T)$ under mixed strategy $(m, 1 - m)$ exceeds $E_S(\overline{T}) = 10 - 10p$ under tit-for-tat iff $p > 8/11 = 0.73$.

Given that S chooses T, D's expected pay-off from using his mixed strategy is

$$E_D(m) = 10m + 7(1 - m) = 7 + 3m;$$

when $m = 3/11^-$,

$$E_D(3/11^-) = 7 + 3(3/11^-) = 86/11^- = 7.82^-.$$

Clearly, these expected pay-offs for S (2.73^+) and D (7.82^-) are better than their expected pay-offs under tit-for-tat (2.50 and 6.00, respectively), illustrating Proposition 1 (when $0.73 < p < 0.78$). Also note that the (3,7) outcome in the Figure 7.2 game is Pareto-superior to the tit-for-tat expected pay-offs, but this outcome is not in equilibrium, as noted earlier.

The mixed-strategy expected pay-offs for S and D are based on the assumption that D chooses $m < 3/11$ to induce S to tell the truth. What are the consequences for D if he chooses $m > 3/11$ to induce S to lie? In this case, given that S rationally chooses $\overline{T}$, D's expected pay-off is

$$E_D(m) = 0(m) + 8(1 - m) = 8 - 8m;$$

when $m = 3/11^+$,

$$E_D(3/11^+) = 8 - 8(3/11^+) = 64/11^- = 5.82^-,$$

which is substantially less than the expected pay-off that D obtains (7.82^-) when he makes it advantageous for S to be truthful. Moreover, 5.82^- is less than the 6.00 that D obtains from tit-for-tat, so Proposition

1 does not hold if D randomizes his choices between B and $\bar{B}$ to induce S to lie.

In sum, we have shown that both players lose when D sticks punctiliously to a policy of tit-for-tat which makes it advantageous for S to lie. Both can do better, by comparison, when D ignores his detection equipment entirely and randomizes his choices between B and $\bar{B}$ to induce S to be truthful.

This mixed-strategy calculation raises the question of how D might persuade S that it is indeed in both players' interest that D randomize his choices — in the prescribed manner — to elicit truth-telling from S. Before addressing this question, however, we shall demonstrate that it is not in general optimal for D totally to ignore the signal his detection equipment gives him. Instead, he should incorporate this information into his inducement calculations, which will be described next using a more sophisticated model.

Optimal Inducement Strategies

We begin by complicating the previous model. Let

q = probability that D chooses B if his detector indicates T;
r = probability that D chooses B if his detector indicates $\bar{T}$.

Previously we assumed that $q = 1$ and $r = 0$ when D followed tit-for-tat, but now we want to show that it is optimal in the Figure 7.2 Truth Game for D to respond to his detector (still assumed to have reliability $p = 3/4$, whatever S chooses) probabilistically rather than deterministically.

Let

$$s = \text{probability that S chooses T.}$$

Then for $0 \le q, r, s \le 1$, S's and D's expected pay-offs are

$$
\begin{aligned}
E_S &= sE_S(T) + (1 - s)E_S(\bar{T}) \\
&= s[p\{qa_2 + (1 - q)a_3\} + (1 - p)\{ra_2 + (1 - r)a_3\}] + (1 - s) \\
&\quad [p\{ra_4 + (1 - r)a_1\} + (1 - p)\{qa_4 + (1 - q)a_1\}]; \\
E_D &= sE_D(T) + (1 - s)E_D(\bar{T}) \\
&= s[p\{qb_4 + (1 - q)b_2\} + (1 - p)\{rb_4 + (1 - r)b_2\}] + \\
&\quad (1 - s)[p\{rb_1 + (1 - r)b_3\} + (1 - p)\{qb_1 + (1 - q)b_3\}].
\end{aligned}
$$

For the pay-offs given in the Figure 7.2 game, the expected pay-offs (after considerable simplifications) are

$$
\begin{aligned}
E_S &= (1/4)\{s(12 - 13q - 31r) + 30r + 10q\}; \quad &(1) \\
E_D &= (1/4)\{s(-4 + 17q + 27r) - 24r - 8q + 32\}. \quad &(2)
\end{aligned}
$$

Now, by keeping $(12 - 13q - 31r)$ positive, D can induce S to tell the truth, because this will raise E_S, given that $s > 0$.

In particular, if $r = 0$ and $q = 12/13^-$, S should always tell the truth $(s = 1)$, yielding

$$E_S = 30/13^+ = 2.31^+.$$

Similarly, D's expected payoff will be

$$E_D = 118/13^- = 9.08^-.$$

The fact that 9.08^- is greater than what D would obtain from his "straight" mixed strategy (7.82^-) — independent of what he detects — or tit-for-tat (6.00) — described in the previous section — seems a good reason for adopting it. That S's expected pay-off of 2.31^+ is less than what he obtains from D's mixed strategy (2.73^+) or tit-for-tat (2.50) means that S suffers when he (rationally) responds to the incentive D offers him to be truthful.

D's inducement strategy in this case is a more sophisticated policy than simply tit-for-tat. That is, when D makes his strategy choices probabilistic — according to q and r given above — he can do considerably better and, at the same time, decrease S's expected pay-off.

The key to this optimality calculation is that D can induce S to choose T over $\overline{T}$ — but not just by choosing a (straight) mixed strategy, unrelated to what he detects: rather, D should only selectively follow the signals of his detector, according to the calculated q and r optimality values given earlier, though it has a relatively high reliability $p = 3/4$. Thus, if his detector indicates that S chose T, it is optimal for D always to choose B (as expected), but if it indicates that S chose $\overline{T}$, it is optimal for D to choose $\overline{B}$ only about $12/13 = 92$ percent of the time.

Of course, when $p = 1$ and D's detection capability is perfect, he should strictly adhere to tit-for-tat. But then S should always tell the truth, because his pay-off will be 2 versus 0 for lying; this, in turn, gives D his highest pay-off of 10, so — as indicated earlier — the strategies T and $B/\overline{B}$ are in equilibrium when detection is certain. In reality, however, this is never the case.

This example illustrates the following proposition:

> *Proposition 2:* When D follows a sophisticated inducement strategy (mixed), based on his detection probability, he can raise his expected pay-off and lower S's, over what the players would obtain from tit-for-tat or a straight mixed strategy.

Note that this sophisticated inducement strategy, dependent on whether D detects T or $\overline{T}$, is itself mixed. If D detects $\overline{T}$, he should always choose $\bar{B}$ (as with tit-for-tat); the mixing comes in only when D detects T — and 8 percent of the time does not respond with B.

This deviation by D from tit-for-tat simultaneously lowers $E_S(\bar{T})$, and raises $E_S(T)$, for S in order to induce him to choose T. But this means that S receives less than tit-for-tat would give him at the same time that D gains more. This reasoning applies generally to the Truth Game, whatever the numerical pay-offs are that are consistent with the Figure 7.1 rankings, so Proposition 2 is not specific to the Figure 7.2 pay-offs but characterizes all Truth Games in which lying is rational when D follows tit-for-tat. A sophisticated inducement strategy, by incorporating D's detection probability in the expected pay-off calculations, entices S to be truthful — to his detriment and D's benefit.

One might think, in the earlier optimality calculation for E_S, that one could keep the factor $(12 - 13q - 31r)$ in equation (1) positive by letting $q = 1$ instead of $r = 0$. But if $q = 1$, the factor becomes $(-1 - 31r)$, which can be made positive only if $r < 0$; this strategic choice by D, however, is ruled out by the fact that r is a probability and, therefore, cannot be negative. (As shown in the appendix to Brams (1985), in order to maximize E_D, D should choose q and r, which are in an inverse linear relationship to each other, so that the former is as large, and the latter as small, as possible, given that certain conditions are met.) In the Figure 7.2 example, setting $r = 0$ means that only q is allowed to vary, so optimal mixing can occur only when D detects T and not when he detects $\bar{T}$.

But if D can take advantage of his detection capability to induce S to be truthful in order to help himself (D), why cannot S, who we assume also knows this capability, choose a mixed strategy to induce D to believe *him* — and in the process raise his own expected pay-off? The answer is that he can. We shall illustrate how, after stating a proposition analogous to Proposition 2:

Proposition 3: When S follows a sophisticated inducement strategy (mixed) based on D's detection probability, he can raise his expected pay-off and lower D's over what the players would obtain from tit-for-tat or a straight mixed strategy.

Consider equation (2) for E_D. It can be rewritten as

$$E_D = (1/4)\{q(17s - 8) + r(27s - 24) + (-4s + 32)\}. \tag{3}$$

Clearly, when $s = 8/17^+$, D will have an incentive to set $q = 1$ (and $r = 0$) so as to maximize E_D; but when $s = 24/27^+ = 8/9^+$, he will now have an incentive to set $r = 1$ as well. In the former case, $E_S = 81/34^+ = 2.38^+$, and in the latter case $E_S = 26/9^+ = 2.89^+$, so S would prefer the latter. This gives D an expected pay-off of $E_D = 65/9^- = 7.22^-$, compared with $128/17^- = 7.53^-$ in the former case.

Thus, to induce D always to choose B — whether S chooses T ($q = 1$) or $\overline{T}$ ($r = 1$) — S should adopt a mixed strategy $(t, 1 - t)$ over T and $\overline{T}$, where $t > 8/9 = 0.89$. In other words, if S is truthful about 90 percent of the time, it is in D's interest always to believe S, whatever signal he detects.

This is the sophisticated inducement strategy (mixed), alluded to in Proposition 3, that is optimal in the Figure 7.2 example. If $t > 8/9$, we showed above that it is better for S than tit-for-tat (which is optimal when $8/17 < p \leqslant 8/9$), so it remains only to show that it is better for S than a straight mixed strategy.

Such a strategy is one in which S would choose probability t of telling the truth such that $E_D(B) > E_D(\overline{B})$ for D, or

$$10t + 0(1 - t) > 7t + 8(1 - t)$$
$$t > 8/11.$$

If, for example, $t = 8/11^+ = 0.73^+$, and D rationally responds by always choosing B, the expected pay-off to S will be

$$E_S = 2t + 10(1 - t) = 10 - 8t,$$

or $10 - 8(8/11^+) = 24/11^- = 2.18^-$, which is well below the 2.89^+ expected pay-off S obtains when his detection capability is incorporated into the calculation of an optimal inducement strategy.

In summary, we have shown that, when D induces S always to be truthful,

$$E_S = 2.31^+, E_D = 9.08^-;$$

when S induces D always to believe,

$$E_S = 2.89^+, E_D = 7.22^-.$$

There is obviously a value to "leading" the other player with a sophisticated inducement strategy, which in general will be mixed.

If both players choose their inducement strategies simultaneously, both suffer compared with what each's inducement strategy would yield when the other player optimally responds to it (D suffers less because S, by being truthful 89 percent of the time, comes close to doing what D would like him to do):

$$E_S = 2.31, E_D = 8.96.$$

These results suggest that, should one player not be able successfully to assert his leadership, it may not be in that player's best interest to pursue an inducement strategy. Instead, he may prefer to guarantee himself an expected pay-off independent of what the other player does. This is the topic explored in the following section.

Optimal Guarantee Strategies and Overall Comparisons

Strategies that guarantee each player an expected pay-off not dependent on the other player's strategy choice in the Truth Game (with detection) are analogous to minimax/maximin strategies that guarantee the value in two-person constant-sum games (without detection). The difference lies in the fact that *either* player's guarantee strategy in a constant-sum game guarantees the other player's (guarantee) pay-off, for the guarantee — and all other — pay-offs to the players must sum to the constant. In the Truth Game, by contrast, the guarantee strategy of one player does not determine the other player's pay-off: it depends on the latter's choice. This leads to the fourth (and last) proposition:

> *Proposition 4:* S and D can guarantee themselves expected pay-offs, independent of the strategy choices of the other player, which are in general lower than the expected pay-offs they obtain from their sophisticated inducement strategies.

Starting with D, he can make his expected pay-off independent of S in equation (2) by letting

$$-4 + 17q + 27r = 0.$$

In particular, if $r = 0$, then $q = 4/17$, giving $E_D = 128/17 = 7.53$, a security value of which D can be assured whatever strategy S chooses. In this case, S does best to pick strategy T and obtain an expected pay-off of $48/17 = 2.82$. Note that D's security value of 7.53 is substantially below his inducement value of 9.08^-.

Now consider the game from S's perspective. To make his expected pay-off independent of the choice of q and r by D, rewrite equation (1) as follows:

$$E_S = (1/4)\{q(-13s + 10) + r(-31s + 30) + 12s\}. \qquad (4)$$

This equation is analogous to equation (3) — which itself is a rewrite of equation (2) — in the previous section.

Now S can make E_S independent of q by choosing $s = 10/13$, or independent of r by choosing $s = 30/31$. In the former case, his expected pay-off will be

$$E_S = (1/4)\{r(-310/13 + 30) + 120/13\}$$
$$= r(20/13) + 30/13.$$

Clearly, if $r = 0$ — its minimum value — S can guarantee himself $30/13 = 2.31$. By comparison, in the latter case,

$$E_S = (1/4)\{q(-390/31 + 10) + 360/31\}$$
$$= q(-20/13) + 90/31.$$

If $q = 1$ — its maximum value — S can guarantee himself $70/31 = 2.26$. Hence, S can do better by making E_S independent of q by choosing $s = 10/13$. Then, as we showed in the previous section, D will have an incentive to set $q = 1$ and $r = 0$, yielding an expected pay-off for D of $17/2 = 8.50$. As with D's security value, S's security value of 2.31 is well below his inducement value of 2.89^+.

Since security values are independent of the other player's strategy choice (i.e., of a choice of s by S, and choices of q and r by D), they are the same for S (2.31) and D (8.50) whatever their opponents do. As with optimal mixed strategies in two-person, constant-sum games, a player's choice of a guarantee strategy means that he may not benefit from possible "mistakes" by his opponent. This is always true of D but not of S, who benefits if $r > 0$ when $s = 10/13$.

A more general picture emerges when one compares the expected pay-offs of the two players in the Truth Game for their different strategy pairs shown in Table 7.1. To begin with, D's adherence to tit-for-tat hurts both players in this game, as was shown in the earlier section on the Truth Game, despite D's relatively high detection probability of $p = 3/4$ and S's knowledge of it. The tit-for-tat policy is less desirable because this p is not high enough to encourage truth-telling by S, whereas a straight mixed strategy by D — ignoring what he detects — that makes it rational for S to be truthful in fact benefits both players. Thus, tit-for-tat by D, coupled with lying by S, is Pareto-inferior to the second set of strategies shown in Table 7.1 (straight mixed strategy by D, truth-telling by S), so rational players would presumably not subscribe to the first strategies.

At the same time, it would seem foolish for D to throw away the information he obtains from his detection capability to concoct a sophisticated inducement strategy that, while making it rational for S still to tell the truth, benefits him (D) even more, though now at S's expense.

But there is no rule in the Truth Game that says that only D can be the initiator. If S can turn the tables, inducing D always to believe by being truthful approximately 90 percent of the time, S now benefits at D's expense.

TABLE 7.1 **Expected Pay-offs to Different Strategy Pairs in the Truth Game**
($p = 3/4$)

Strategy Pair	Signaler (S)	Detector (D)	Pareto-inferior[a]
Tit-for-tat by D, lying by S	2.50	6.00	Yes
Straight mixed by D, truth-telling by S	2.73^+	7.82^-	No
Sophisticated inducement by D, truth-telling by S	2.31^+	9.08^-	No
Sophisticated inducement by S, always believing by D	2.89^+	7.22^-	No
Sophisticated inducement by S and D	2.31	8.96	Yes
Guarantee by D, truth-telling by S	2.82	7.53	No
Guarantee by S, tit-for-tat by D	2.31	8.50	Yes
Guarantee by S and D	2.31	7.53	Yes

a. Pareto-inferiority is based only on the numerical pay-offs, not on the pluses or minuses.

Both players achieve their highest expected pay-offs (2.89^+ for S, 9.08^- for D) by exploiting the known reliability of the detection equipment and using mixed strategies to induce the other player to make a particular choice favorable to themselves. It is not surprising that D wants S to be truthful, nor is it surprising that S wants D to ignore his detection equipment completely and believe, regardless of the signal he detects.

What *is* unexpected is that S, by being truthful almost all the time, can make it rational for D always to believe him, even when he (D) detects lying. Manifestly, there is a value in S's establishing a record of honesty, because then his reputation may sustain D's belief even when D's detector indicates lying. Thereby *implicit* belief, or trust, in S — believing S regardless of what he detects — may be a rational response for D.

The major problem we see with inducement strategies — even sophisticated ones that incorporate detection information to induce rational responses — is that the putative responder may not want to be induced. Indeed, as the expected pay-offs demonstrate, it is always better for him to seize the initiative himself than passively to respond to the incentives the other player sets up for him with his mixed strategy.

Unless one player can lay valid claim to being the initiator rather than the responder, we suspect that there will be a conflict over proper roles — as well there should be, since it is rational for the players to fight for the initiative. The issue of who defers to whom can partially be circumvented by the guarantee strategies, but they limit the players to relatively low fixed expected pay-offs (2.31 for S, 7.53 for D). Curiously, the other player's optimal response to these strategies — tit-for-tat by D, truth-telling by S — provides each of them with higher expected pay-offs (2.82 for S, 8.50 for D) than were they the guarantors. When both players try simultaneously to induce or guarantee, the resulting outcomes are Pareto-inferior, though inducement is better for D than guarantee in this case.

In summary, it pays to be responsive to a guarantor but not to an inducer, who will capitalize on your responsiveness. In the latter case, you can do at least as well and generally better as a guarantor yourself (7.53 versus 7.22$^-$ for D, 2.31 in either case for S).

The fact, however, that S's sophisticated inducement strategy yields him at least as much as his guarantee strategy, and sometimes more (if D is responsive), means that it is dominant and should always be chosen. D, in turn, does best by responding with his own inducement strategy, yielding 2.31 and 8.96 for S and D, respectively, which is a Pareto-superior pair. On the other hand, if S should be responsive to D's sophisticated inducement strategy, D does even better (9.08), making his inducement strategy dominant as well.

Note that four strategy pairs in Table 7.1 are Pareto-superior and four are Pareto-inferior. The former are the best candidates for *both* players, though D's straight mixed strategy (second row in Table 7.1) ignores information it seems unlikely the players would eschew. For reasons given in the previous paragraph, however, the fifth-row pair seems particularly attractive since each player has an incentive to induce the other, regardless of how the other responds. Unfortunately for D, however, this is a Pareto-inferior pair because he suffers somewhat (8.96 versus 9.08) when S, who has no incentive to switch from sophisticated inducement, is not truth-telling.

In the next section we turn to the question of interpreting these theoretical results. We shall argue that the verification problem in arms control, particularly between the superpowers, very much involves inducements and guarantees that, as in the Truth Game, may require paying only selective attention to one's detection equipment by D, and occasional lying by S.

Interpretation and Conclusions

We have established four propositions that give better and worse strategies for a signaler and a detector — as measured by their expected pay-offs — in the Truth Game. The last three propositions hold generally, whatever the cardinal utilities associated with the preference rankings in the Truth Game, as long as D's detection probability is low enough to make lying rational for S when D follows a tit-for-tat policy. The first proposition also requires that this detection probability be within a certain range.

Patently, policy-makers in some area of national defense have considered lying and other forms of less-than-forthcoming behavior rational, presumably because they thought the chances of detection were sufficiently low that the risk of being discovered made it worthwhile. We believe that the Truth Game, insofar as it mirrors the goals of a policy-maker choosing between telling and not telling the truth, illustrates why this may be the case.

The Truth Game also illustrates how a detector might try to coax out the truth. In general, he (D) should *not* always believe his detection equipment, and respond accordingly (i.e., with tit-for-tat), even if it is fairly reliable. It is better instead to pay only selective attention to it, sometimes believing it when it indicates a lie, sometimes not believing an indication of the truth. Only the latter denial, however, is rational in the illustrative game, but it makes the point that this apparently errant behavior may be what is required to make truth-telling rational for S.

Optimal guarantee strategies that elicit the truth are also mixed, as are inducement and guarantee strategies that S may invoke. Perhaps the strangest result is that largely honest behavior on S's part may make it rational for D not to trust his detection equipment, even when it indicates lying, but instead always to believe S (at least until S's impeccable reputation for truthfulness is undermined).

In the superpower arms race, it seems, both sides have, by and large, been willing to give each other the benefit of the doubt — at least until recently (Wicker, 1983; Gwertzman, 1984) — despite the contrary indications they sometimes receive (Buchheim and Caldwell, 1983) (and which are considered by the US–USSR Standing Consultative Commission). This is an example of paying only selective attention to one's detection equipment, especially when the other side is viewed as a mostly honest signaler.

It also seems that both sides occasionally disbelieve what are perceived to be truthful signals, perhaps to generate better evidence from the other side. As optimal inducement and guarantee strategies of

D in the Truth Game suggest, this behavior is eminently rational when it makes S more forthcoming.

It appears, then, that the superpowers probably do not always play it "straight" about what they detect (Richelson, 1984; Steinberg, 1983). Whether they deliberately mix things up or act as if they do, their sometimes capricious behavior seems consistent with optimal mixed strategies in the Truth Game.

Of course, fine-grained optimality calculations, based on the cardinal utilities of the players and their detection probabilities, cannot be made with any exactitude in most real-world applications. Yet, these calculations do show up important qualitative differences between, say, inducement and guarantee strategies. The fact that both kinds of optimal strategies are mixed in a nonconstant-sum game such as the Truth Game seems to us most significant.

At a normative level, it says that one should always act probabilistically — randomizing one's choices within certain constraints — though this behavior is, in a fundamental sense, arbitrary. Anomalously, arbitrariness may be required to satisfy exemplary goals, such as discovering the truth. Hence one should not shun it if optimal achievement of these goals is desired. At the same time, arbitrary behavior may clash with well-known ethical principles; and, in a theological context, it raises the distressing problem of evil in the world (Brams, 1983).

In the secular arena of arms control, non-adherence to tit-for-tat — under prescribed conditions — may be viewed as a kind of deliberate deception or clandestine behavior, which has been previously analyzed in 2 × 2 ordinal games using a different model (Brams, 1977).[4] The moral issue, we believe, is whether the need of seeking the truth, or protecting oneself in an arms race, provides sufficient justification for occasional lying by S, or for D's faking his response (by departing from tit-for-tat) to the signal of S that he detects (Bok, 1978).

The issue seems to us not clear-cut, especially given the fact that detection is never perfect. This compromises any attempt to benefit from always being truthful (S), or adhering meticulously to a reciprocity principle like tit-for-tat (D). More generally, simple ethical positions in an uncertain world become more tenuous.

NOTES

1. This game is adapted to the problem of monitoring environmental pollution, in a repeated-game extension, in Russell (1984).

2. Raymond Dacey and Donald Wittman, in personal communications (July 1983), have indicated that p must be defined with respect to specific events or actions and not

just to S's strategy choices of truth-telling and lying. In the context of arms control, this can easily be done with a plausible scenario. Let S's first strategy of T be interpreted to mean that S reduces his arms (R) *and* tells the truth about his reduction; and let T̄ be interpreted to mean that S does not reduce his arms (R̄) *and* lies that he has. Then *p* is the probability that D correctly detects R or R̄, which, by assumption, are actions invariably associated with T and T̄, respectively. Since S will always claim that he chose R/T, *p* defines *the probability that D correctly detects whether this claim is truthful or not.* This probability depends not on whether S claims to be truthful — he always does — but instead on his actions R and R̄, which we assume are equivalent to T and T̄ in the arms control scenario.

3. For different analyses of this policy, see Brams, Davis, and Straffin (1979); Dacey (1979, 1982); and Axelrod (1984).

4. Other game-theoretic and related models relevant to problems of deception are Axelrod (1979a, 1979b) and Reese (1982).

REFERENCES

AXELROD, R. (1984) The Evolution of Cooperation. New York: Basic Books.

AXELROD, R. (1979a) "Coping with deception" pp. 390-405 in S. J. Brams et al. (eds.) Applied Game Theory: Proceedings of a Conference of the Institute for Advanced Studies, Vienna, June 13-16, 1978. Würzburg: Physica-Verlag.

———(1979b) "The rational timing of surprise." World Politics 31 (January): 228-246.

BOK, S. (1978) Lying: Moral Choice in Public and Private Life. New York: Pantheon Books.

BRAMS, S. J. (1977) "Deception in 2 × 2 games." Journal of Peace Science 2 (Spring): 171–203.

——— (1982) "Omniscience and omnipotence: how they may help — or hurt — in a game." Inquiry 25 (June): 217–231.

——— (1983) Superior Beings: If They Exist, How Would We Know? Game-Theoretic Implications of Omniscience, Omnipotence, Immortality, and Incomprehensibility. New York: Springer-Verlag.

——— (1985) Superpower Games: Applying Game Theory to Superpower Conflict. New Haven, Conn.: Yale University Press.

——— and M. P. HESSEL (1982) "Absorbing outcomes in 2 × 2 games." Behavioral Science 27 (October): 393–401.

——— and M. P. HESSEL (1983) "Staying power in 2 × 2 games." Theory and Decision 15 (September): 279-302.

BRAMS, S. J., M. D. DAVIS, and P. D. STRAFFIN Jr (1979) "The geometry of the arms race." International Studies Quarterly 23 (December): 567-588; and "A reply to 'Detection and Disarmament,'" 599-600.

BRAMMS, S. J. and D. WITTMAN (1981) "Nonmyopic equilibria in 2×2 games." Conflict Management and Peace Science 6 (Fall): 39–62.

BUCHHEIM, R. W., and D. CALDWELL (1983) "The US–USSR standing consultative commission: description and appraisal." Providence, RI: Brown University, Center for Foreign Policy Development (mimeographed).

DACEY, R. (1979) "Detection and disarmament." International Studies Quarterly 23 (December): 589-598.

———(1982) "Detection, inference and the arms race," pp. 87-100 in M. Bradie and K. Sayre (eds.), Reason and Decision. Bowling Green, Ohio: Bowling Green State University, Bowling Green Studies in Applied Philosophy, iii: 1981.

FISHBURN, P. C. (1974) "Lexicographic orders, utilties and decision rules: a survey." Management Science 20 (July): 1442–1471.

GWERTZMAN, B. (1984) "Reagan is said to find breaches by Soviets of agreements on arms." New York Times (14 January): 1.

MEYER, S. M. (1984) "Verification and risk in arms control." International Security 8 (Spring): 111–126.

NASH, J. (1951) "Non-cooperative games." Annals of Mathematics 548: 286–295.

POTTER, W. C. (ed.) (1980) Verification and SALT: The Challenge of Strategic Deception. Boulder, Colo.: Westview Press.

REESE, W. (1982) "Deception in a game theoretic framework," pp. 115–135 in D. C. Daniel and K. L. Herbig (eds.) Strategic Military Deception. New York: Pergamon Press.

RICHELSON, J. T. (1984) "The Keyhold satellite program." Journal of Strategic Studies 7 (June): 121–153.

RUSSELL, C. S. (1984) "Monitoring sources of pollution: lessons from single and multiple play games." Washington, DC: Resources for the Future, Quality of the Environment Division, Discussion Paper 121.

SCHELLING, T. C. (1960) The Strategy of Conflict. Cambridge, Mass.: Harvard University Press.

SNOW, D. M. (1983) The Nuclear Future: Toward a Strategy of Uncertainty. University: University of Alabama Press.

STEINBERG, G. M. (1983) Satellite Reconnaissance: The Role of Informal Bargaining. New York: Praeger.

US ARMS CONTROL AND DISARMAMENT AGENCY (1976) Verification: The Critical Element in Arms Control. Washington, DC: US Government Printing Office, publication 85 (March).

WICKER, T. (1983) "Cheating on SALT." New York Times (3 May): A27.

CHAPTER 8

AMBIGUOUS INFORMATION AND THE ARMS RACE AND MUTUAL DETERRENCE GAMES

RAYMOND DACEY

The superpowers employ rhetoric to manipulate each other's behavior in plays of the arms race and mutual deterrence games. This chapter presents an account of the use of ambiguous rhetoric as a manipulative device within the context of decision-theoretic play of the games. More specifically, it presents an account of ambiguous bribes and threats to manipulate the adversary to engage in cooperative behavior.

The arms race and mutual deterrence games can be seen as instances of the prisoner's dilemma game. A decision-theoretic analysis of prisoner's dilemma, if it is to be interesting, requires a theory of decision with more power than the standard (e.g., Savage) theory, since the latter yields the usual game-theoretic stalemate. The first novelty of this paper is the introduction of Richard Jeffrey's (1983) theory of decisions to model decision-theoretic play of the arms race and deterrence games.[1]

The rhetoric used by the superpowers is usually subtle. A superpower does not usually simply threaten or bribe the other power. Rather, the rhetoric employed by the superpowers is usually ambiguous, that is, purposefully uncertain. There is nothing novel here in the analysis of ambiguous rhetoric. We shall adopt Shepsle's (1972a, 1972b) notion of ambiguity as a lottery. However, the resulting notions

AUTHOR'S NOTE: I wish to acknowledge the helpful criticisms made by Steven J. Brams and Richard Toelle, and the very fine editorial comments of Claudio Cioffi-Revilla.

of (1) a probabilistic bribe, (2) a probabilistic threat, (3) probabilistic tit-for-tat — and (4) the surprising conclusion that all three manipulative devices are risk-free to the user — constitute the second novelty of the paper.

Finally, probabilities revised on the basis of (purposefully) uncertain information cannot be revised via the standard process of probability conditionalization based on Bayes's theorem. The third novelty of this chapter is the introduction of Jeffrey's probability kinematics as the proper method for revising probabilities on the basis of ambiguous information.

The chapter proceeds as follows. The first section introduces and applies Jeffrey's theory of decision in the arms race/deterrence game. The following section introduces the notions of a probabilistic bribe, a probabilistic threat, and probabilistic tit-for-tat, and presents the arguments that support the conclusion that all three manipulative devices are risk-free to the user. A third main section introduces Jeffrey's probability kinematics and presents an example of the application of probability kinematics. The final section discusses various open issues surrounding the analysis presented in the chapter.

Throughout, the USSR is treated as the manipulative player and the USA is treated as the object of manipulation. This device is employed for ease of exposition. Since the prisoner's dilemma game is symmetric, anything that can be said about one player can be said about the other. Also please note that the mathematics required to state and prove results is simple and straightforward, and involves only analytical geometry.

General Framework

The arms race and the state of mutual deterrence between the two superpowers is best modeled as a prisoner's dilemma game (Brams, 1976; Dacey and Toelle, 1982; Zagare, 1983). Standard game-theoretic and decision-theoretic resolutions of the game yield "degenerate" solutions wherein the dominance present in the game dictates the well-known stalemate.[2] This section of the chapter presents the rudiments of the (nonstandard) decision-theoretic resolution of the game based upon Jeffrey's (1983) theory of act-state-dependent decisions.

The arms race/deterrence game, seen as a decision problem for the USA, involves two acts, a_1 = cooperate and a_2 = do not cooperate,[3] and two states of nature, b_1 = the USSR cooperates and b_2 = the USSR does not cooperate. The payoffs to the USA are as follows:

USA

	a₁	a₂

where $1 > U > V > 0$. The USA holds two act-dependent probability distributions, one for a_1, with $\Pr(b_1/a_1) = P$ and $\Pr(b_2/a_1) = 1 - P$, and one for a_2, with $\Pr(b_1/a_2) = Q$ and $\Pr(b_2/a_2) = 1 - Q$. The expected pay-off for a_1 is $E(a_1) = PU + (1 - P)0 = PU$ and the expected pay-off for a_2 is $E(a_2) = Q1 + (1 - Q)V$. The decision tree for the problem is shown in Figure 8.1. The cooperative act a_1 is preferred to the noncooperative act a_2 if and only if $PU > Q + (1 - Q)V$.[4] If the probabilities are treated as parameters, then the set of points (V, U) at which a_1 is preferred to a_2 is graphically represented as the shaded region in Figure 8.2.

The square in Figure 8.2 includes all those points (V, U) for which $0 < V < 1$ and $0 < U < 1$. The broken line separates the square into the feasible upper triangle, where $0 < V < U < 1$, as is required by the prisoner's dilemma pay-off table, and the infeasible lower triangle, where $0 < U < V < 1$. The solid line is the set of points (V, U) where the acts are indifferent, and it divides the feasible region into the shaded region, where a_1 is preferred to a_2, and the unshaded region, where a_2 is preferred to a_1. The equation of the solid line is

$$U = \frac{1 - Q}{P} V + \frac{Q}{P} . \tag{1}$$

The slope of the line, $(1 - Q)/P$, and the intercept, Q/P, are positive, since $0 < Q < 1$ and $P > 0$. Note that the specific values of the slope and the intercept are undetermined. Thus Figure 8.2 represents the case where the slope is greater than, and the intercept is less than, unity. The graph also can take either of the interesting forms shown in Figure 8.3(a) and (b).

From equation (1) it is clear that, if $Q > P$, then the intercept is greater than unity and the solid line would not enter the feasible upper triangle. That is, if $Q > P$, then a_2 is preferred to a_1 at all feasible points (V, U). Thus, Jeffrey's theory of decisions yields a non-degenerate solution to the arms race-deterrence game only if $P > Q$. To avoid trivialities, we shall limit our attention to those situations where $P > Q$.[5]

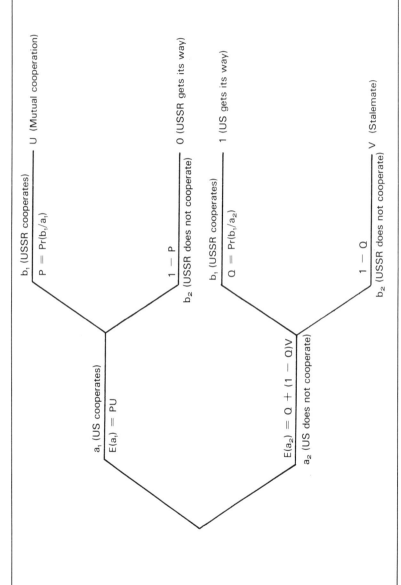

Figure 8.1

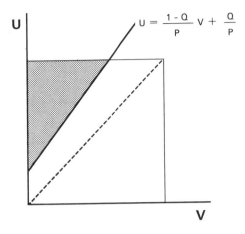

Figure 8.2

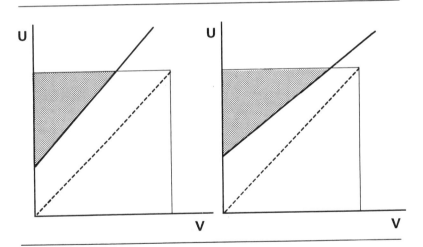

Figure 8.3a   Figure 8.3b

Furthermore, note that, if the intercept becomes 0 and the slope becomes 1, then a_1 is preferred to a_2 in the whole of the feasible region. Thus, if the USSR can manipulate the values of P and Q so that the intercept moves toward 0 and the slope moves toward 1, then the USSR will have manipulated the USA toward cooperation.

The Effects of Probability Manipulation

The USSR can manipulate the partial beliefs of the USA in three interesting ways. First, we shall say that the USSR *probabilistically bribes* the USA if and only if the USSR communicates a message E_B to the USA that increases P and leaves Q unchanged. Thus E_B "says" that, while the probability that the USSR will cooperate given that the USA will not cooperate is unchanged, the probability that the USSR will cooperate given that the USA will cooperate is increased. Second, we shall say that the USSR *probabilistically threatens* the USA if and only if the USSR communicates a message E_T that leaves P unchanged and decreases Q. Thus, E_T "says" that, while the probability that the USSR will cooperate given that the USA will cooperate is unchanged, the probability that the USSR will cooperate given that the USA will not cooperate is decreased. Finally, we shall say that the USSR engages in *probabilistic tit-for-tat* (TFT) if and only if the USSR communicates a message E_{TFT} that increases P and decreases Q. Thus, E_{TFT} "says" that the probability that the USSR will cooperate given that the USA will cooperate is increased and the probability that the USSR will cooperate given that the USA will not cooperate is decreased.

The effects of probabilistic bribes, threats, and tit-for-tat are surprising. We shall say that a message E puts the USSR *at risk* if and only if there are feasible pay-offs at which the shift in the probabilities P and/or Q due to E induces an otherwise cooperative USA to be noncooperative. Similarly, we shall say that a message E is *risk-free* to the USSR if and only if it does not put the USSR at risk. Intuition and naive geometry suggest that a probabilistic bribe would be risk-free whereas probabilistic threats and probabilistic tit-for-tat would put the USSR at risk. It is easy to establish, however, the surprising theorem:

The messages E_B, E_T, and E_{TFT} are all risk-free to the USSR.

CASE 1: BRIBES

Consider first a probabilistic bribe. Recall that the indifference curve is the set of points (V, U) that lies on equation (1). A probabilistic bribe increases P to $\hat{P}$ and leaves Q unchanged. The slope of the line, therefore, is reduced from $(1 - Q)/P$ to $(1 - Q)/\hat{P}$, and the intercept is reduced from Q/P to $Q/\hat{P}$.

The geometry of a probabilistic bribe is given in Figure 8.4. Recall that at points (V, U), which lie above an indifference curve, a_1 is preferred to a_2; at points below an indifference curve a_2 is preferred to a_1. Therefore, in area I, a_1 is preferred to a_2 before and after the bribe.

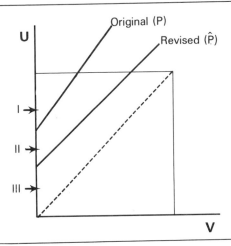

Figure 8.4

In area II, a_2 is preferred to a_1 before the bribe and a_1 is preferred to a_2 after the bribe. Finally, in area III a_2 is preferred to a_1 before and after the bribe. There are, accordingly, no points in the feasible region where the USA shifts from cooperation (a_1) to noncooperation (a_2). That is, a probabilistic bribe does not put the USSR at risk, and is therefore risk-free to the USSR.

CASE 2: THREATS

Now consider a probabilistic threat. A probabilistic threat decreases Q to $\hat{Q}$ and leaves P unchanged. The slope of the indifference curve is therefore increased from $(1 - Q)/P$ to $(1 - \hat{Q})/P$ and the intercept is reduced from Q/P to $\hat{Q}/P$. Thus, the (naive) geometry of a probabilistic threat suggests two possible cases which are illustrated in Figures 8.5(a) and (b).

Figure 8.5(a) is similar to the graph for a probabilistic bribe (Figure 8.4). In area I, a_1 is preferred to a_2 before and after the bribe. In area II, a_2 is preferred to a_1 before the bribe and a_1 is preferred to a_2 after the bribe. In area III a_2 is preferred to a_1 before and after the bribe. Clearly, by Figure 8.5(a), a probabilistic threat is risk-free to the USSR. Figure 8.5(b) includes area IV, which lies above the original indifference curve and below the revised curve. Thus, in area IV the effect of a threat is to induce the USA to switch from a_1 to a_2. Therefore, the USSR would be at risk if the actual pay-offs lie in area IV.

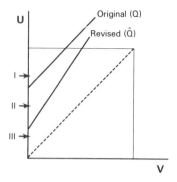

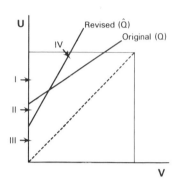

Figure 8.5a   **Figure 8.5b**

The conclusion that a probabilistic threat can put the USSR at risk is based on naive geometry and is incorrect. Let (V^*, U^*) denote the point at which the original and revised indifference curves intersect. Then, at (V^*, U^*),

$$\frac{1-Q}{P} V^* + \frac{Q}{P} = \frac{1-\hat{Q}}{P} V^* + \frac{\hat{Q}}{P}.$$

Solving for V^* and substituting back into the expression yields $V^* = 1$ and $U^* > 1$ (see Figure 8.6(a) and (b)). Note that the area IV is now outside the feasible region, leaving areas I, II, and III as before. Thus, contrary to the conclusion based on naive geometry, we can properly conclude that a probabilistic threat does not put the USSR at risk. That is, a probabilistic threat is risk-free to the USSR.

CASE 3: TIT-FOR-TAT

Finally, consider probabilistic tit-for-tat. Probabilistic tit-for-tat increases P to $\hat{P}$ and decreases Q to $\hat{Q}$. The shift in the slope of the indifference curve is indeterminate; that is, $1 - \hat{Q} > 1 - Q$ and $\hat{P} > P$, which leaves the relationship between $(1 - \hat{Q})/\hat{P}$ and $(1 - Q)/P$ undetermined. The intercept of the indifference curve is reduced from Q/P to $\hat{Q}/\hat{P}$. Thus, the (naive) geometry of probabilistic tit-for-tat suggests three possible cases, which are illustrated by Figures 8.7(a)–(c). Figures 8.7(a) and 8.7(b) are like the graph for a probabilistic bribe (Figure 8.4); in these cases probabilistic tit-for-tat is risk-free to the

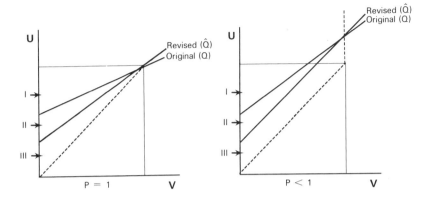

Figure 8.6a   **Figure 8.6b**

USSR. Figure 8.7(c) is like Figure 8.7(b) for a probabilistic threat; it suggests that there is a subregion, area IV, of the feasible region where the USSR is at risk.

However, the conclusion that probabilistic tit-for-tat can put the USSR at risk, again based on naive geometry, is incorrect. Let (V^*, U^*) be the point at which the original and revised indifference curves intersect. Then, at (V^*, U^*) we have

$$\frac{1-Q}{P} V^* + \frac{Q}{P} = \frac{1-\hat{Q}}{\hat{P}} V^* + \frac{\hat{Q}}{\hat{P}}.$$

Simple rearrangement of the terms yields

$$\hat{P}Q - P\hat{Q} = V^* \{(\hat{P}Q - P\hat{Q}) - (\hat{P} - P)\}.$$

Now $\hat{P} > P$ and $\hat{Q} < Q$, so that $\hat{P}Q - P\hat{Q} > 0$ and $\hat{P} - P > 0$. Furthermore, for the case illustrated in Figure 8.7(c), $(1 - Q)/P < (1 - \hat{Q})/\hat{P}$, so that $(\hat{P}Q - P\hat{Q}) - (\hat{P} - P) > 0$. Thus,

$$V^* = \frac{\hat{P}Q - P\hat{Q}}{(\hat{P}Q - P\hat{Q}) - (\hat{P} - P)} > 1.$$

Now, (V^*, U^*) must satisfy equation (1). For $V^* > 1$, clearly

$$U^* > \frac{1-Q}{P} + \frac{Q}{P} = \frac{1}{P} > 1.$$

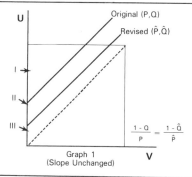

Figure 8.7a

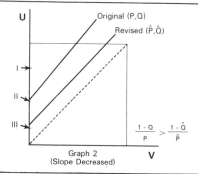

Figure 8.7b

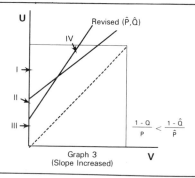

Figure 8.7c

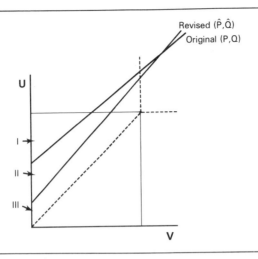

Figure 8.8

Therefore, $V^* > 1$ and $U^* > 1$, and the correct geometry for Figure 8.7(c) is shown in Figure 8.8. Area IV is outside the feasible region, leaving areas I, II, and III as before. Thus, contrary to the conclusion based on naive geometry and intuition, we can properly conclude that probabilistic tit-for-tat is risk-free to the USSR.

The surprising theorem has been proved. The three-part analytical geometry argument has established that E_B, E_T, and E_{TFT} are all risk-free to the USSR.

Manipulation of Probabilities via Ambiguous Information: Jeffrey's Probability Kinematics

The analysis presented in the previous section reveals that the USSR, without risk, can manipulate the behavior of the USA by manipulating the partial beliefs held by the USA. This section presents an analysis of the use of ambiguous information as a device to manipulate the partial beliefs held by the USA and thereby the behavior of the USA.

Following Shepsle (1972a, 1972b), we shall say that a message is ambiguous if it is purposefully uncertain. More specifically, a message E is ambiguous if E is a disjunction $e_1 \lor e_2 \lor \ldots \lor e_n$ (where $\lor$ denotes disjunction), presented so that the receiver can adduce the true disjunct only up to a probability. Thus, if the USSR presents E ambiguously, then the USA possesses the probability distributions $P(E) = \{P(e_1/a_1), \ldots, P(e_n/a_1)\}$ given a_1 and $Q(E) = \{Q(e_1/a_2), \ldots, Q(e_n/a_2)\}$ given a_2. The USSR manipulates the partial beliefs of the USA by manipulating the probability distributions $P(E)$ and $Q(E)$. That is, the USSR instantiates the message E as E_B, E_T, or E_{TFT} so that the USA adduces new probability distributions $\hat{P}(E) = \{\hat{P}(e_1/a_1), \ldots, \hat{P}(e_n/a_1)\}$ and $\hat{Q}(E) = \{\hat{Q}(e_1/a_2), \ldots, \hat{Q}(e_n/a_1)\}$.

The logic of the manipulation process is provided by Jeffrey's (1983) probability kinematics. The important point to note is that the logic of the manipulation process is not provided by the usual logic of probability conditionalization, that is, the revision of probabilities via Bayes's theorem. The fundamental tenet of probability conditionalization is given by C. I. Lewis (1946: 186; as cited and discussed in Jeffrey, 1983: 167–168): "If anything is to be probable, then something must be certain. The data, which themselves support a genuine probability, must themselves be certain."

Genuine probabilities, in Lewis's sense, are conditional probabilities generated from prior probabilities and *certain* data via Bayes's theorem. Ambiguous information is (purposefully) *uncertain*, and therefore probabilities based upon ambiguous information are not genuine, in Lewis's sense, and are not generated via probability conditionalization. Jeffrey's probability kinematics provides the logic of probability revision that supplants probability conditionalization.

For ease of exposition we shall consider only dichotomous ambiguous information $E = e \vee \bar{e}$, where the overbar denotes negation. Then the kinematic revisions are as follows. The initial probability of b_1 given as a_1 is revised from

$$P = P(b_1/e\&a_1)P(e/a_1) + P(b_1/\bar{e}\&a_1)P(\bar{e}/a_1)$$

to

$$\hat{P} = P(b_1/e\&a_1)\hat{P}(e/a_1) + P(b_1/\bar{e}\&a_1)\hat{P}(\bar{e}/a_1)$$

and the initial probability of b_1 given a_2 is revised from

$$Q = Q(b_1/e\&a_2)Q(e/a_2) + Q(b_1/\bar{e}\&a_2)Q(\bar{e}/a_2)$$

to

$$\hat{Q} = Q(b_1/e\&a_2)\hat{Q}(e/a_2) + Q(b_1/\bar{e}\&a_2)\hat{Q}(\bar{e}/a_2).$$

The revisions involve the (genuine) conditional probabilities $P(b_1/e\&a_1)$, $P(b_1/\bar{e}\&a_1)$, $Q(b_1/e\&a_2)$, and $Q(b_1/\bar{e}\&a_2)$. These are the conditional probabilities that the USSR will cooperate, given (i.e., on the hypothesis) that either e or $\bar{e}$ is certain. The probabilities are analogous to the conditional probabilities encountered in preposterior analysis in standard decision theory. Note, however, that the revised state probabilities $\hat{P}$ and $\hat{Q}$ are not generated from P and Q, respectively, via probability conditionalization.

An example of kinematic probability revision is in order. The following example concerns only probabilistic tit-for-tat and is based on the familiar policy of conditional cooperation. The policy is stated simply as: "I'll cooperate if you will; otherwise, I won't." As before, we shall let the USSR be the manipulative player. Suppose, then, that the USSR announces that it will adhere to the policy of conditional cooperation.

The statement of the policy is a conjunction of two conditional statements. The former says, "If you'll cooperate, then I'll cooperate," whereas the second says, "If you won't cooperate, then I won't cooperate."[6] Formally the former statement is $a_1 \Rightarrow b_1$, and the latter is $a_2 \Rightarrow b_2$, where $\Rightarrow$ is the usual "if . . ., then . . ." connective.

Now, let $e_{\text{TFT}} = (a_1 \Rightarrow b_1)\&(a_2 \Rightarrow b_2)$. Then, we shall show, $E_{\text{TFT}} = e_{\text{TFT}} \vee \overline{e_{\text{TFT}}}$ is an instance of probabilistic tit-for-tat. To show that this is the case we must show that $\hat{P} > P$ and $\hat{Q} < Q$ in accordance with the kinematic equations given above.

Suppose the USA, in an effort to test the adherence of the USSR to the policy, performed a cooperative act, for example by dismantling some missiles in Western Europe, to which the USSR responded by performing a cooperative act, such as dismantling some missiles in Eastern Europe. The two cooperative acts constitute a positive instance of the $a_1 \Rightarrow b_1$ part of the policy. Suppose, further, that the USA also performed an uncooperative act, for example by placing new, more sophisticated tanks in Western Europe, to which the USSR responsed by also performing an uncooperative act, such as placing new, more sophisticated antitank weapons in Eastern Europe. The two uncooperative acts constitute a positive instance of the $a_2 \Rightarrow b_2$ part of the policy.

Suppose that, before the performance of the two pairs of acts, the USA held the probabilities $P(e_{\text{TFT}}/a_1)$ and $P(\overline{e_{\text{TFT}}}/a_1)$ for a_1 and $Q(e_{\text{TFT}}/a_2)$ and $Q(\overline{e_{\text{TFT}}}/a_2)$ for a_2. Then the initial state probabilities P and Q are, by the kinematic equations,

$$P = P(b_1/e_{\text{TFT}}\&a_1)\,P(e_{\text{TFT}}/a_1) + P(b_1/\overline{e_{\text{TFT}}}\&a_1)\,P(\overline{e_{\text{TFT}}}/a_1)$$

and

$$Q = Q(b_1/e_{\text{TFT}}\&a_2)\,P(e_{\text{TFT}}/a_2) + Q(b_1/\overline{e_{\text{TFT}}}\&a_2)\,Q(\overline{e_{\text{TFT}}}/a_2),$$

respectively. These equations reduce to

$$P = P(e_{\text{TFT}}/a_1)$$

and

$$Q = Q(\overline{e_{\text{TFT}}}/a_2),$$

since $P(b_1/e_{\text{TFT}}\&a_1) = 1$ and $P(b_1/\overline{e_{\text{TFT}}}\&a_1) = 0$, $Q(b_1/e_{\text{TFT}}\&a_2) = 0$ and $Q(b_1/\overline{e_{\text{TFT}}}\&a_2) = 1$.[7]

The state probabilities are revised on the basis of the two pairs of acts, as follows. The probability P is revised, via the kinematic equations, to $\hat{P}$:

$$\hat{P} = P(b_1/e_{\text{TFT}}\&a_1)\,\hat{P}(e_{\text{TFT}}/a_1) + P(b_1/\overline{e_{\text{TFT}}}\&a_1)\,\hat{P}(\overline{e_{\text{TFT}}}/a_1),$$

where $\hat{P}(e_{\text{TFT}}/a_1)$ is the probability, held by the USA, that the USSR will adhere to the policy of conditional cooperation given the two pairs of acts. Clearly, the two pairs of acts are positive instances of the policy, so that $\hat{P}(e_{\text{TFT}}/a_1) > P(e_{\text{TFT}}/a_1)$. As before, $P(b_1/e_{\text{TFT}}\&a_1) = 1$ and $P(b_1/\overline{e_{\text{TFT}}}\&a_1) = 0$, so $\hat{P}$ reduces to $\hat{P}(e_{\text{TFT}}\&a_1)$. Therefore, $\hat{P} > P$.

Likewise, the probability Q is revised, on the basis of the kinematic equations, to $\hat{Q}$ as follows:

$$\hat{Q} = Q(b_1/e_{\text{TFT}}\&a_2)\hat{Q}(e_{\text{TFT}}/a_2) + Q(b_1/\overline{e_{\text{TFT}}}\&a_2)\hat{Q}(\overline{e_{\text{TFT}}}/a_2),$$

where $\hat{Q}(\overline{e_{\text{TFT}}}/a_2)$ is the probability, held by the USA, that the USSR will *not* adhere to the policy of conditional cooperation given the two pairs of acts. Clearly, the two pairs of acts are positive instances of the policy, so that $\hat{Q}(\overline{e_{\text{TFT}}}/a_2) < Q(e_{\text{TFT}}/a_2)$. As before, $Q(b_1/e_{\text{TFT}}\&a_2) = 0$ and $Q(b_1/\overline{e_{\text{TFT}}}\&a_2) = 1$, so $\hat{Q}$ reduces to $\hat{Q}(\overline{e_{\text{TFT}}}/a_2)$. Therefore, $\hat{Q} < Q$.

Thus, the policy of conditional cooperation, instantiated by the two pairs of acts, constitutes an example of probabilistic tit-for-tat. That is, the USSR has uttered a statement E_{TFT} with components e_{TFT} and $\overline{e_{\text{TFT}}}$ such that the USA can tell which of e_{TFT} and $\overline{e_{\text{TFT}}}$ holds only up to a probability; *and* the USSR has responded to US initiatives so as to manipulate the USA to alter its state probabilities so that $\hat{P} > P$ and $\hat{Q} < Q$. This concludes the example.

Conclusion

The foregoing account of the role of purposefully uncertain (i.e., ambiguous) rhetoric in manipulating the play of a superpower in the arms race/deterrence game involves the following novelties:

(1) the application of Jeffrey's nonstandard theory of decisions as the proper decision-theoretic account of plays of the game;

(2) the introduction of the concepts of a probabilistic threat, a probabilistic bribe, and probabilistic tit-for-tat as manipulative devices;

(3) the establishment of the surprising result that all these manipulative devices are risk-free to the user;

(4) the application of Jeffrey's probability kinematics as the proper procedure for probability revision, given purposefully uncertain (i.e. ambiguous) information.

The foregoing analysis admits of two open issues. First, the ambiguous information used as a manipulative device was formulated as the simple dichotomy $E = e \vee \bar{e}$. It remains to provide an analysis of the role of ambiguous information as a manipulative device where the information has the more general form of an n-ary disjunction — that is, where $E = e_1 \vee e_2 \vee \ldots \vee e_n$.

Second, the foregoing analysis is based upon the presumption that Jeffrey's theory of decisions is the proper theory for decision-theoretic plays of the arms race/deterrence game. It remains to establish this presumption.

NOTES

1. Jeffrey (1983: 15–17, 20) has applied his theory to the prisoner's dilemma, and Dacey and Toelle (1982) have applied the theory to the arms race game.

2. Brams and Wittman (1981) present a nonstandard game-theoretic resolution of the game which yields a non-degenerate solution, but provides no mechanism of information transfer.

Steven J. Brams (private communication) has pointed out that the game treated in the Brams-Wittman analysis is a game of complete information which becomes, under their nonstandard resolution procedure, a game of perfect information. Thus, there is no mechanism for the transfer of private (or strategic) information because there is no such information in a perfect information game. Please note that the formalities of game theory are avoided in the present analysis because it is a decision-theoretic analysis, and also that the present analysis does provide a mechanism of information transfer.

3. For the arms race game, $a_1 = b_1 =$ "continue to arm" and $a_2 = b_2 =$ "begin to disarm." For the mutual deterrence game, $a_1 = b_1 =$ "is deterred" and $a_2 = b_2 =$ "is not deterred."

4. To see that the standard decision theory yields a degenerate solution, simply remove the act-dependence of the probabilities and let $Q = P$. Then a_1 is preferred to a_2 if and only if $PU > P + (1 - P)V$. But $PU < P$ since $0 < U < 1$. Further, $(1 - P)V > 0$ since $0 < P < 1$ and $V > 0$. Thus, $PU < P + (1 - P)V$ for all values of P, U, and V, and, therefore, a_1 is never preferred to a_2.

5. Note that this is a reasonable presumption. Since P is the probability that the USSR will cooperate given that the USA cooperates and Q is the probability that the USSR will cooperate given that the USA will not cooperate, it seems reasonable that $P > Q$.

6. See Brams, Davis, and Straffin (1979) for the initial statement of the policy of conditional cooperation.

7. The proofs are as follows.

To show:
$$P(b_1/e_{TFT}\&a_1) = 1$$

Proof:

$P(b_1/e_{TFT}\&a_1)$	$= P[b_1/(a_1{\Rightarrow}b_1)\&(a_2{\Rightarrow}b_2)\&a_1]$	by substitution
	$= P[b_1/b_1\&(a_2{\Rightarrow}b_2)]$	by $\Rightarrow$ elimination
	$= \dfrac{P[b_1\&b_1\&(a_2{\Rightarrow}b_2)]}{P[b_1\&(a_2{\Rightarrow}b_2)]}$	by definition of conditional probability
	$= \dfrac{P[b_1\&(a_2{\Rightarrow}b_2)]}{P[b_1\&(a_2{\Rightarrow}b_2)]}$	since $p\&p$ is equivalent to p
	$= 1$	

To show:
$$P(b_1/\overline{e_{TFT}}\&a_1) = 0$$

Proof:

$P(b_1/\overline{e_{TFT}}\&a_1)$	$= P[b_1/\{\overline{(a_1{\Rightarrow}b_1)\&(a_2{\Rightarrow}b_2)}\}\&a_1]$	by substitution
	$= P[b_1/\{\overline{(\overline{a}_1{\vee}b_1)\&(\overline{a}_2{\vee}b_2)}\}\&a_1]$	since $p{\Rightarrow}q$ is equivalent to $\overline{p}{\vee}q$
	$= P[b_1/[(\overline{\overline{a}_1{\vee}b_1}){\vee}(\overline{\overline{a}_2{\vee}b_2})]\&a_1]$	by DeMorgan's law
	$= P[b_1/[a_1\&\overline{b}_1){\vee}(a_2\&\overline{b}_2)\}\&a_1]$	by DeMorgan's law
	$= P[b_1/(a_1\&a_1\&\overline{b}_1){\vee}(a_1\&a_2\&\overline{b}_2)]$	by the distribution law
	$= P[b_1/(a_1\&\overline{b}_1){\vee}(a_1\&a_2\&\overline{b}_2)]$	by the conjunction law
	$= P[(b_1/a_1\&\overline{b}_1)$	by *modus tollendo ponens*
	$= \dfrac{P(b_1\&a_1\&\overline{b}_1)}{P(a_1\&\overline{b}_1)}$	by definition of conditional probability
	$= \dfrac{0}{P(a_1\&\overline{b}_1)}$	by assignment of 0 axiom of probability theory
	$= 0$	

To show:
$$Q(b_1/e_{TFT}\&a_2) = 0$$

Proof:

$Q(b_1/e_{TFT}\&a_2)$	$= Q[b_1/[(a_1{\Rightarrow}b_1)\&(a_2{\Rightarrow}b_2)]\&a_2]$	by substitution
	$= Q[b_1/(a_1{\Rightarrow}b_1)\&b_2]$	by $\Rightarrow$ elimination
	$= \dfrac{Q[b_1/b_2\&(a_1{\Rightarrow}b_1)]}{Q[(a_1{\Rightarrow}b_1)\&b_2]}$	by definition of conditional probability
	$= \dfrac{0}{Q[(a_1{\Rightarrow}b_1)\&b_2]}$	by assignment of 0 axiom of probability theory
	$= \qquad 0$	

To show:
$$Q(b_1/\overline{e_{\text{TFT}}}\&a_2) = 1$$

Proof:

$$Q(b_1/\overline{e_{\text{TFT}}}\&a_2) = Q[b_1/[\overline{(a_1 \Rightarrow b_1)\&(a_2 \Rightarrow b_2)}]\&a_2] \qquad \text{by substitution}$$

$$= Q[b_1/\overline{[(\overline{a}_1 \vee b_1)\&(\overline{a}_2 \vee b_2)]}\&a_2] \qquad \begin{array}{l}\text{since } p \Rightarrow q \text{ is equivalent} \\ \text{to } \overline{p} \vee q\end{array}$$

$$= Q[b_1/[\overline{(\overline{a}_1 \vee b_1)} \vee \overline{(\overline{a}_2 \vee b_2)}]\&a_2] \qquad \text{by De Morgan's law}$$

$$= Q[b_1/[(a_1\&\overline{b}_1) \vee (a_2\&\overline{b}_2)]\&a_2] \qquad \text{by De Morgan's law}$$

$$= Q[b_1/(a_2\&a_1\&\overline{b}_1) \vee (a_2\&a_2\&\overline{b}_2)] \qquad \text{by the distribution law}$$

$$= Q[b_1/(a_1\&a_2) \vee (a_2\&\overline{b}_2)] \qquad \text{by the conjunction law}$$

$$= Q(b_1/a_2\&\overline{b}_2) \qquad \text{by } \textit{modus tollendo ponens}$$

$$= \frac{P(b_1\&a_2\&\overline{b}_2)}{p(a_2\&\overline{b}_2)} \qquad \begin{array}{l}\text{by definition of} \\ \text{conditional probability}\end{array}$$

$$= \frac{P(a_2\&\overline{b}_2)}{P(a_2\&\overline{b}_2)} \qquad \text{since } b_1 = \overline{b}_2$$

$$= 1$$

REFERENCES

BRAMS, S. J. (1976) Paradoxes in Politics. New York: Free Press.

———, M. D. DAVIS, and P. D. STRAFFIN Jr (1979) "The geometry of the arms race." International Studies Quarterly 23 (December): 567–588; and "A reply to 'Detection and disarmament,'" 599–600.

BRAMS, S. J. and D. WITTMAN (1981) "Nonmyopic equilibria in 2 × 2 games." Conflict Management and Peace Science 6 (Fall): 39-62.

DACEY, R. and R. TOELLE (1982) "Decision-theoretic resolutions of the arms race game." Unpublished paper presented at the University of Illinois meeting of the Institute for the Study of Conflict Theory and International Security, Urbana, Ill., September 22–24.

JEFFREY, R. (1983) The Logic of Decision. Chicago, Ill.: University of Chicago Press.

LEWIS, C. I. (1946) An Analysis of Knowledge and Valuation. La Salle, Ill.: Open Court.

SHEPSLE, K. (1972a) "The paradox of voting and uncertainty" and "Parties, voters and the risk environment: a mathematic treatment of electoral competition under uncertainty," pp. 252–270 and 273–287 in R. G. Niemi and H. F. Weisberg (eds.), Probability Models of Collective Decision-Making. Columbus, Ohio: Charles Merrill.

——— (1972b) "The strategy of ambiguity: uncertainty and electoral competition." American Political Science Review 66 (June): 555–568.

ZAGARE, F. (1983) "Toward a reconciliation of game theory and the theory of mutual deterrence." Unpublished paper presented at the UCLA meeting of the Institute for the Study of Conflict Theory and International Security, Los Angeles, Calif., June 23–25.

PART III

Social and Political Communication

CHAPTER 9

LANGUAGE AND COMMUNICATION: THE RISE OF THE MONOLINGUAL STATE

J. A. LAPONCE

Language is not, of course, the sole or always the major carrier of information. In some circumstances — an intimate conversation between two lovers or among three heads of state — it may indeed be the least important. Gestures, body movements, clothes, or, in different circumstances, rituals, dances, and music may have a greater density of meaning than the spoken or written word. Overall, however, language is for most people the primary means of communication. We do not know of communities that do not use language to integrate (or segregate) their functions. Even the Trappist monks are not totally speechless, and, although they may not speak much, most read or write. Language is among the major social forces, one strangely overlooked by Mosca, that bind masses, relate them to specific elites, and connect these elites together. Whether or not they share a common language makes a difference for the society and its members.

Languages also play a crucial role in the conduct of international relations. World politics in a monolingual world would be quite different from the conduct of international affairs in a world of a few quasi-dominant languages or one in which many languages enjoy equal status. The world's linguistic structure — which languages play what roles — shapes the habits of and facilities for communication, the mobility of individual citizens and their ability to link themselves to a worldwide information system (hence the permeability of national boundaries), the function and training of diplomats, and the diversity of sociocultural patterns. Hence the status of individual languages in the global communications network is important.

How stable is the world's current linguistic structure? One perspective suggests that the present situation — a multiplicity of languages — is likely to continue indefinitely, possibly forever. Linguistic change on a massive level is sufficiently difficult, this argument continues, as to make it highly improbable. Hence the babel of tongues in today's world is likely to persist even if one or another minor language disappears. Some proponents of this pluralist perspective argue that such inertia is a good thing. It permits people to express themselves in their native tongue and thus does not deny them their creative potential.

An alternative perspective sees the world moving either haphazardly or inexorably toward monolingualism. In a Darwinian struggle for survival, pockets of resistance notwithstanding, the stronger languages will drive out the weaker. Some argue that the expansion of a global communications network will make inevitable the world's eventual use of but a few languages, perhaps only one. Some see this as the path toward peace: a common world language would facilitate communication and lead to conflict resolution among most of the world's peoples. A few, such as Esperantists, are at work creating artificially a language that in their view could serve as a common tongue.

Such widely varying perspectives pose some interesting puzzles for students of international relations. This chapter approaches change in the world's linguistic structure in two ways. First of all, it explores the *general conditions of language change*. A background question concerns the extent to which the number of languages is growing or declining worldwide. Another question concerns which "natural" factors make a language's survival more or less likely. More specifically, we consider the role of the modern state as language planner, as an active participant in the process by which some languages within its territorial domain die while others persist and even grow stronger. Second, the chapter investigates the *conditions for global language change*. Is today's multiplicity of languages likely to persist? Or are we witnessing a trend toward the emergence of a few "dominant" languages or even global monolingualism? Again, a crucial question is the role of the state in furthering or retarding such global language change.

The Life and Death of Languages

Is the universe expanding or contracting? Are there more or fewer species today than yesterday? Do social systems have entropic or syntropic tendencies? In recent decades astronomy has alternated between believing that the world of stars is growing and believing that it is contracting. Today's predominant thought sees it expanding, and the universe becoming more varied. Not so the world of pears. At the beginning of the nineteenth century there were 4,000 different types of pears in North America—4,000 types assumed to derive from a common ancestor. Today, of these 4,000 kinds, only 600 still exist and nearly all of these belong to only 12 varieties. The world of pears may well be contracting at a time when that of stars is expanding, but one day it may expand again, if only because of the success of gene banks in using radiation to create hybrids and new strands.

What of the world of languages? In looking at the birth, persistence, and death of languages, three interrelated issues are relevant. The first is change in the sheer *number* of languages. Is their number growing or diminishing? The second is their *growth rate*, that is, the net rate at which new languages are being born while others are dying. The birth rate of languages may in turn be increasing or decreasing, just as the death rate or disappearance of languages may be proceeding more slowly or rapidly. The third issue is the *life expectancy* of languages. How long do languages live?

The absence of agreement on the definition of what constitutes a language means that the answers to key questions are subject to considerable variation. But definitional uncertainty is not peculiar to sociolinguists. Biologists have a similar problem when they define species and their varieties. How many different characteristics must there be before two flies can be said to be of different types? What level of non-intelligibility must exist before two languages can be said to be foreign to each other? In the case of flies, the fact that the flies' opinions are not taken into consideration simplifies the problem; in the case of languages, by contrast, the speakers' own perceptions cannot so easily be ignored. Thus we usually treat Slovak and Czech as two distinct tongues although they are mutually intelligible, while the upper- and lower-class English speakers studied by Labov (1968) are typically considered to belong to the same language group even though their mutual intelligibility is not so great as that of Slovaks and Czechs.

Any enumeration of the total number of languages, any measure of their growth rate or life span, is hence bound to be very rough. Estimates of the number of languages spoken today range anywhere from 2,500 to 7,000 (Muller, 1964; Laponce, 1984).[1] Such estimates pose problems of measurement. While one can speak of a single French language, can one speak of a single Chinese language or even of a single Mandarin tongue? Are Nynorsk and Bokmal to be counted separately? Using a cut-off figure of 1 million speakers, Culbert (1984) tallied 165 separate languages (excluding dialects). Muller's (1964) higher level of aggregation (at least 5 million speakers), which also ignores the distinctiveness of dialects, results in the ranking of the 82 languages shown in Table 9.1 (data from Culbert, 1984). Depending on whether one retains Muller's 2,500 as the total number of languages spoken today or Ferguson's 7,000. These 82 languages represent either 3 or 1 percent of the total number of existing languages. They nevertheless account for 96.4 percent of the world's population.

The life span of a language is even less subject to precise measurement. Considering the sole languages of major cultures (French, English, German, Chinese, and so forth) to the exclusion of their dialectical variations, Cailleux (1953) estimates that, from prehistory to present times, languages have lived for an average of 2,000 to 3,000 years and that, for every language that died, two languages were born. (Thus Latin, now considered a dead language, spawned at least nine well-established offspring.) Such figures, however imprecise, at least suggest the direction of past trends.

Now, in the era of what Valery (1945) calls *le monde fini*, that long trend toward diversification has apparently come to an end. In Africa, Asia, South and North America, as well as in Europe, sociolinguists and ethnographers make concordant observations: the number of effective languages is diminishing. (Concern for the survival of these languages is, to be sure, often exaggerated for political reasons, but the fears are not unreasonable.) This fact prompts us to ask why some languages persist while others die.

The Survival of Languages

What factors enhance the likelihood that a language will survive? What factors contribute to its death? The previous section treated the birth, persistence, and death of languages as actuarial statistics, as random events occurring in a complex world. In fact, we can identify specific characteristics of that complex world that in the past have made a difference for the survival of languages. This in turn can be a first step toward a more data-based analysis of the correlates of language survival.

SIZE OF LINGUISTIC COMMUNITY

Implicit in the earlier discussion is the proposition that the number of speakers using a language affects its durability. There is *ceteris paribus* doubtless some threshold, a minimum number of native speakers required to give what they speak the formal status of a living language.

TABLE 9.1 Languages with at least Five Million Speakers, 1984

Rank	Language	No. (m.)	% of World Population	Rank	Language	No. (m.)	% of World Population
1	Chinese[a]	935	19.6	42	Hungarian	13	0.3
2	English	409	8.6		Ibo	13	0.3
3	Hindi-Urdu[b]	352	7.4	44	Sinhalese	12	0.3
4	Russian	280	5.9	45	Czech	11	0.2
5	Spanish	275	5.8		Greek	11	0.2
6	Arabic	166	3.5		Nepali	11	0.2
7	Bengali	160	3.4		Sindhi	11	0.2
8	Portuguese	157	3.3	49	Amharic	10	0.2
9	Malay/Indon.	122	2.6		Fula	10	0.2
10	Japanese	121	2.5		Zhuang	10	0.2
11	German	118	2.5		Uzbeck	10	0.2
12	French	110	2.3	53	Afrikaans	9	0.2
13	Punjabi	69	1.4		Berber	9	0.2
14	Korean	63	1.3		Bulgarian	9	0.2
15	Italian	62	1.3		Byelorussian	9	0.2
16	Tamil	60	1.3		Madurese	9	0.2
	Telegu	60	1.3		Malagasy	9	0.2
18	Marathi	59	1.2		Swedish	9	0.2
19	Javanese	50	1.0	60	Azerbaijani	8	0.2
20	Turkish	48	1.0		Galla	8	0.2
	Vietnamese	48	1.0	62	Kurdish	7	0.1
22	Thai	42	0.9		Malinke	7	0.1
	Ukrainian	42	0.9		Quechua	7	0.1
24	Polish	39	0.8		Rwanda	7	0.1
25	Kannada	36	0.8		Tatar	7	0.1
26	Gujurathi	35	0.7	67	Catalan	6	0.1
	Swahili	35	0.7		Kazakh	6	0.1
28	Malayalam	31	0.7		Khmer	6	0.1
29	Persian	29	0.6		Tibetan	6	0.1
30	Burmese	28	0.6		Tui-fante	6	0.1
	Oriya	28	0.6		Uighur	6	0.1
	Tagalog	28	0.6		Zulu	6	0.1
33	Hausa	27	0.6	74	Danish	5	0.1
34	Rumanian	24	0.5		Finnish	5	0.1
35	Dutch	20	0.4		Norwegian	5	0.1
	Serbo-Croatian	20	0.4		Rundi	5	0.1
37	Pashto	19	0.4		Shona	5	0.1
38	Sundanese	17	0.4		Slovak	5	0.1
39	Assamese	15	0.3		Somali	5	0.1
	Visayan	15	0.3		Sotho	5	0.1
	Yoruba	15	0.3		Xhosa	5	0.1

a. Mandarin 81%, Wu 6%, Cantonese 6%, Min 5%, and Hakka 3%.

b. Hindi 78% and Urdu 22%; if Punjabi is added to Hindi/Urdu, it moves ahead of English in the rank order.

SOURCE: Culbert (1984: 245).

How precisely to indicate the magnitude of this threshold nevertheless poses a serious research task.

Available evidence (Dressler and Wodak-Leodolter, 1977; Foster, 1982) indicates that the viability of a language is linked to the size of the community using it: small languages are dying out. If disappearance were to be the fate of the languages spoken today by fewer than 1 million people, then 93-98 percent of all contemporary languages would vanish. There is even doubt about the possibility of survival enjoyed by some of the 165-odd languages spoken by more than 1 million people. Will Latvian, spoken by 2 million, will Berber, spoken by 9 million, will Ukrainian, spoken by 42 million, be able to resist the assimilative pressure of their politically more powerful competitors? And, if they do, will they survive as anything more than home or kitchen languages, as amputated or dumb languages not used for the higher social and cultural functions?

Such evidence must be interpreted with caution. Setting the threshold at 5 million for our estimate reduces to 82 the number of those languages to which we would assign some probability of survival (Table 9.1). And yet we must note that much smaller languages, such as Icelandic, which only half a million speak, sustain themselves without great problem. These considerations suggest that, while the size of the linguistic community may be important, that variable alone will not go far toward an explanation of which languages live and die. We must look at other factors as well.

LINGUISTIC TRADITION

Social traits acquired by large masses of people are slow to change. Accordingly, as a first approximation we may predict (again, *ceteris paribus*) that the major languages of today will persist into tomorrow. This is not to say that they will not evolve in the course of time. We may, for instance, view Latin as a dead language, one that "died." It is more appropriate to view it as a language that, because of other circumstances, evolved to the point that, should Cato come back to life today, he would be unable to understand the residents of the same Roman street in which he lived in his own day; nor could he understand the residents of any other street in the world (yet at all major universities in the world he would find somebody to talk to, or at least somebody with whom to exchange written messages).

No major language is frozen for all times. This fact suggests two additional points. First, whether or not we consider a language stable depends on the time frame we use in the analysis. A language may be relatively unchanging over the span of a century, but if our time frame is a millenium then we may find striking change. Any prediction about the future of a language must thus specify temporal conditions. Second, we must consider both the inertia of language and its rate of change when we try to assess the future prospects of a given tongue. If we would understand the probability of its persistence, we must look beyond linguistic tradition toward the rate at which native speakers are assimilating foreign words and expressions into their everyday speech, the rate of change exhibited in principles of grammar, and other dynamic elements of language. These elements depend in turn on the language community's social setting.

LINGUISTIC RICHNESS

In their competition for speakers, languages depend for their success to some measure on their richness. By this I mean two things. The first is quantitative: the number of words spoken, written, or printed at a given point in time, that is, the *size* of the language (as opposed to the size of the language community using it). The second aspect is qualitative. Although "quality" refers sometimes to semantic precision, we shall use it to refer to the *importance* of the linguistic communication. Importance is determined both at the *individual* level, by the hierarchy that people establish among their various social roles (work, family, church, etc.), and at the *social* level, by the consequences of the message — ordering a meal, writing a scientific paper, or issuing a military command.

While a language's quantitative and qualitative richness contributes to its ability to compete successfully with other languages, this characteristic by itself is insufficient to guarantee survival. Linguistic richness did not prevent classical Greek and Latin from transformations that rendered them obsolete.

BOUNDARIES

Boundaries between languages are more or less porous. Porosity conditions the likelihood that a language will undergo transformation over time. What kinds of boundaries exist, and what kind of impact do they have? First, if one linguistic community is separated from another by some sharp *physical* discontinuity, such as an ocean passage or high mountains, it is normally easier for both to retain their linguistic distinctiveness. Where there is physical proximity, there will in all likelihood be some language crossing in the borderlands. A reasonable proposition for research is that the degree of linguistic border-crossing varies inversely with the impermeability of the physical boundary.

The same is true if the boundary is not physical but *linguistic*. Two communities with separate languages stemming from the same root (e.g. French and Italian) will have more permeable linguistic boundaries than communities with languages derived from different roots (e.g. French and German). If we could somehow control for the effect of physical factors, we might also hypothesize that the geographic extent of the borderlands will vary directly with the closeness of the languages. More generally, linguistic gradients (measured by the degree of mutual comprehension), together with other communications gradients, such as the power gradient suggested by Boulding (1962), should help plot and understand the way in which states protect or project themselves within or across their borders (Starr and Most, 1976).

Third, *social* boundaries can on occasion be even more important. Where the ruling classes speak one tongue and the ruled another, the differentiation serves a social function that quickly spills over into political, economic, and other roles. We may hypothesize that the greater the congruence between linguistic and status differentiation, the more asymmetrical will be the future prospects of the two languages, with the high-status language likely to be more persistent. Alternatively, as Deutsch (1953) has shown, if the low-status language community is numerically superior to the high-status language community, and if the former becomes socially mobilized, then its language may eventually become the dominant one.

COMMUNICATION DENSITY

Critical to the viability of a language is the nature of the communication network that sustains it. In *open systems*, characterized by low levels of communication, languages tend to diverge. The human ear and brain are good at distinguishing sounds but not so good at remembering and fixing them precisely. We do to words what we do to the images of people we seek to remember in the absence of pictures: we modify them; we change them, sometimes beyond recognition. To retain a single, universally understandable language, the speakers of that language need to remain huddled together within a dense system of communication.

Inversely, in a *closed system*, characterized by high levels of communication among different languages, the trend is toward unilingualism. This occurs either through convergence and the creation of creoles, or through the dominance of one language over another. In the latter case the dominant language gains control of socially strategic roles and functions before eliminating its competitors.

Papua-New Guinea and the USA contrast sharply in their communication density. The former has 700-odd languages of full capacity, languages that cover all the social roles of the individuals who live in many isolated villages, tribes, and islands. The USA, with a population more than 70 times and a territory more than 20 times that of Papouasia, has only one (possibly two) universal languages that serve all the needs of all the roles of the community, of the family, of the church, of the school, of work, politics, shopping, joking, and so forth. Papua-New Guinea is an illustration of an older state of affairs. It illustrates the tendency of languages to diverge when their speakers are not in close contact. The USA, the most industrial of industrial societies, a society so densely packed with communication networks that it well deserves the MacLuhan qualifier of a "global village" — this huge state, on the contrary, notwithstanding recent legislation favoring bilingual education, exemplifies the trend toward unilingualism.

The tendency of high-communication-density systems toward unilingualism is not, of course, equally pronounced in all societies. But even when it is stopped or reversed temporarily, that tendency is identifiable. In less than two centuries, France was transformed from a country where less than half of its population spoke French into a state where very few of its citizens do not speak it. In Switzerland, however, the decline of the minority languages, Romanche excepted, has been very slow. Ethnic and local pride, helped by protective cantonal policies (those of unilingual education in particular), have enabled French and Italian to maintain themselves in their respective territorial niches. But in the past two centuries Switzerland, like France, has simplified its linguistic map, mostly at the expense of the local patois, particularly on the French side of the linguistic divide.

Any thorough examination of the birth and death of languages, then, must consider several variables: size of linguistic community, linguistic tradition, linguistic richness, various kinds of boundaries, communication density, and quite possibly others. Consider one of the first questions asked in this section: Is there a minimum size required for a language's survival? The answer, we now see, depends on the level of a society's integration in the worldwide networks of economic, social, and political exchanges. As long as they remain isolated in their dense tropical forests, the many Indian languages of Venezuela can survive with only a few hundred or even a few dozen speakers. By contrast, the Indian languages of British Columbia can no longer survive the pressure of English because the Indian tribes of the Pacific Northwest are becoming increasingly integrated, especially religiously and politically, into the dominant society.

Let us, accordingly, rephrase the question to read: Is there a minimum number of speakers needed for a language to survive the competition of other languages once the society carrying that language has entered the phase of what we often call modernity, with its attendant industrialization and urbanization? Even this question requires sharpening. If we operationalize "modernity" to mean that any society having at least one full-fledged university is modern, then the question becomes: What is the population size needed to sustain a university that teaches chemistry as well as history in a given language? The Swedes of Finland with 400,000 speakers cannot quite do it; and the 600,000 Franco-ontarians have not been able to do it either. But the Israelis, with 3 million speakers of Hebrew, have been able to turn a religious into a scientific language. Let us, somewhat arbitrarily, set at 1 million the minimum population needed to sustain a modern university. This cutting point distinguishes approximately 165 languages as "university-capable." This figure, higher in fact than the number of languages operating a full university curriculum today, still represents only 2–7 percent of all spoken tongues.

If smallness is an obstacle to cultural power, it is also, although not so obviously, an obstacle to political independence. At the top of the quantitative hierarchy, population size is clearly related to the likelihood of a language controlling (even if only partially) an independent state. Among the first ten languages of Table 9.1, each of these is the official language of at least one state. Among the successive groups of ten, the proportions are, respectively, 50, 60, 30, 60, and 40 percent. If our list had gone below the 5 million or, even better, the 1 million mark, however, then we would have found that, with few exceptions (such as Dzougkha), small numbers are clearly associated with non-sovereign status. Of the world's 63 official languages used as the dominant language in the central administration of at least one independent state, only three (Divehi, Icelandic, and Maltese) are spoken by fewer than 500,000 people. Revealingly, these exceptions are small, well-isolated "island" languages.[2]

The interaction among these factors and their relationship to political variables suggest that we look more closely at the role of the state in matters of language survival.

The State as Language Planner

In the previous section we considered a number of what might be termed "natural" causes for the life and death of a language. Our

argument led to the conclusion that one of the more important determining factors in language survivability in contemporary times may be
the nation-state. Whether by design or indirection, the modern state
acts as a language planner.

The policies of states strongly influence the survival of the languages
within their borders. The modern state is typically one that assimilates
its peripheral languages. In the words of Calvet (1974), it is "glot-
tophagic" — whether it be a fast "eater," such as France and the USA in
the nineteenth century, or a slow but patient consumer, such as the
Soviet Union since the 1930s. Some states have consciously tried to
hasten this process. Others, by contrast, have aimed at protecting their
multilingualism. What political purposes do such policies serve?

A main purpose derives from the state's goals vis-à-vis its international environment. States that project their power beyond their
borders and beyond their immediate neighbors have sought, through
unilingualism, to strengthen their internal system of communication,
hence giving themselves a secure home base. They see linguistic
fragmentation as an obstacle to mobility and/or communication. They
may even see it as a threat to the state's territorial integrity if educated
minorities are concentrated at the periphery of that state and if the
leaders of these minorities resent being controlled by central
authorities.

Given the fact that almost two-thirds of all independent states (65
percent in 1984) have linguistic minorities accounting for at least a
tenth of their population, such an argument seems both counterfactual
as historical description and improbable as a policy guideline.
Moreover, the statistical relationship (Pool, 1972) between linguistic
fragmentation and political or economic development shows that,
although multilingualism is a frequent characteristic of the poorer and
unstable polities, it is not, per se, an obstacle to either wealth, stability,
or power. The cases of Canada, Switzerland, and the Soviet Union
indicate the latter possibility.

Since languages typically protect themselves by concentrating their
speakers in homogeneous territorial niches, since the state is an essentially territorial institution, and since the modern state, with few exceptions, uses a single dominant language to mobilize and integrate its
populations, the conjunction of these factors leads to the proposition
that the languages best able to survive in an era of accelerated language
death are those whose fate is linked inextricably to that of a sovereign
state. There should thus be an increase in the coincidence of two
obstacles to communication: state and linguistic borders.

Recasting the data nonetheless reveals less *politically effective*
multilingualism than the above figure implies. If we classify states no

longer according to the number of speakers of their various languages, or according to the number of languages spoken by at least a certain percentage of the population, or according to the likelihood that two citizens of the same state matched at random will have the same dominant language (Lieberson, 1981; Greenberg, 1971), but rather according to the number of languages given the rank of *official language* and *actually used* in the administration and governance of the *central authorities* of the state, then an interesting picture emerges (Table 9.2). The Vatican excepted, multilingual states fit into either of two categories: (1) states formerly ruled by either France or Britain, and (2) small buffer states. Canada, India, and Kiribati are examples of the first type, Afghanistan, Switzerland, and Belgium of the second. *None* of the old and powerful states, even if its level of linguistic fragmentation is as high as that of the Soviet Union or China, operates its central institutions in more than one language.

In fact, only 15 percent of the world's independent states recognize officially more than one language as the language of their central government and actually use these languages in more than symbolic

TABLE 9.2 Politically Effective Multilingualism

States that are Multilingual in the Operation of their Central Government[a]	
Afghanistan(?)[b]	Mauritania
South Africa	Pakistan
Belgium	Papua-New Guinea
Burundi	Philippines(?)[c]
Cameroon	Western Samoa
Canada	Seychelles
Cyprus	Singapore(?)[c]
Czechoslovakia	Sri Lanka
Finland	Swaziland
India	Switzerland
Kiribati	Tanzania
Lesotho	Vanuatu
Madagascar	Vatican
Malta	Yugoslavia

a. Ireland, Israel, and Norway are excluded on the grounds that, in the first two cases, the second official language is hardly used in the central administration, while, in the third, Nynorsk can be considered a mere variation of Bokmal; inclusion of these states would not affect our observations.

b. Lack of recent information.

c. These states are *politically* close to being unilingual English.

fashion. Even fewer are the states that, in addition to being multilingual at the center, allow the minority languages to have secure geographical niches protected by rigid boundaries of the Swiss and Belgian kind. Less than 5 percent of independent states are in that category and, as already noted, none of them belongs to the group of major world powers.

States that opt to support multilingualism do so for a variety of reasons. One is some notion of justice, the feeling that people must be able to express themselves in their native tongues to realize their full cultural, political, or other potential. In other cases, language segregation between elites and masses may be a means of reducing access to the ruling class. When Latin was a prerequisite to entry into the government bureaucracy, the overwhelming majority of the European population was put, by means of a linguistic divide, on a de facto political reservation. The same is true today of the African masses that do not speak either Arabic, French, or English. It may thus be that the interest of the ruling class is in maintaining language fragmentation. That strategy, whether conscious or not, characterizes the pre-modern state. Its successor, being urban, industrial, and increasingly in need of a large white-collar stratum, requires a relatively high level of education.

Educational mobilization of peripheral populations, national communication systems (especially television), and economic development are all likely to lead, under the control of the central state, to reduced levels of linguistic fragmentation. The exception may be those states with open immigration policies or highly porous boundaries, in which the increase in the number of immigrants speaking a foreign language outstrips the effectiveness of linguistic assimilation policies. Even so, the dominant trend is toward politically effective monolingualism. There is a growing coincidence of state and linguistic boundaries.

CONSEQUENCES OF INCREASED MONOLINGUALISM WITHIN STATES

In sum, a significant trend affecting the global communications structure is the diminishing number of languages together with the enhanced monolingualism of states. The trend arises from a variety of circumstances, but the state's role as de facto language planner, pushing toward monolingualism, is one of, if not *the*, key ingredient.

The replacement of multi- by monolingual states is likely to have consequences more obvious at the internal than at the international level. Conflicts resulting from language contact should increase in number and intensity as more states become more urban and more industrial. Such ethnic conflicts should make it more unlikely that the multinational authoritarian states will liberalize their existing structures. In the long run, however, the linguistic and hence, usually, ethnic homogenization of a country should have a profound effect on its political system if such homogenization reduces the fear that communities settled at the borders of the state would secede should power be transferred from a central bureaucracy or a ruler to the people at large (in the Soviet Union or Kenya, for example).

The economic advantages of state monolingualism, as indicated by Pool's (1972) analysis, are not obvious when one compares monolingual states to those that either have few languages (such as Canada or Switzerland) or are highly fragmented but have a clearly dominant and well-known lingua franca (such as the Soviet Union and Singapore). The advantage of the unilingual state becomes more obvious if one compares it to the highly linguistically fragmented states that lack a well-known lingua franca. A simplification of their linguistic map should be of most obvious benefit to such states; it should facilitate geographic and social mobility and make internal communications more effective.

What of the cultural costs associated with the disappearance or crippling of the small languages that lack the political institutions needed to ensure their survival? For some, including myself, the disappearance of a language, which means almost certainly the disappearance of a culture, is a sad event. This reaction is admittedly emotional and prejudiced when responding to a question put in the abstract, that is, without knowing the specifics of the culture that disappears and the specifics of the culture that replaces it. In matters of language, as in the concern for the ecology, one tends to have favorite personal causes — Frisian, whales, Romanche, or bald eagles — unless, of course, and this is the more common attitude, one does not particularly care one way or the other. Those who, while not fanatical conservationists of all languages at all costs, would regret a reduction in the number of existing languages and the disappearance of the multilingual state, will find some comfort in one of the paradoxes of the modern state: while it is one of the main agents of linguistic assimilation (particularly through its schools and universities), the modern unilingual state is the main protector and guarantor of global multilingualism since, typically, it jealously protects its own language against foreign competitors.

Globally, the trend summarized here means the interaction of ever more monolingual states. Should these states insist on the primacy of their own languages in international discourse, then we might anticipate a stabilization or even proliferation of the number of languages in use internationally. Is such an expectation borne out by the evidence?

Dominant International Languages

Throughout the course of history, a small number of languages, sometimes only one, has been dominant. In earlier times this was true largely for political reasons. Through force of arms, the Romans established Latin as the lingua franca across their empire; and for centuries after the empire disappeared Europeans, for administrative as well as other practical reasons, maintained Latin as the language of political, cultural, scholarly, and religious discourse. In more recent times, although language dominance continues to be a function of power and politics, science and technology have also become important factors. An intriguing and significant question, particularly for students of world politics, concerns the number and growth rate of dominant languages. Here we shall look at the extent to which some languages dominate global distributions in terms of population, scientific productions, and military power, and then we shall turn to the question of whether or not particular languages are consolidating their dominance across various areas to attain the status of an internationally dominant language.

LANGUAGES AND THEIR SPEAKERS

The data in Table 9.1 reveal an interesting pattern about the distribution of people according to the language they speak. The fact that over 96 percent of the world's population communicate in only 82 languages does not imply an equal distribution across the various tongues. If we cut the rank-ordered languages into five equal population slices, then we find that the first tier belongs to a single language, Chinese, and that the second comprises only three additional languages (English, Hindi/Urdu, and Russian). The third quintile includes five more: Spanish, Arabic, Bengali, Portuguese, and Malay/Indonesian. Thus, nine languages account for about 60 percent of the people of the world. The remaining quintiles contain 14 and 59 languages, respectively.

The strength of a language in terms of the number of people speaking it, however, is only one measure of its overall strength or significance. Languages also have strengths as a consequence of the type of information being communicated. If the information is of considerable importance, then the language used to communicate those ideas gains in significance. From a somewhat different perspective, if individuals using a language become important for other reasons, such as scientific eminence or military power, then the languages they speak will gain in strength.

LANGUAGES OF SCIENCE

To ascertain which languages dominate in science, we may use as an indicator the language of original articles (as distinct from translations) included in *Chemical Abstracts* between 1960 and 1980 (Laponce, 1984). Forty-five languages accounted for all but nine of more than 3 million articles so identified (Table 9.3). Again, the degree of hierarchy is impressive. Some 95 percent of the world's production of chemical knowledge occurs in only six languages: English, Russian, Japanese, German, French, and Polish. If we had similar data from previous centuries — which, regrettably, do not exist — then a comparison would doubtless show:

> (1) fluctuations at the top of the hierarchy (with, for example, the first-place ranking going from Latin to French to German to English);
> (2) an overall increase in the number of languages used in scientific publications (with primary use of Latin being followed by a diffusion that in turn gave way in the mid-twentieth century to *some* consolidation);
> (3) the relatively quick rise, to the very top, of languages such as Japanese and Russian.

Table 9.3 offers two different interpretations. On the one hand, the list of languages used for scientific communication in the field of chemistry gives the impression of an abundance of actors. A closer reading, on the other hand, leads us to note that only six languages account for 95 percent of the total production and that two alone account for more than 82 percent.

A corpus other than *Chemical Abstracts* — the *Index Medicus*, for example, or UNESCO statistics (incomplete, unfortunately) on the world production of books by language — would give us slightly different rankings. The overall structure of dominance would nevertheless remain similar: a few, very few, dominant languages, all politically sovereign, and a few dozen very minor languages.

LANGUAGES OF POWER

Measuring the military power of a language imposes a change in the unit of analysis. We can no longer use individual statistics since we lack data on the language actually spoken in barracks or in the field by

TABLE 9.3 Articles Abstracted in *Chemical Abstracts*, **by Language, 1980**

Rank	Language	No.	%	Rank	Language	No.	%
1	English	263,430	64.7	24	Byelorussian	101	—
2	Russian	72,843	17.8	25	Slovenian	96	—
3	Japanese	21,180	5.2	26	Norwegian	88	—
4	German	16,155	4.0	27	Greek	86	—
5	French	8,310	2.0	28	Vietnamese	78	—
6	Polish	4,559	1.1	29	Persian	68	—
7	Italian	3,126	0.8	30	Malay/Indonesian	55	—
8	Chinese	3,118	0.8	31	Hebrew	47	—
9	Spanish	2,542	0.6	32	Afrikaans	43	—
10	Czech	1,960	0.5	33	Albanian	40	—
11	Bulgarian	1,680	0.4	34	Armenian	23	—
12	Rumanian	1,478	0.4	35	Thai	17	—
13	Hungarian	1,159	0.3	36	Georgian	14	—
14	Portuguese	928	0.2	37	Hindi	13	—
15	Korean	890	0.2	38	Macedonian	12	—
16	Serbo-Croatian	886	0.2	39	Azerbaijani	8	—
17	Slovak	817	0.2		Latvian	8	—
18	Ukrainian	588	0.1		Lithuanian	8	—
19	Dutch	381	0.1	42	Arabic	7	—
20	Swedish	307	0.1	43	Estonian	3	—
21	Turkish	207	0.1	44	Esperanto	2	—
22	Danish	123	—		Swahili	2	—
23	Finnish	102	—	46	Punjabi	1	—

NOTE: Other languages in which one article was written in 1980 or in the previous 19 years are Gaelic, Icelandic, Interlingua, Kazakh, Mongolian, Sindi, Turkmen, and Welsh.

soldiers and their commanders; the study of what language commands or kills what other language in the heat of battle or in the quiet of treaty-making remains to be done. Table 9.4 instead assigns the military expenditures of states to their sole *official* languages — provided that these languages are *actually* used in the central administration of the state. In the case of multilingual societies, such as Switzerland or South Africa, the expenditures are assigned proportionally to each language according to its population size. Such a measure advantages the languages that happen to be at or near war. In 1980 there were more soldiers in uniform who spoke Vietnamese than soldiers in uniform who spoke French or German, but Switzerland alone could, within 48 hours, redress the balance by increasing its army from 3,000 to 600,000.

The hierarchy of military strength (Table 9.4) shows a more even geographic distribution than does the hierarchy of scientific

TABLE 9.4 Language and Military Power: Language Hierarchy according to
Military Expenditures, 1980 (US$ m.)

Rank	Language	Military Expenditures	%	Rank	Language	Military Expenditures	%
1	English	177,422	30.7	26	Rumanian	1,470	0.3
2	Russian	152,000	26.4	27	Danish	1,350	0.2
3	Chinese	59,595	10.3	28	Bulgarian	1,140	0.2
4	Arabic	36,129	5.3	29	Slovak	1,127	0.2
5	German	27,525	4.8	30	Hungarian	1,106	0.2
6	French	24,027	4.2	31	Finnish	610	0.1
7	Spanish	12,032	2.1	32	Tagalog	577	0.1
8	Japanese	8,960	1.5	33	Swahili	490	0.1
9	Vietnamese	8,500	1.5	34	Amharic	385	0.1
10	Dutch	7,334	1.3	35	Albanian	371	0.1
11	Italian	6,760	1.2	36	Slovene	324	0.1
12	Hindi/Urdu	5,492	0.9	37	Macedonian	201	—
13	Korean	4,760	0.8	38	Burmese	198	—
14	Polish	4,670	0.8	39	Klalkla (Mong.)	127	—
15	Hebrew	4,420	0.7	40	Bengali	115	—
16	Persian	4,227	0.7	41	Thai	109	—
17	Malay	3,887	0.7	42	Tamil	108	—
18	Swedish	3,636	0.6	43	Somali	95	—
19	Serbo-Croatian	2,838	0.5	44	Malagasy	89	—
20	Portuguese	2,788	0.5	45	Pashto	47	—
21	Turkish	2,590	0.4	46	Laotian	38	—
22	Czech	2,393	0.4	47	Singhalese	25	—
23	Greek	1,806	0.3	48	Nepali	19	—
24	Norwegian	1,570	0.3	49	Maltese	5	—
25	Afrikaans	1,536	0.3				

NOTE: For lack of information the following are not included: Bislama, Chichewa, Comorean, Divehi, Dzonkla, Icelandic, Khmer, Kiribati, Lesotho, Nauruan, Samoan, Siswati, Tongan, and Tswana.
SOURCE: International Institute for Strategic Studies (1981: 96–7).

knowledge. The first 12 languages, which account for 90 percent of total world military expenditures, cover all continents. Four (Chinese, Japanese, Vietnamese, and Hindi/Urdu) have their base located exclusively in Asia; another four (Russian, German, Dutch, and Italian) are based in Europe; one (Arabic) is in North Africa and the Middle East; one (French) is in Europe, North America, and Africa, although its main base is in Europe; one (Spanish) is in Europe and Latin America, with its main base in the latter; and the most widely spread language,

English, appears on all continents, even South America. Were we to give to atomic power a multiplier commensurate with its military importance, then the concentration of military power would be greatly increased. It would nonetheless remain true that, compared with the scientific hierarchy, the military hierarchy of the various sovereign languages shows greater equality. Compared with the mid-nineteenth century, the second part of the twentieth century has many more languages that satisfy Lyautey's definition of a language — a patois backed by an army.

PATTERN OF CHANGING DOMINANCE

The evidence on the distribution of languages according to the number of people speaking them, their scientific productivity, and military strength suggests two points of interest. First, the world has seen dramatic changes in the relative status of various languages. Until, say, the fifteenth century and the subsequent flowering of the territorial state system, Latin served as the primary language of communication among princes, ecclesiastics, scholars, and others. Even afterwards, communication across boundaries remained restricted to one or two key languages — French for diplomacy, for instance, and (later) German for science. The nineteenth century, which ushered in an era of nationalism, saw nation-states beginning to compete for primacy or at least equal status for their national languages. Previously dominant languages gave up their place of honor as language hierarchies began to crumble. Today we are witnessing the emergence of new hierarchies. More people are speaking fewer languages, and a few languages account for a large proportion of science and military expenditures. If we take the long-term view, the world of a single dominant language has given way, after a preliminary process of diffusion, to one in which a handful of languages enjoy dominant positions.

But, second, no single language and no set of languages is currently able to consolidate its overweening dominance. The top languages in terms of size are not necessarily the highest-ranking ones in terms of science or military might. Were we to extend the analysis to indicators of other values, such as wealth, or cultural and other skills, we would anticipate finding similar distributions on each one but a continued dispersion across the entire range of values. It is not likely that in the foreseeable future any single language will be able to consolidate its position to become *the* dominant language of global interaction. In what circumstances might a language accomplish such a goal? Or, more broadly, what circumstances might enhance the likelihood that a language will attain or maintain status as a dominant language globally?

The State and International Linguistic Dominance

Again, we have first looked at patterns of international linguistic dominance as a "natural" phenomenon, and again we must ask: What role does the state play in establishing and maintaining such patterns? Does the fact of increasing monolingualism within states have an effect on international language usage? Will the nation-states that share one of the few remaining multi-state languages be at an advantage over those that do not?

Implicit in our earlier discussion of language dominance is the *centrality of the state*. The effect of a language's "official" status can be seen in the data on chemical knowledge. Over three-quarters (78 percent) of the languages listed in Table 9.3 are official languages used in the central administration of at least one state; and, among the languages that account individually for more than 0.1 percent of the world's production of chemical knowledge, *all* are "sovereign" languages in the political sense of the term. Thus Slovak, however small its number of speakers, is used in fact as well as in law in the administration of a sovereign country's central government. It ranks ahead of such languages as Ukrainian, which has a much larger number of speakers but is not used in the central administration of the Soviet Union.

A comparison of the percentages in Tables 9.1 and 9.3 shows that, although their overall curves may be similar (resembling a negative exponential distribution), the individual languages occupy often markedly different positions on these curves. Chinese is the first in terms of population but only eighth in the chemical hierarchy; Hebrew is ninety-third in the former but thirty-first in the latter. The ratio of the percentage of language of chemical abstracts to the percentage of world speakers is 7.5 for English, 2.5 for Czech, 2.1 for Japanese, and 2.0 for Slovak, but only 0.10 for Spanish and 0.04 for Chinese.[3] Being the language of an independent state does not guarantee a good position in the hierarchy of production of chemical knowledge, but *not* being the language of a sovereign state guarantees a ratio of below 1.0 (Table 9.5).

In short, the growth in the number of scientific languages (notwithstanding the overwhelming dominance of two of them) and the trend toward the reduction in the total number of world languages

TABLE 9.5 Languages without Governments as Scientific Communicators

Ratio of (percentage language of abstracts)/(percentage of world speakers) for the languages in Table 9.2 that are not used as official languages in the central administration of a single national state

Armenian	0.55
Ukrainian	0.15
Byelorussian	0.12
Georgian	0.04
Latvian	0.04
Lithuanian	0.04
Estonian	0.03
Esperanto	0.02
Azerbaijani	0.01
Punjabi	0.00

both find their explanation in the linguistic policies of the modern state: eliminating minority languages internally and promoting one's dominant language externally.

Much the same can be said about power, as indicated by military expenditures. More generally, we might note that English is the language of 42 states and French the language of 28, while Russian is the language of only one. Barring reversals of power suffered by the USA in a major war, English is likely to continue well into the twenty-first century in its role as the first major language of world communication. Are there measurable political consequences of this probability?

Is language a factor in, for instance, the formation of international alliances? The historical data on language and alliance formation are far from clear on this point. On the one hand, as Table 9.6 shows, neither French nor English crosses the major political division that separates communist from non-communist states: is that due, in part, to the effects of a common language? (German, Korean, and Spanish can be used to argue the negative case since they do cross the divide — however, one could also argue that, at least with respect to German and Korean, the overlap does not result from the wishes of the populations concerned.) On the other hand, the Western alliance is an alliance of many languages.

In searching for an answer to the question, it is easier to deduce from the psychological evidence than to induce from historical events contaminated by many intervening factors (geography, economic necessities, and so forth). That psychological evidence suggests that a common language will facilitate collaboration (as de Gaulle also assumed), since people have difficulty trusting someone whose

TABLE 9.6 Language and Political Régime: The Classification of Speakers of Multi-State Languages by Political Régime

Language	Democratic/ Pluralist (%)	Non-communist Authoritarian (%)	Communist (%)
German	80	—	20
English	80	20	—
Korean	—	70	30
Spanish	35	60	5
French	75	25	—
Hindi/Urdu	90	10	—
Mandarin	—	2	98
Portuguese	10	90	—
Tamil	—	100	—

NOTE: The category "democratic/pluralist" corresponds to that of "free states," as used by Russett and Starr (1981), except in the cases of Gambia, Surinam, Botswana, and Sri Lanka, which are categorized here as "non-communist authoritarian." Should Sri Lanka be put in the democratic/ pluralist category, then the distribution would be democratic/pluralist 5%, non-communist authoritarian 95%. Cuba has been counted as a communist state, but the African states claiming adherence to Marxism/Leninism have been put — following the views of most Africanists — in the category of non-communist authoritarian regimes.

language they do not understand (Zuckerman, 1964; Steyn, 1972).[4] If so, then the replacement of English or French by native languages such as Malay, Kiribati, Sinhalese, Arabic, or Swahili in former African or Asian colonies should weaken the links among states and societies now joined by a common language. But English, Spanish, Arabic, and French, especially the first three, should — assuming that we are prepared to induce from the psychological to the social — continue holding the advantage over mono-state languages with regard to the formation of alliances and the creation of what Karl Deutsch (1954) calls "security communities."

A more general question focuses on the role that states seek to play as *international language planners*. Most leaders of powerful states would doubtless welcome the installation of a single global language — provided that it was their own. Occasionally, a state in recent times has even acted on the assumption that, whether it wished to or not, the world was by necessity moving toward the adoption of its own language as the international lingua franca. Not since the fall of Latin from that status, however, has any state been able to achieve such a dream. Certainly no state today is powerful enough to impose its own national language on the rest of the world.

Yet several states are sufficiently powerful in one respect or another to ensure that their national languages will not be relegated to the dustbin of the global communications network. Most chemists, especially those in the West, who have something important to say will in all probability publish it in English. The scholar who chooses to publish in, say, Norwegian must recognize that the work will not capture much attention. Not so chemists in the Soviet Union, who, encouraged by the state, are concerned with other values in addition to having their work universally read and understood. A result is that serious chemists outside the socialist world must learn sufficient Russian to keep abreast with important developments, or else must rely on abstracting and translating services: they cannot afford to ignore research simply because it is published in Russian rather than English.

Thus we find a paradox in international language developments. On the one hand, the world appears set on a course already traveled by the old, powerful states of Europe, a course that leads to the increased coincidence of political and linguistic boundaries. It seems likely that many "lesser" languages will disappear. Only their official status as languages of a central governmental administration will prevent others from following the same route. In this sense the world will move away from its multiplicity of languages toward monolingualism.

On the other hand, given the probability of continuing international political and other forms of competition, global monolingualism is not likely to result. A "new" state or region with a single language may well achieve significant political status (for example, China) or economic status (for example, the Arab oil-producers), enabling it to advance its own language as *a* dominant international language. To the three or four dominant languages of today may thus be added several more. Concurrent with the diminished number of languages used internationally, then, is the probability of growth in the number of dominant international languages.

These two trends — increased monolingualism within states, and uneven competition internationally among languages for a position of dominance—ensure that language, in addition to race, religion, and national origin, will remain a major, often *the* major, ethnic force affecting domestic and international politics.

NOTES

1. Muller's estimates are more conservative than those of Culbert because they refer only to knowledge of a language as first language. Thus, while Muller estimates French to have 65 million speakers, Culbert assigns it 95 million.

2. Other small "island" languages such as Tongan, Samoan, and Bislama may one day achieve similar status.

Obviously, minor languages have a greater chance of becoming a central government language if the state is small. Barring the fragmentation of the Indonesian, Indian, and Soviet states, Javanese, Telegu, Gujarati, and Ukrainian are most unlikely ever to become "sovereign" languages, unlikely ever to control an independent state. Very small languages such as Icelandic and Siswati have been able to do so in very small countries. Not all small nations enjoy linguistic homogeneity, however. Among the states that in 1980 had less than 1 million inhabitants, 34 percent had a low level of linguistic homogeneity (that is, their official language, if they had only one, or their dominant official language if they had more than one, was normally used by less than 50 percent of the population). By contrast, among the large states, those with more than 50 million inhabitants, the number of such cases amounted to only 14 percent. Possessing a state structure is more likely for a small language if the state is small, but small languages are endangered in small as in large states. Many of the languages of India, Indonesia, and the USSR have a most uncertain future, but so have many of the languages of Papua-New Guinea (Laponce, 1984).

3. French has a ratio below 1.0 if we use Culbert's population estimate, a ratio of 1.0 if we use Muller's.

4. The assumption that mutual intelligibility is of importance to alliance formation implies, of course, that alliance-making is not exclusively in the hands of multilingual elites — diplomats, for example, who bridge easily the linguistic divide by means of a lingua franca such as English or French. It assumes that the populations of the states concerned have an impact on these alliances. Since that impact is more likely to be felt in democratic than in non-democratic systems, one should perhaps distinguish between the two as well as between "state alliances" and "societal alliances."

REFERENCES

BOULDING, K. E. (1962) Conflict and Defense: A General Theory. New York: Harper & Brothers.

CAILLEUX, A. (1953) "L'evolution quantitative du langage." Bulletin de la Société Préhistorique Française 50: 505–514.

CALVET, L. J. (1974) Linguistique et Colonialisme: Petit Traité de Glottophagie. Paris: Payot.

CULBERT, S. S. (1984) "The principal languages of the world," p. 245 in The World Almanac and Book of Facts 1985. New York: Newspapers Enterprise Association.

DEUTSCH, K. W. (1953) Nationalism and Social Communication: An Inquiry into the Foundations of Nationality. Cambridge, Mass.: MIT Press; and New York: John Wiley.

——— (1954) Political Community at the International Level: Problems of Definition and Measurement. Garden City, NY: Doubleday.

DRESSLER, W., and R. WODAK-LEODOLTER [eds.] (1977) "Language death." International Journal of the Sociology of Language, no. 12.

FOSTER, M. K. (1982) "Canada's first languages." Language and Society no. 7 (Winter/Spring): 7–16.

GREENBERG, J. H. (1971) Language, Culture, and Communication: Essays. Stanford, Calif.: Stanford University Press.

International Institute for Strategic Studies (1981) The Military Balance 1980-1981. London: International Institute for Strategic Studies.

LABOV, W. (1968) "The reflection of social processes in linguistic structures," pp. 240–251 in J. A. Fishman (ed.), Readings in the Sociology of Language. The Hague and Paris: Mouton.

LAPONCE, J. A. (1980) "Le comportement spatial des groupes linguistiques: solutions personnelles et solutions territoriales aux problèmes de minorités." International Political Science Review 1, 4: 478–494.

——— (1984) Langue et territoire. Quebec: Les Presses de l'Université Laval.

LIEBERSON, S. (1981) Language Diversity and Language Contact. Stanford, Calif.: Stanford University Press.

MULLER, S. H. (1964) The World's Living Languages: Basic Facts of Their Structure, Kinship, Location and Number of Speakers. New York: Frederick Ungar.

POOL, J. (1972) "National development and language diversity," pp. 213–230 in J. A. Fishman (ed.), Advances in the Sociology of Language, v. ii: Selected Studies and Applications. The Hague and Paris: Mouton.

RUSSETT, B. M. and H. STARR (1981) World Politics: The Menu for Choice. San Francisco, CA: W. H. Freeman.

STARR, H. and B. A. MOST (1976) "The substance and study of borders in international relations research." International Studies Quarterly 20 (December): 581–620.

STEYN, R. W. (1972) "Medical implications in polyglottism." Archives of General Psychiatry 27 (August): 245–247.

VALERY, P. (1945) Regards sur le Monde Actuel et Autres Essais. Paris: Gallimard.

ZUCKERMAN, M. (1964) "Perceptual isolation as a stress situation: a review." Archives of General Psychiatry 11 (September): 255–276.

CHAPTER 10

EUROPEAN COMMUNITY AND INTRA-EUROPEAN COMMUNICATIONS: THE EVIDENCE OF MAIL FLOWS

CAL CLARK
RICHARD L. MERRITT

The European Economic Community, formalized in 1957 by the Treaty of Rome, brought revolutionary change to the politics and economics of West Europe. The EEC, to be sure, has not achieved the full integration which many of its advocates initially envisioned. Substantial progress nonetheless has occurred on many fronts. Politically, the EEC has brought together into a "security community," where bargaining and accommodation among allies have replaced the threat of war among enemies, countries whose hostility had ravaged Europe twice in our century. Economically, the Community has encouraged among its members a substantial growth of trade and more subtle economic linkages (Deutsch et al., 1957; Haas, 1958; Kitzinger, 1963; Etzioni, 1965; Puchala, 1966; Deutsch et al., 1967; Lindberg and Scheingold, 1970; Caporaso, 1972; Morgan, 1973). Along with these developments came a sea-change in mass attitudes: the West European publics moved toward mutual friendliness and at least passive support for supranational integration among the "Six" (Inglehart, 1967; 1977: Ch. 12; Merritt, 1968; Lindberg and Scheingold, 1970: Chs. 2 and 8).

Such changes in mass attitudes are part of a puzzle that has greatly intrigued theorists of political integration (Merritt, 1983). Are they the consequence of institutionalization? Are they the result of patterns of social communication (cf. Deutsch, 1953) that must exist before significant steps toward institutionalization make sense? Or are popular attitudes, patterns of social communication, and institutionalization so intertwined that we cannot separate them for analysis? In the case of the EEC, we might argue that the effort to unite its member states, incomplete as it has been, has stimulated increased communications among the member populations through business contacts, student exchanges, and so forth, and that enhanced communication across an ever wider range of concerns in turn has changed popular attitudes.

This paper explores such a possibility by testing the hypothesis that the formation of the EEC has had a significant impact upon one major type of international communication: mail flows among West European countries. Because the structure of international mail exchanges in Europe has traditionally remained very stable and unresponsive to even spectacular political and economic events and crises (Clark, 1973a; Merritt and Clark, 1977), any effects on European mail patterns that are associated with the formation of the EEC would be especially significant in understanding the political integrative process.

Analyzing International Mail Flows

For some seven decades before the Treaty of Rome was signed, and during the first four years of the EEC's existence, the Universal Postal Union (1886–1961) collected and published data on the international mail exports of member countries and their colonies. Reliance on national reporting, of course, meant some missing data and variations in reporting, but the data collection is sufficiently systematic to warrant serious attention by scholars today. The mail analyzed here consists of the UPU's basic category of all "ordinary and registered mail"—which is the category used in most such quantitative studies (Deutsch, 1956; Russett et al., 1964; Puchala, 1966) — plus "ordinary parcel post," because of its prominence in many overseas mail exchanges (for details, see Merritt and Clark, 1979).

The level of postal interaction between any two states can be indicated by a coefficient of Relative Sending (RS), which is a slight modification of the Relative Acceptance coefficient (RA) developed by Savage and Deutsch (1960). In essence, the RS statistic measures real-world deviations from a "null model"; that is, it measures by how much the actual mail flow between two countries departs from the "null" amount that would be expected were all mail in the international system randomly sent and received. (See Puchala, 1970; Caporaso, 1971; Russett, 1971; Clark and Welch, 1972; Hughes, 1972; and Merritt and Clark, 1979, for discussions on how this index compares with other potential measures of international interactions and transactions.)

The computation of the null model of world transactions (of mail, trade, or whatever) rests on two assumptions: (1) that a country's percentages of world imports and exports represent its "propensities" to import and export, respectively; and (2) that the exportation or importation of any item is an independent event. The probability that any particular transaction (letter, trade consignment, etc.) goes from country I to country J, then, is, according to probability theory, the product of their respective propensities to export and import. Because by definition countries cannot send international transactions to themselves, however, a complex statistical model must be applied to distribute among the pairs of importers and exporters in the system the products of potential self-trade — that is, the product of I's proportion of world exports and its proportion of world imports (Savage and Deutsch, 1960, with various elaborations by Chadwick and Deutsch, 1973, and Goodman, 1963). (See Merritt and Clark, 1979 for a description of how the original Savage–Deutsch null model was modified for this analysis of mail flows.)

Once we have calculated the probability of any specific transaction going from country I to country J, we can derive the level of transactions *expected* under null-model conditions (E_{ij}) by multiplying this probability by the number of world transactions. The strength or intensity of relative interaction is then measured by the normalized deviation of E_{ij} from the *actual* level of transactions (A_{ij}) going from I to J according to the formula:

$$RA_{ij} \text{ or } RS_{ij} = \frac{A_{ij} - E_{ij}}{E_{ij}}$$

where:

RA_{ij} and RS_{ij} are coefficients of relative interaction
A_{ij} is the actual amount of transactions going from I to J
E_{ij} is the expected amount of transactions going from I to J under null-model conditions.

From this formula, it is easy to see that RS_{ij} or $RA_{ij} = 0$, when $A_{ij} = E_{ij}$. Thus, above-average transaction linkages are denoted by positive values of the index, while negative values signify below-average interactions. The magnitude of the coefficient may be conceived as a percentage measure of how greatly actual transactions depart from expected values. For example, an RS_{ij} score of $+1.00$ indicates that actual transactions are twice as great as expected, while one of -0.50 shows that actual interactions are only half of "normal expectations."

The above formulation poses two practical problems. For one thing, it creates an asymmetrical scale. The lower limit of the index is -1.00, which occurs when there are no transactions between the states in question. Its positive range goes upward to a varying maximum determined by the transactors' shares of world mail or trade flows. Using the above example, how can we generalize when I sends J twice as many transactions as expected ($RS_{ij} = +1.00$) and J sends I only half as many as expected ($RS_{ji} = -0.50$)? A mean score ($RS = +0.25$) suggests a more positive relationship than our intuition tells us exists. For another thing, as Clark (1973b) has shown, the smaller the proportion of world transactions accounted for by any pair of transacting parties, the higher their mutual RA or RS score can potentially be. If two states each have 20 percent of world transactions, then the maximum value of their RA or RS score is about $+3.00$, while this maximum is $+79.00$ if the two partners each account for 1 percent of world trade or mail flows. This variability makes comparison somewhat difficult when the pairs of countries involved account for widely differing proportions of world transactions.

One method of handling this problem is to transform the RA and RS scores to create distributions with limited ranges, let us say, from -1.00 through 0.00 to $+1.00$. This can be done by compressing disproportionately the high values on the *positive* end of the scale by means of a trigonometric transformation:[1]

let y = the *original* (positive) RS score

and

let x = the *transformed* (positive) RS score, or RS^t.

As x varies from 0 to $\pi/2$, y = tangent (x) would vary from 0 to ∞. If this is transformed to

$$y = \text{tangent} \left(x \frac{\pi}{2} \right),$$

then x varies from 0 to 1 as y varies from 0 to ∞. This formula can then be manipulated algebraically to get x in terms of y:

$$x = \frac{2}{\pi} \text{tangent}^{-1} (y)$$

$$= \frac{(2 \arctan\text{gent} [y])}{\pi}.$$

Our procedure thus transforms an *RS* score of $+1.00$, which analysts have usually considered quite strong, into an RS^t value of $+0.50$, an *RS* score of $+5.00$ into an RS^t score of $+0.84$, an *RS* score of $+10.00$ into an RS^t score of $+0.94$, and so forth. Negative *RS* scores are not subjected to this transformation. The result is a symmetrical distribution with values ranging from -1.00 to $+1.00$, which has the conceptual advantage that the greatest possible positive and negative deviations from null-model conditions are equal in value. Using RS^t scores in statistical analyses, such as computing means, vitiates problems connected with the usual *RS* (or *RA*) index such as its highly asymmetrical range and its restriction of very high scores to only small transacting partners.

The RS^t coefficient was used to measure the level of mail interaction among all reporting countries and colonies for selected years between 1890 and 1961, when, unfortunately, the UPU terminated its program of systematically collecting and reporting international mail transactions. The next section examines the changes over this 72-year period in relative mail flows among the EEC Six to see whether or not significant changes are associated with the formation of the EEC. We shall then apply multivariate analysis to the mail RS^t scores among all West European nations in 1928 and 1961 to see whether or not, once other potential causal factors are controlled, the creation of the EEC affected the direction of West European mail flows.

Historical Development of Mail Communications among EEC Members

From the late nineteenth century until the outbreak of World War II, the pattern of European international mail flows was very stable. It consisted of several tightly integrated regions at the periphery — Anglo-America, Scandinavia, East and Southeastern Europe, and a loose grouping of Latin countries in the south — but no cohesive regional grouping in the core of central and western Europe (although in the 1920s and 1930s Germany appeared to be emerging as the communications hub in the core). Even such catastrophic events as World War I and the Great Depression had little impact on this overall structure (Clark, 1973a; Merritt and Clark, 1977).

In view of such long-term stability in overall European mail patterns, any change apparently associated with the European Economic Community would be of great interest. We can make an initial assessment of the possibility that the creation of the EEC stimulated increased mail communications among its members by examining Table 10.1, which presents the mutual RS^t scores for the six countries

TABLE 10.1 Relative Mail Interactions of EEC States: RS^t Scores

Exporting State

1890

Importing State	Ger.	Neth.	Lux.	Bel.	Fr.	It.
Ger.	—	0.389	0.497	*	-0.244	-0.279
Neth.	0.677	—	-0.242	*	-0.260	-1.000
Lux.	0.463	-0.616	—	*	-0.141	-0.721
Bel.	-0.139	0.773	0.806	—	0.650	-0.554
Fr.	0.057	0.000	0.393	*	—	0.456
It.	-0.414	-0.851	-0.798	*	0.459	—

1928

Importing State	Ger.	Neth.	Lux.	Bel.	Fr.	It.
Ger.	—	0.585	0.385	-0.110	-0.541	-0.287
Neth.	0.628	—	-0.385	0.814	-0.372	-0.613
Lux.	0.393	-0.609	—	0.939	0.536	-0.654
Bel.	0.126	0.841	0.958	—	0.676	-0.389
Fr.	-0.549	-0.259	0.558	0.686	—	0.269
It.	0.025	-0.543	-0.051	-0.476	0.406	—

1949

Importing State	W. Ger.	Neth.	Lux.	Bel.	Fr.	It.
W. Ger.	—	0.362	0.573	-0.261	0.044	0.242
Neth.	0.655	—	0.339	0.497	0.231	-0.341
Lux.	-0.076	-0.834	—	0.854	0.547	-0.827
Bel.	0.138	0.677	0.948	—	0.622	0.330
Fr.	-0.552	-0.616	0.506	0.038	—	0.285
It.	-0.123	-0.722	0.203	-0.093	0.676	—

1958

Importing State	W. Ger.	Neth.	Lux.	Bel.	Fr.	It.
W. Ger.	—	0.473	0.433	0.310	0.132	-0.054
Neth.	0.542	—	0.315	0.788	-0.209	-0.431
Lux.	0.253	-0.620	—	0.936	-0.021	-0.628
Bel.	0.120	0.721	0.935	—	0.663	0.038
Fr.	-0.239	-0.073	0.580	0.775	—	0.609
It.	-0.008	-0.294	0.550	0.264	0.680	—

Exporting State

1913

Importing State	Ger.	Neth.	Lux.	Bel.	Fr.	It.
Ger.	—	0.527	0.666	*	-0.021	-0.409
Neth.	-0.624	—	-0.635	*	-0.110	-0.689
Lux.	0.783	-0.731	—	*	0.006	-0.386
Bel.	0.063	0.816	0.758	—	0.671	-0.573
Fr.	-0.129	-0.024	0.633	*	—	0.456
It.	0.032	-0.840	0.253	*	0.599	—

1937

Importing State	Ger.	Neth.	Lux.	Bel.	Fr.	It.
Ger.	—	0.777	0.748	0.330	-0.500	0.660
Neth.	0.596	—	0.051	0.849	-0.401	-0.111
Lux.	0.295	-0.479	—	0.960	-0.062	-0.611
Bel.	0.044	0.823	0.946	—	0.658	0.150
Fr.	-0.410	0.057	0.796	0.809	—	0.500
It.	0.242	-0.378	-0.436	-0.041	0.150	—

1955

Importing State	W. Ger.	Neth.	Lux.	Bel.	Fr.	It.
W. Ger.	—	0.459	0.530	-0.108	0.044	0.063
Neth.	0.575	—	0.138	-0.677	0.032	-0.358
Lux.	0.509	-0.547	—	0.934	0.132	-0.621
Bel.	0.063	0.722	0.920	—	0.676	0.044
Fr.	-0.212	-0.293	0.596	0.733	—	0.320
It.	0.000	-0.278	0.448	-0.101	0.704	—

1961

Importing State	W. Ger.	Neth.	Lux.	Bel.	Fr.	It.
W. Ger.	—	0.558	0.430	0.264	0.025	0.349
Neth.	0.694	—	0.070	0.779	-0.230	0.013
Lux.	0.325	-0.529	—	0.948	0.025	-0.402
Bel.	0.242	0.762	0.953	—	0.568	0.017
Fr.	0.162	-0.273	0.550	0.714	—	0.516
It.	0.367	-0.303	0.500	0.573	0.641	—

* Belgium did not report mail exports in 1890 or 1913.
NOTE: Data after 1949 are for the Federal Republic alone; in 1949, German exports are from West Germany alone, while German imports are to all zones (including the Soviet zone).

TABLE 10.2 Proportion of EEC Dyads by Strength of Relationship[a]

Years	Extreme Disengagement		Noncommunication		Indifference		Positive Attraction		Strong Engagement	
	No.	%	No.	%	No.	%	No.	%	No.	%
Pre-World War I										
1890	5	20	6	24	4	16	6	24	4	16
1913	4	16	3	12	7	28	4	16	7	28
Interwar years										
1928	3	10	9	30	4	13	7	23	7	23
1937	1	3	6	20	8	27	5	17	10	33
Post-World War II: before Treaty of Rome										
1949	4	13	3	10	6	20	11	37	6	20
1955	1	3	5	17	10	33	7	23	7	23
Post-World War II: after Treaty of Rome										
1958	2	7	4	13	7	23	9	30	8	27
1961	0	0	5	17	6	20	12	40	7	23
$N =$	20		41		52		61		56	

a.   *Definitions of column categories:*
     Extreme disengagement: $-1.000 \leq RS^t \leq -0.600$
     Noncommunication: $-0.599 \leq RS^t \leq -0.200$
     Indifference: $-0.199 \leq RS^t \leq +0.199$
     Positive attraction: $+0.200 \leq RS^t \leq +0.599$
     Strong engagement: $+0.600 \leq RS^t \leq +1.000$
NOTE: Because of rounding errors, rows may not add to 100 %.

that signed the Treaty of Rome.[2] Table 10.2 summarizes the data for each year by grouping the RS^t scores into five levels of interaction, ranging from extreme disengagement at one end of the scale to strong engagement at the other:

Extreme disengagement: $-1.000 \leq RS^t \leq -0.600$
Noncommunication: $-0.599 \leq RS^t \leq -0.200$
Indifference: $-0.199 \leq RS^t \leq +0.199$
Positive attraction: $+0.200 \leq RS^t \leq +0.599$
Strong engagement: $+0.600 \leq RS^t \leq +1.000$

Finally, the mean or average RS^t scores of each country with the other five are displayed in Table 10.3. This table also shows linear regression and correlation coefficients for the changes over time in each country's mean RS^t scores.

TABLE 10.3 Mean Dyadic Scores with the Rest of the Six, by Country

Year	Germany	Neth.	Lux.	Belgium	France	Italy	Overall
1890	+0.113	−0.132	−0.036	+0.308	+0.153	−0.411	+0.028
1913	+0.235	−0.117	+0.149	+0.358	+0.199	−0.171	+0.136
1928	+0.065	+0.009	+0.207	+0.335	+0.141	−0.231	+0.100
1937	+0.278	+0.178	+0.221	+0.551	+0.160	+0.013	+0.234
1949	+0.100	+0.025	+0.222	+0.376	+0.179	−0.037	+0.141
1955	+0.193	+0.112	+0.303	+0.457	+0.274	+0.022	+0.227
1958	+0.195	+0.121	+0.274	+0.555	+0.290	+0.072	+0.251
1961	+0.352	+0.154	+0.287	+0.582	+0.272	+0.227	+0.307
Linear regression							
$R =$	+0.51	+0.82	+0.85	+0.82	+0.82	+0.94	+0.89
Slope[a]	+0.020	+0.040	+0.038	+0.037	+0.020	+0.076	+0.034
Sig. level	0.10	0.007	0.004	0.007	0.007	0.003	0.002

a. Increment per year in RS score.

PRE-WORLD WAR I ERA

In the years before World War I, the future EEC states clearly fell far short of resembling a cohesive or distinctive communications region. In fact, taken as a whole, the Six manifested a pattern of indifference. In 1890 the percentage of RS^t scores in Table 10.2 stronger than indifference (40 percent) approximately equals those below indifference (44 percent); and the overall mean RS^t score for that year of +0.228 (Table 10.3) is very close to the absolute null model. In terms of the linkages of individual states, Belgium, with a mean RS^t score of +0.308, had by far the strongest mail ties with the rest of the group and was the only one to average more than the indifference point of +0.200. France (+0.153) and Germany (+0.113) also gave some indication of positive attraction to the group. On the other end of the scale, Italy, with a mean RS^t score of −0.411, displayed substantial disengagement from the rest of the Six (except France). The fact that the Netherlands also had a negative mean RS^t score (−0.132) is somewhat surprising in view of its central geographic position.

The mean RS^t score for the region jumped from +0.028 in 1890 to +0.136 in 1913. All of the Six had their averages rise, and four of these increases were quite significant: Luxembourg enjoyed a spectacular overall growth, from −0.036 to +0.149; France and Germany increased to +0.199 and +0.235, respectively; and Italy had the largest absolute increase of 0.240 (that is, from −0.411 to −0.171) although it still remained estranged from the rest of the Six (except France, with which Italy enjoyed a mean RS^t score of +0.528). This increase in mean transaction scores resulted primarily from an intensification of many of the positive relationships (with the proportion of strongly positive ones increasing from 16 to 28 percent) and from an upgrading of "noncommunication" dyads to "indifferent" ones. It did not constitute a substantial movement toward regional communications integration, however, because the number of positively attracted dyads in Table 10.2 remained almost constant (40 percent in 1890 and 44 percent in 1913) at a level that included less than half of the intra-regional interactions, and because the proportion of pairs of countries in the "extreme disengagement" category remained fairly high (20 percent in 1890 and 16 percent in 1913).

Moreover, the pattern of individual relationship (Table 10.1) reveals overlapping groups of two or three states rather than a single, cohesive region. Thus, Germany was linked to the Netherlands and Luxembourg; the Netherlands to Germany and Belgium; Luxembourg to Germany, Belgium and perhaps France; Belgium to the Netherlands, Luxembourg, and France; France to Belgium and Italy; and Italy to France. Several pairs of countries are conspicuous by their relative lack of communications: (1) Italy with Germany, the Netherlands, Belgium, and for the most part Luxembourg; (2) somewhat surprisingly, perhaps, the Netherlands and Luxembourg; and (3) to a lesser extent France and the Netherlands.

An examination for these years of the EEC countries' RS^t scores with the rest of the world (data not presented here) shows that only the three Benelux countries enjoyed their strongest European mail contacts with their future EEC partners. Germany's primary ties, by contrast, were with the northern portion of central Europe, while France and Italy had strong ties in southern Europe. These data provide another indication that before World War I the future Six were far from being an integrated communications region.

INTERWAR ERA

The situation remained much the same after World War I. Changes between 1913 and 1928 were fairly small and offset each other. The proportion of positive RS^t scores rose slightly, from 44 to 50 percent, but this was more than offset by the rise of significantly negative dyads, from 28 percent in 1913 to 40 percent in 1928, thus causing decline (from +0.136 to +0.100) in the mean RS^t score for the Six as a whole. In particular, the aftermath of World War I resulted in a precipitous drop of Franco-German mail ties. The mean RS^t scores for the individual countries remained fairly stable. The main exception was a tremendous drop in Germany's mean (from +0.235 to +0.065), which manifested the communications cost of the war. Otherwise, there were small and offsetting increases in the means for Luxembourg and the Netherlands and decreases for France and Italy.

The same set of separate but overlapping groups that existed before the war was still in evidence. In fact, we even find some decline in regional cohesiveness: Italy's ties with France, Belgium, and Luxembourg decreased; and France's mail relations with Germany and the Netherlands went from relatively neutral to strongly negative. Germany's linkages with almost all other parts of Europe were significantly stronger than with its future EEC partners; and France and Italy still had stronger ties with southern Europe than with the other members of the Six.

The looming of World War II, we might suppose, would have created closer relations among the allies on each side and diminished communications between the two groups of future belligerents. These hypotheses are at best only partially verified by the data. By 1937 there had been a dramatic growth in Italo-German mail linkages. Mail bonds among the other four countries, however, increased only slightly; and, if anything, there was a slight but appreciable increase in Allied mail with the two Axis powers.

That there was nevertheless some movement toward greater regional cohesion can be seen in Tables 10.1–10.3. The mean RS^t score for the Six as a whole jumped from +0.100 to +0.234; the proportion of positive RS^t scores rose slightly from 46 to 50 percent (the percentage of dyads characterized by strong engagement showed a large increase from 23 to 33 percent); and, at the other end of the scale, there was also a substantial decline (from 40 to 23 percent) in the pairs of countries manifesting significant communications disengagement. The emergence of Germany during the interwar period as the communications hub of Europe (Clark, 1973a) provided a major stimulus for this growth. Germany's average leaped over fourfold from +0.065 to +0.278 and went from fourth to second among the Six. There were also very substantial increases in the mean RS^t scores of the Netherlands (from +0.009 to +0.178), Belgium (+0.335 to +0.551), and Italy (−0.231 to +0.013). Thus, on the eve of World War II, five of these six countries appeared at least minimally integrated in their patterns of mail communications (with mean RS^t scores of +0.160 and above); and even Italy advanced from estrangement from the regional grouping to indifference toward it.

POST-WORLD WAR II ERA

World War II and the dozen years from 1937 to 1949 saw a slight decline in the level of mail communications among future members of the EEC, although, as after World War I, some contradictory movements can be discerned. On the one hand, the proportion of positive mail linkages in Table 10.2 increased appreciably (from 50 to 57 percent); the number of pairs of countries whose mutual RS^t scores were both negative fell from three (out of 15) to only one (Italy–Netherlands); and France's exports (but not imports) of mail became substantially more concentrated in the EEC region. These changes were more than balanced, on the other hand, by a drop (from 33 to 20 percent) in the dyads displaying strong engagement ($RS \geqslant + 0.60$); and a rise (from 3 to 13 percent) in the dyads in extreme disengagement. As a result, the mean RS^t score for the Six as a whole dropped from +0.234 in 1937 to +0.141 in 1949. As at the end of World War I, Germany had by far the most precipitous drop (from +0.278 to +0.100) in mail communications with the rest of the Six, again showing the communications cost of its war policy. Significant decreases also occurred for Belgium, which nevertheless remained the most strongly integrated member of the group, and the Netherlands.

By 1955, after the beginnings of the movement toward European economic integration (such as the formation in 1952 of the European Coal and Steel Community) but before the Treaty of Rome, the trend of growing social communication among the Six had resumed. The mean RS^t score for the group rose again to +0.227, almost equal to the level of 1937; and the individual averages for all the Six except Italy increased substantially. There were also positive changes in the extreme scores: the proportion of very high RS^t scores rose from 20 to 23 percent and that of very low RS^t scores fell from 13 to 3 percent.

The next half-dozen years, especially between 1958 and 1961, witnessed further growth in the cohesiveness of intra-EEC mail patterns. The overall mean RS^t score for the Six increased from +0.227 in 1955 to +0.251 in 1958 and +0.307 in 1961. Concomitantly, the proportion of positive relationships ($RS^t \geqslant + 0.200$) rose from 46 to 63 percent; and for the first time there were no pairs of countries in 1961 whose RS^t scores fell into the lowest category of extreme disengagement.

A glance at the patterns of individual countries reinforces this view of growing cohesiveness. Italy enjoyed the greatest growth in mail communications with the other members of the Six. The leap of its average RS^t score from +0.072 in 1958 to +0.227 in 1961 indicates that, for the first time in modern history, Italy had integrated itself into a communications region with the other members of the EEC. West Germany also manifested a strong increase in mail links with its EEC partners (from +0.195 in 1958 to +0.352 in 1961). The rank order of average scores indicates that Belgium (+0.582) continued to have by far the strongest communications linkages; Germany (+0.352) was second, followed by Luxembourg and France (averaging near +0.280); and even Italy (+0.227) and the Netherlands (+0.154) enjoyed mean scores that were higher than any of the states except Belgium in 1890.

Of particular interest in this respect are the changing linkages between individual countries and their EEC partners. The crucial relationship between France and Germany, the largest EEC countries in terms of economic potential and in many ways the linchpin of any effort to unite West Europe economically or in any other way, was considerably strengthened. The year 1961 marked the first time that both their mutual RS^t scores were positive, even though French exports to Germany still ranked in the category of indifference. (Russett, 1965: 42–46, using per capita international mail data, reaches the same conclusion regarding growing Franco-German ties.) Equally noteworthy is the fully fledged entrance of Italy into the intra-EEC postal network.

An examination of the global matrix of RS^t scores substantiates the trend of growing communications integration among the Six. By 1961 the Benelux countries had few significant mail linkages outside the EEC region, and Italy had dissolved its ties with southern Europe. France's relationship with southern Europe was still somewhat stronger than that with the EEC countries, but this difference was much less than in the interwar period. West Europe, although remaining far from being the most important focus of the German Federal Republic's postal span of attention, had gained in importance over previous decades.

CONCLUSION

By 1961 the EEC states had finally emerged as a fairly distinct and cohesive region in terms of international mail flows, and they seemed to be moving toward greater regionalization. Their growing mail ties are clearly indicated by the regressions against time of mean RS^t scores (Table 10.3). For the Six as a whole, transaction strength grew in a generally linear fashion over time ($r = 0.89$; $b = 0.034$; significance level = 0.002). Except for Germany, whose cyclical expansion and contraction of mail relations with the region resulted in only a moderate relationship between its average RS^t scores and time ($r = 0.51$; significance level $= 0.10$), similarly strong linear growth patterns, with correlation coefficients ranging from 0.82 to 0.94, characterized the individual countries as well. Figure 10.1 presents these results graphically. Using each country's mean scores with respect to the other five, it shows that an upward trend was under way throughout the entire three-quarters of a century between 1890 and 1961.

It is difficult to sort out the effect of institutionalization on the trends in intra-EEC mail flows. On the one hand, the steady growth of mail linkages over the entire time span suggests that, disruptive wars notwithstanding, patterns of mutually rewarding interaction preceded the development of economic and eventually political institutions. We might carry this argument further to state that such patterns of interaction created a basis in community for the subsequent institutionalization. On the other hand, even taking into account the long-time growth in postal interactions, a substantial leap toward communications regionalization came only after World War II, most especially after 1955. Italian mail links with the rest of the EEC, for example, became significant only after the Treaty of Rome went into effect.

Influences on Mail Interactions

An appropriate way to move from descriptions of changes over time in international mail flows to an assessment of their determinants is multivariate analysis. Here we shall focus on two years: 1928, representative of the halcyon era between the wars, the era before the world economic system crashed and before Nazi Germany and Fascist Italy forged the Axis alliance; and 1961, the year (at least among those for which data are available) in which mail linkages among the Six reached their peak. The *dependent variables* of our analysis — that is, what we want to explain — are thus:

(1) *1928 RS^t scores*, or the relative levels of international mail interaction during a period of economic prosperity but well before there were any concrete moves toward a European economic community;
(2) *1961 RS^t scores*, the latest date for which we have mail flow data;
(3) *RS^t score change, 1928–61*, or the difference between the 1961 and 1928 values, taken as an indicator of the degree of change in mail interactions.

Sixteen countries were included in the analysis: the six original EEC members (Belgium, France, Italy, Luxembourg, the Netherlands, and

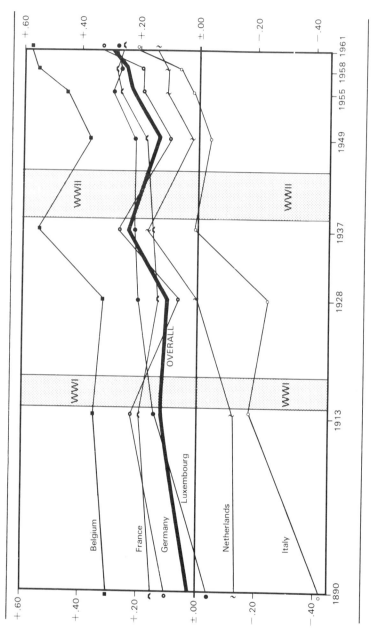

Figure 10.1 Mean Dyadic Scores with the Rest of the Six, by Country

West Germany), the seven West European countries that made up the European Free Trade Association, or EFTA (Austria, Denmark, Norway, Portugal, Sweden, Switzerland, and the United Kingdom), and the three other major West European countries (Finland, Ireland, and Spain). The interactions among these 16 countries (e.g. German exports to Austria, Finland, etc.; Austrian exports to Germany, Finland, etc.; and so forth) form 240 dyadic pairs for analysis for each of the two years.

Five *predictor variables* were posited to explain the level of mail interaction among the West European states. The first two indicate membership in West European supranational organizations:

(1) *Common EEC membership:* If the states comprising a particular dyad were both members of the European Economic Community (e.g. France and West Germany), we coded the dyad as 1. Otherwise (e.g. West Germany and Austria), the dyad was coded 0.

The analysis in the previous section suggests that common EEC membership should be strongly associated with increasing levels of mail flows over time and should have a positive association with 1961 RS^t scores of mail interaction (and something similar should hold for trade as well). The language, geographic, and political divisions that existed among these six countries in 1928, however, argue that there should be little, if any, relationship between group membership and interaction strength.

(2) *Common EFTA membership:* The same coding procedure was used here as for common EEC membership.

Since the founding of EFTA in 1959–60 occurred too close to 1961 to be likely to have produced any major effects by our last data point, little significant change over time would be expected. Also, given the greater heterogeneity of the EFTA members compared with EEC members in terms of geographic and linguistic dispersion, mail and trade interactions among them should be somewhat weaker. EFTA is thus included in this model as a "control" group for explaining European communication patterns, since EFTA membership is not expected to affect mail flows while, according to our earlier analysis, EEC membership might very well do so.

Two additional factors which many writers have asserted influence the degree of interaction between two countries are spatial and social distance. "Gravity" models of various types of interactions have persuasively shown that distance possesses a very strong negative relationship with the strength of interactions (Zipf, 1949; Isard et al.,

1960: Ch. 11; Deutsch and Isard, 1961; Tinbergen, 1962: 262–263; Merritt, 1964, 1974; Linnemann, 1966).

(3) *Common border:* Given the relatively compact nature of Europe, distance was measured here by whether or not the countries in a particular dyad share a common border. We scored the dyad 1 if its members are contiguous to each other, and 0 otherwise.

Contiguity should be strongly correlated with opportunities for interaction, as well as indicating the possibility (and usually the actuality) of overlapping ethnic populations which produce especially high levels of communications. By the same token, peoples in different countries who speak the same language might be expected to communicate much more with each other than those who do not.

(4) *Language similarity:* Language similarity was measured on a three-point scale (in descending order): (i) same language, (ii) similar language group, and (iii) dissimilar language. We focused on four major language groups: (i) English, (ii) Romance (French, Portuguese, Spanish, Italian), (iii) German–Dutch–Flemish, and (iv) Scandinavian (excluding Finnish). We treated Belgium, Luxembourg, and Switzerland as multilingual states (e.g., Switzerland was coded as having the same language as West Germany, Austria, France, and Italy).

The final explanatory factor is another measure of interaction: the level of trade between the members of each dyad. Economic interactions might well be expected to spur broader ties of communication. Accordingly, the level of trade at any one time between members of a dyad should have a strong influence on their mail communications; and changes in trade should produce corresponding shifts in mail transactions.

(5) *Trade RA^1:* Trade interaction is indicated by the RA statistic discussed earlier (Savage and Deutsch, 1960), as transformed according to the same algorithm applied to the RS statistics. Data for 1928 RA scores were provided by Richard W. Chadwick of the University of Hawaii,[3] while the 1961 RA scores were calculated from the United Nations *Yearbook of International Trade Statistics* (1967) using exchange rates reported in the United Nations *Statistical Yearbook* (1969: 594–595) to convert trade figures into US dollars.

There were unfortunately some missing data for the trade and mail interaction indices. For one thing, trade reports for Belgium and Luxembourg were combined for both 1928 and 1961. For another, mail data were missing for Spanish exports in 1928 and for Swedish and

Swiss exports in 1961. Because excluding countries from the analysis might well bias the results, estimates of these missing data were made and substituted into the analysis. The same RA^t scores were given for both Belgium's and Luxembourg's trade with other West European states; and their mutual RA^t scores were assumed to be equal to their mutual RS^t scores for mail interaction. For the three countries with missing mail export data, RS^t scores were estimated by their import RS^t scores with their various partners. (Although the RS^t statistic is not a symmetrical measure, in that RS^t_{ij} seldom equals RS^t_{ji}, import and export RS^t scores between the two countries are usually of the same magnitude.) Since there were missing data for both Sweden and Switzerland in 1961, Sweden's RS^t score for exports to Switzerland in 1958 was used to estimate their mutual RS^t scores in 1961.

Multiple regression analysis was applied to estimate the combined impact and relative influence of the independent variables on the strength of mail ties among the West European nations. Tables 10.4–10.6, presenting the regression results, contain three principal types of statistical information. First, the multiple R indicates the overall combined impact of the predictor items on the dependent variable. Second, standardized regression or beta (b) coefficients measure the relative impact of each independent variable after the effects of other predictors have been controlled. Third, the correlation coefficient r shows the strength of the bivariate association of each independent variable with the dependent variable in question, and thus indicates the changes in these relationships produced in the multivariate analysis.

One potential problem in multiple regression analysis, called multicollinearity, occurs when two or more independent variables are highly intercorrelated (Blalock, 1972: Ch. 19). Two of the independent variables used here — language similarity and geographic proximity — have an intercorrelation high enough ($r = 0.64$) to be in the danger zone for multicollinearity. However, examination of such evidence of multicollinearity as the beta coefficients and standard errors of the predictors in the regression equation, and changes in the multiple R when independent variables are added to or removed from the analysis, indicates that multicollinearity is not a problem.

Three sets of regressions were run — for 1928, for 1961, and for changes in mail and trade ties between the two years. Each regression included all dyads with no missing data.

1928 AND 1961: A GEOGRAPHIC DETERMINISM OF TRANSACTION FLOWS

Table 10.4 presents for 1928 the results of the regression of mail RS^t scores on all five independent variables described above and of trade

TABLE 10.4   **Influences on West European Transactions, 1928**

	Mail RS^t		*Trade RA*^{t}	
Multiple R	0.82		0.61	
Relative Influence	Beta	r	Beta	r
Common EEC membership	−0.05	0.22	−0.01	0.21
Common EFTA membership	0.00	0.04	0.08	0.07
Common border	0.38	0.70	0.50	0.60
Language similarity	0.03	0.51	0.16	0.47
1928 Trade *RA*^{t}	0.53	0.76	—	—

RA^t scores on the other four predictors. Both multiple R's are very high (0.82 for mail and 0.61 for trade).

The results of these two regressions demonstrate that geographic contiguity played a central role in 1928 in shaping West European transactions. It was the predominant determinant of the strength of trade ties ($r = 0.60$; $b = 0.50$) and had a strong effect on mail flows as well — both directly ($r = 0.70$; $b = 0.38$) and indirectly, through its impact on trade relations, which exerted the strongest independent influence on mail interactions ($r = 0.76$; $b = 0.53$). The two types of transactions were thus very strongly related. Physical distance exercised a very pronounced influence and constraint on the pattern of West European communications and interactions.

Otherwise, the predictor variables had only a marginal effect at best. Despite a moderately strong relationship with the two dependent variables ($r = 0.47$ with trade RA^t and 0.51 with mail RS^t), language similarity had little independent influence on either type of transaction once the effects of geographic proximity were controlled. There was a slight positive tendency for trade to be conducted between countries with similar languages ($b = 0.16$), but, surprisingly, language similarity had no independent influence whatever on mail flows.

As expected, future membership in the EEC and EFTA trading groups bore little relationship to international transactions in 1928. EEC membership had a slight bivariate correlation with trade ($r = 0.21$) and mail ($r = 0.22$). Once the moderate relationship between EEC membership and both common borders ($r = 0.38$) and language similarity ($r = 0.31$) is taken into account, however, these positive relationships are erased; and both betas, while not statistically significant, are slightly negative (-0.05 for mail and -0.01 for trade). EFTA membership had no significant association at all with these two types of international transactions in either the bivariate or the multivariate results. In short, the data for 1928 support most of the original hypotheses, with the exception that language similarity had a somewhat weaker relationship than anticipated.

Data for the 1961 regressions for the mail RS^t scores and trade RA^t scores are presented in Table 10.5. Both the explanatory impact of the independent variables (multiple $R = 0.80$ for mail and 0.63 for trade) and the causal pattern of the relative influence of the predictor variables are quite similar to the situation in 1928. Our major hypothesis that EEC membership would have a positive impact on mail and trade flows in West Europe in 1961 is decisively disconfirmed. To be sure, the bivariate correlations of EEC membership with mail and trade rose from 0.22 to 0.34 for mail and from 0.21 to 0.26 for trade, but the multiple regression shows that these bivariate associations stemmed from the effects of other explanatory factors. Unlike the situation in 1928, although the betas for EEC membership were slightly positive (0.06 for mail and 0.05 for trade), they were far from being statistically significant. In sum, interactions among the Six of the EEC were clearly stronger in 1961 than in 1928, but they were not nearly so high as we had anticipated. The EFTA variable, in contrast, followed expectations in that in 1961 it had no association whatever with West European mail and only a slight one with trade ($r = 0.12$; $b = 0.14$).

Turning to the primary causes of West European transaction flows, having a common border ($r = 0.60$; $b = 0.46$) remained the strongest influence on trade, although its predominance was slightly less than in 1928. Again, as in 1928, language similarity had a secondary but still significant influence on the strength of trade relations ($r = 0.49$; $b = 0.18$). The results for the mail flow regression are similar to 1928 as well. Trade RA^t score ($r = 0.71$; $b = 0.44$) again exerted the most

TABLE 10.5   Influences on West European Transactions, 1961

	Mail RS^t		Trade RA^t	
Multiple R	*0.80*		*0.63*	
Relative Influence	*Beta*	*r*	*Beta*	*r*
Common EEC membership	0.06	0.34	0.05	0.26
Common EFTA membership	−0.04	−0.01	0.14	0.12
Common border	0.36	0.70	0.46	0.60
Language similarity	0.09	0.55	0.18	0.49
1961 Trade RA^t	0.44	0.71	—	—

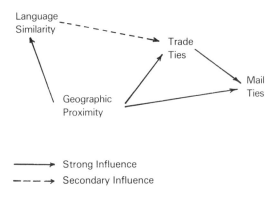

Figure 10.2 Cross-Sectional Model of Influences on West European Transactions

influence on mail flows, with geographic proximity ($r = 0.70; b = 0.36$) a close second, while the bivariate association between mail ties and language similarity ($r = 0.55$) disappeared in the multivariate results once the effects of distance and trade relations were controlled.

The cross-sectional results for both 1928 and 1961 suggest the causal pattern outlined in Figure 10.2. The strength of trade ties is determined primarily by geographic distance, with language similarity having a secondary effect. In turn, both a common border and the magnitude of the trade scores exert about equal influence on mail flows. The strength of intra-European transaction flows thus appears to be essentially the result, either directly or indirectly, of geographic factors.

FROM 1928 TO 1961: IMPACT OF THE EEC ON MAIL FLOWS

Table 10.6 presents the multiple regression results from the analysis of changes in European trade and mail linkages between 1928 and 1961. Unlike the cross-sectional relationship for 1961, a cross-temporal study indicates a very significant strengthening of the EEC communications network after World War II. In fact, among the explanatory variables, EEC membership had the strongest impact on mail relations and was one of two significant influences on trade ties. With multiple R's of 0.31 for mail and 0.22 for trade, the overall impact of the

TABLE 10.6   Influences on West European Transactions, 1928–1961

	*Mail RS*ᵗ		*Trade RA*ᵗ	
Multiple R	0.31		0.22	
Relative Influence	Beta	r	Beta	r
Common EEC membership	0.25	0.22	0.09	−0.01
Common EFTA membership	−0.06	−0.10	0.06	0.05
Common border	−0.18	−0.05	−0.22	−0.20
Language similarity	0.09	0.04	−0.02	−0.13
Change in Trade RA^t	0.16	0.17	—	—

independent variables, although much less than in the cross-sectional regressions, remains statistically significant.

The regression results for explaining changes over time in the trade RA^t scores strongly indicate that, during the third of a century between our two time points, European trade spread away from concentrations between neighboring states. Geographic proximity had by far the strongest impact on changes in the strength of trade relations ($r = -0.20$; $b = -0.22$). The negative direction of this relationship shows that, as might well be expected, advancing technology and communications between the late 1920s and early 1960s resulted in the growing geographic dispersion of West European trade patterns. Although there was no bivariate association between EEC membership and changes in trade strength ($r = -0.01$), belonging to the EEC became the second strongest predictor once the other independent variables were controlled ($b = 0.09$), and at a level that is marginally significant statistically ($p = 0.12$). This finding supports the hypothesis that the formation of the European Economic Community stimulated the growth of international transactions among the participating states. EFTA membership and language similarity were completely unrelated to changes in the trade RA^t scores.

The predicted impact of the EEC's formation emerged in the data on changes in the strength of mail linkages between 1928 and 1961. Common membership in the EEC had the strongest relationship to change in the mail RS^t scores in both the bivariate and multivariate results ($r = 0.22$; $b = 0.25$). Also, it should be noted that the formation of the EEC was more strongly associated with increasing mail than trade transactions, despite the EEC's principal concern with economic institutions and cooperation. Although the temporal data are not complete enough to support a firm conclusion about the causal sequence in the relationship between growing social communications and EEC institutionalization, this certainly demonstrates the importance of social communications, as indicated by international mail flows, in the process of European economic integration.

As in the case of changes in trade relations, West European mail flows became more dispersed geographically between 1928 and 1961. This trend is indicated by the fact that the presence of a common border was the second most important predictor ($r = -0.05; b = -0.18$). There was also some tendency for mail to increase between countries with similar languages ($b = 0.09$) and growing trade ties ($b = 0.16$). This latter relationship between changes in mail and trade flows is surprisingly low in view of the very strong cross-sectional correlations between these two variables (averaging 0.75 for 1928 and 1961) and of changes in both being influenced primarily by EEC membership and distance. Evidently, while both trade and mail linkages became more dispersed geographically, these dispersions moved in somewhat different directions, as is suggested by the fact that language similarity had some influence on changes in mail, but not trade, relations.

The multivariate analysis of changes over time in the strength of West European mail linkages thus shows that communications among the Six grew significantly after the formation of the European Economic Community — even after other potential causal factors are controlled. Somewhat weaker but still significant results emerged in the multiple regression for trade RA^t scores. Together these findings support the conclusion that the formation of the EEC did indeed exercise a significant effect on communication and transaction flows in West Europe. The formation of EFTA, by way of contrast, produced no such immediate increase in mail or trade linkages.

Mail Flows and the European Community

The implications of these findings can be divided roughly into analytic conclusions about the empirical relationships examined here and broader speculations about what these relationships might portend for the process of West European integration. The analytic conclusions concern both the general determinants of international transaction flows and the specific impact of the EEC on European communications links.

CAUSES OF SHIFTS IN MAIL FLOWS

While the principal objective of this paper was not to delineate the primary causes of the directions of international transaction flows, the findings nevertheless contain several relevant implications. First, the close relationship that was found between geographic proximity and both mail and trade ties is consistent with previous arguments that transaction flows are primarily a function of the physical distance between any particular pair of senders and receivers (Zipf, 1949; Isard et al., 1960: Ch. 11; Deutsch and Isard, 1961; Tinbergen, 1962: 262–293; Merritt, 1964, 1974; Linnemann, 1966; Hughes, 1972).

Second, two superficially surprising results are that the impact of distance was generally much greater than that of language similarity, and that language similarity had a greater cross-sectional influence on trade than on mail ties. This may be explicable, though, by the mail between minorities in one country and their neighboring national homelands. For example, while strong international communications are commonly assumed to promote mutual understanding and amity, very high levels of international mail existed among warring Balkan countries in the late nineteenth and early twentieth centuries precisely because their conflicts were rooted in overlapping national populations (Clark, 1973a). These findings point to the need to explore levels of transactions within their geopolitical context.

Third, the very strong impact of economic interactions on the level of mail flows, even after the effects of distance and language similarity are controlled, is quite striking. Similarly, Russett and his associates (1964: 315–317) found that, while a nation's propensity to send both domestic and foreign mail is very strongly related to its level of economic development, the extent of its involvement in foreign trade exercises a very important independent effect upon its sending of foreign mail. Thus, economic interactions evidently play a significant role in stimulating broader social communications.

The process of economic and political integration in the European Economic Community, incomplete as it remains, provides a specific example of this more abstract generalization. The emergence of the EEC as a distinct and increasingly cohesive region in terms of its mail communications is especially significant because it represents one of the few appreciable shifts during the twentieth century in the basic structure of West European mail flows. Multivariate analysis, including several other potential causes of international communications patterns, confirms the fact that EEC membership had a positive *independent* impact on change in mail RS^t scores between 1928 and 1961. The expected relationship of EEC membership to the absolute level of mail flows in 1961 nonetheless failed to materialize.

Thus, at least in terms of temporal covariations, the formation of the EEC and the integrative processes that it set in motion evidently stimulated social communication among the mass populations of the member states. This causal sequence between EEC institutionalization and growing social communication among its members is not simply unidirectional. Rather, growing social communications among these countries (Italy excepted) over the first half of the twentieth century may well have constituted a prerequisite for the formation of the European Economic Community.

TRANSACTIONS AND POLITICAL COMMUNITY

We might go further to hypothesize that these changed habits of communication were responsible for the attitudinal shifts noted earlier regarding perceptions of other nations and supranational integration. Numerous observers (e.g. Lindberg and Scheingold, 1970: Chs. 2 and 8) have argued that such changing attitudes provide a "permissive consensus" for elites attempting to promote further integration. As Inglehart (1977) argues, however, the major obstacles, at least at the time he was writing, lie at the elite instead of the mass level:

> In a recent study, West European political leaders and government officials were asked a series of questions about European integration. One of the reasons most frequently cited to explain why European integration had not progressed more rapidly was the claim that the public was not ready for it. In a sense, the very opposite seems to be true. In a number of respects, European publics are quite ready to go beyond the present scope of European integration. They show a growing sense of supra-national identity and a widespread willingness to entrust broader responsibilities to supra-national institutions. In the turmoil following 1973, their leaders were not only failing to move toward the goals they had set themselves, but threatened to undo progress already attained (Inglehart, 1977:362).

There is some reason to believe that public opinion and the international communications which shape it can have some impact on, or can at least constrain, elite foreign policy decision-making. Deutsch and Merritt (1965) argue, for example, that the growing salience of foreign affairs to the publics and business leaders in industrialized democracies has produced relatively stable attitudes toward the external world which greatly inhibit political actions at variance with these perceptions. Merritt and Clark (1977) also found that in early twentieth-century Europe incongruities between nations' social communications linkages, as measured by mail RS scores, and political bloc memberships tended to produce political wavering and sometimes even defection from the blocs.

Such popular pressures seem more negative than positive in the sense that they place limits on the foreign policy behavior of political leaders, rather than providing direct mandates for complex initiatives, such as those required to produce a new spurt of EEC integration. The EEC publics, especially those from the original Six, may be willing to grant a "permissive consensus" for elite activity. They will not, however, exert anywhere near the political pressure necessary to get the current leaderships to transcend the political and bureaucratic interests sustaining the status quo.

In sum, the original activities of European political leaders which set into motion the processes of political and economic integration may have produced the changes in international social communications and national public opinion necessary for any further intensification of the integration movement. This "permissive consensus" nonetheless has emerged in a context of growing resistance by leadership groups to increased supranationalism, which in turn has made the changed state of public opinion superfluous.

NOTES

1. We are indebted to Professor Robert G. Muncaster, Department of Mathematics, University of Illinois at Urbana-Champaign, for suggesting the algorithm of transformation we have used.

2. The scores in Table 9.1 have been extracted from a global matrix. Accordingly, in comparison to the RS^t scores that would result if transactions between the Six and, say, Third World countries were omitted, the intra-European scores are generally higher but more accurate than they would be were we to calculate RS^t scores from just the mail exchanges among the six countries without the global context. See Chadwick and Deutsch (1973) on the importance of using a global matrix.

3. We are indebted to Professor Chadwick for making these data available to us.

REFERENCES

BLALOCK, H. M. Jr (1972) Social Statistics. New York: McGraw-Hill.

CAPORASO, J. A. (1971) "Theory and method in the study of international integration." International Organization 25 (Spring): 228–253.

——— (1972) Functionalism and Regional Integration: A Logical and Empirical Assessment. Beverly Hills, Calif.: Sage.

CHADWICK, R. W. and K. W. DEUTSCH (1973) "International trade and economic integration: further developments in trade matrix analysis." Comparative Political Studies 6 (April): 84–109.

CLARK, C. (1973a) "The evolution of intra-European spans of attention: the evidence of international mail." Paper presented at the 14th Annual Convention of the International Studies Association, New York.

——— (1973b) "The impact of size on the Savage-Deutsch RA statistic." Comparative Political Studies 6 (April): 110–122.

———— and S. WELCH (1972) "Western European trade as a measure of integration: untangling the interpretations." Journal of Conflict Resolution 16 (September): 363–382.

DEUTSCH, K. W. (1953) Nationalism and Social Communication: An Inquiry into the Foundations of Nationality. Cambridge, Mass.: MIT Press; and New York: John Wiley.

———— (1956) "Shifts in the balance of communications flows: a problem of measurement in international relations." Public Opinion Quarterly 20 (Spring): 143- 160.

————, S. A. BURRELL, R. A. KAHN, M. LEE Jr, M. LICHTERMAN, R. E. LINDGREN, F. L. LOEWENHEIM, and R. W. VAN WAGENEN (1957) Political Community and the North Atlantic Area: International Organization in the Light of Historical Experience. Princeton, NJ: Princeton University Press.

———— L. J. EDINGER, R. C. MACRIDIS, and R. L. MERRITT (1967) France, Germany and the Western Alliance: A Study of Elite Attitudes on European Integration and World Politics. New York: Charles Scribner's Sons.

———— and W. ISARD (1961) "A note on the generalized concept of effective distance." Behavioral Science 6 (October): 308–311.

———— and R. L. MERRITT (1965) "Effects of events on national and international images," pp. 132–187 in H. C. Kelman (ed.), International Behavior: A Social-Psychological Analysis. New York: Holt, Rinehart & Winston.

ETZIONI, A. (1965) Political Unification: A Comparative Study of Leaders and Forces. New York: Holt, Rinehart & Winston.

GOODMAN, L. A. (1963) "Statistical methods for the preliminary analysis of transaction flows." Econometrica 31 (January–April): 197–208.

HAAS, E. B. (1958) The Uniting of Europe: Political, Social, and Economic Forces, 1950–1957. Stanford, Calif.: Stanford University Press.

HUGHES, B. B. (1972) "Transaction data and analysis: in search of concepts." International Organization 26 (Autumn): 659–690.

INGLEHART, R. (1967) "An end to European integration?" American Political Science Review 61 (March): 91–105.

———— (1977) The Silent Revolution: Changing Values and Political Styles among Western Publics. Princeton, NJ: Princeton University Press.

ISARD, W., D. BRANHALL, G. O. P. CARROTHERS, J. H. CUMBERLAND, L. N. MOSES, D. O. PRICE, and E. W. SCHOOLER (1960) Methods of Regional Analysis: An Introduction to Regional Science. New York: John Wiley.

LINDBERG, L. and S. SCHEINGOLD (1970) Europe's Would-Be Polity: Patterns of Change in the European Community. Englewood Cliffs, NJ: Prentice-Hall.

LINNEMANN, H. (1966) An Econometric Study of International Trade Flows. Amsterdam: North Holland.

MERRITT, R. L. (1964) "Distance and interaction among political communities." General Systems Yearbook 9: 255–264.

———— (1968) "Visual representation of mutual friendliness," pp. 111–141 in R. L. Merritt and D. J. Puchala (eds.), Western European Perspectives on International Affairs: Public Opinion Studies and Evaluations. New York: Praeger.

———— (1974) "Locational aspects of political integration," pp. 187–211 in K. R. Cox, D. R. Reynolds, and S. Rokkan (eds.), Locational Approaches to Power and Conflict. New York: John Wiley.

——— (1983) "Political integration revisited." Man, Environment, Space and Time 3 (Spring): 1–16.

——— and C. CLARK (1977) "An example of data use: mail flows and the European balance of power, 1890–1920," pp. 169–205 in K. W. Deutsch, B. Fritsch, H. Jaguaribe, and A. S. Markovits (eds), Problems of World Modeling: Political and Social Implications. Cambridge, Mass.: Ballinger.

——— and C. CLARK (1979) Analyzing International Mail Flows. Berlin: Wissenschaftszentrum Berlin, International Institute for Comparative Social Research, Paper IIVG/pr79-3.

MORGAN, R. (1973) West European Politics since 1945: The Shaping of the European Community. New York: Capricorn.

PUCHALA, D. J. (1966) European Political Integration: Progress and Prospects. New Haven, Conn.: Yale University, Political Science Department Research Library (mimeographed).

——— (1970) "International transactions and regional integration." International Organization 24 (Autumn): 732–763.

RUSSETT, B. M. (1965) Trends in World Politics. New York: Macmillan.

———(1971) "Transaction, community, and international political integration." Journal of Common Market Studies 9 (March): 224–245.

———, H. R. ALKER Jr, K. W. DEUTSCH, and H. D. LASSWELL et al. (1964) World Handbook of Political and Social Indicators. New Haven, Conn.: Yale University Press.

SAVAGE, I. R. and K. W. DEUTSCH (1960) "A statistical model of the gross analysis of transaction flows." Econometrica 28 (July): 551–572.

TINBERGEN, J. (1962) Shaping the World Economy: Suggestions for an International Economic Policy. New York: Twentieth Century Fund.

United Nations (1967) Yearbook of International Trade Statistics, 1965. New York: UN Publishing Service.

———(1969) Statistical Yearbook, 1968. New York: UN Publishing Service.

UNIVERSAL POSTAL UNION (1886-1961) Relève des Tableaux Statistiques du Service Postal International. Bern: Bureau International de l'Union Postale Universelle.

ZIPF, G. K. (1949) Human Behavior and the Principle of Least Effort. Cambridge, Mass.: Addison-Wesley.

CHAPTER 11

DISTRIBUTIONAL PATTERNS OF REGIONAL INTERACTIONS: A TEST OF THE POISSON PROCESS AS A NULL MODEL

ALEX MINTZ
PHILIP A. SCHRODT

While the primary focus of quantitative international politics has been the attempt to find statistical order amid the apparent chaos of international behavior, it is equally important to determine the extent to which apparent order may be the product of various patterns of stochastic behavior. This study ascertains the extent to which the Poisson distribution accurately describes the distribution of international interactions in the COPDAB data set. Focusing on two international subsystems — Arab Middle Eastern nations (Iran, Iraq, Jordan, Kuwait, Saudi Arabia, and Syria) and major NATO nations (France, West Germany, the United Kingdom, Italy, and the United States) — for the period 1948–78, we shall examine the degree of fit of the Poisson distribution under a variety of controls for type of interaction, actor and target nation, and level of temporal aggregation of the data.

The Poisson model has been utilized in a number of international relations studies, frequently as a null model against which assumptions of contagion (the occurrence of one event affecting the probability of

AUTHORS' NOTE: The research has been supported by the National Science Foundation (Grant SES 8025053). We wish to thank Yael Assous for her assistance in computer programming. The COPDAB data set used in this research was obtained from the Inter-University Consortium for Political and Social Research, and was originally collected by Edward E. Azar and Thomas Sloan. Neither the original collectors nor the Consortium bear any responsibility for the analyses or interpretations presented here.

237

another) or heterogeneity (the change in the frequency of an event over time) are tested. The initial application of the model was Richardson's (1941, 1945, 1960) modeling of war occurrence; other studies looking at the stochastic distribution of war include Moyal (1949), Weiss (1963), Davis, Duncan, and Siverson (1978), Midlarsky (1981), Singer and Small (1972), Most and Starr (1980), Houweling and Kuné (1984), and Cioffi-Revilla (1985). The topic of alliance formation and disintegration has also generated a number of studies, including Horvath and Foster (1963), Job (1974, 1976), McGowan and Rood (1975), Siverson and Duncan (1976), and Li and Thompson (1978). In addition to these applications, several probability models have been used to analyze the occurrence of coups (Midlarsky, 1970; Laemmle, 1977) and military attacks during the Vietnam war (Chan, 1978).

The Poisson model is important because it provides the simplest definition of randomness over time (see, for a formal discussion, Parzen, 1963; Feller, 1968; or Cinlar, 1975). The model requires only three assumptions:

(1) The probability of one event occurring in a single interval of time is small and constant.
(2) The probability of more than one occurrence within a single interval is very small, and goes to zero as the size of the interval goes to zero.
(3) The occurrence of each event is independent of the occurrence of all other events.

From these assumptions, the equation for the distribution of events generated by a Poisson process can be shown to be:

$$\Pr(N = k) = \frac{e^{-mt}(mt)^k}{k!},$$

where N is the number of events occurring in a time period of length t and m is the "intensity parameter" equal to the average frequency of events per unit of time; the variance of the distribution is also equal to m. When observations are made on units of time of equal duration, then t is equal to 1.00. Note that the distribution will change depending on the length of the time interval being considered; this interval will be called the "level of temporal aggregation" in the discussion. As m becomes large, the Poisson can be approximated by the normal distribution.

While there are many stochastic processes, the Poisson is fundamental and universal because it requires fewer assumptions than any other stochastic process. As Feller notes, there exist a few distributions of great universality which occur in a surprisingly great variety of problems. The three principal distributions, with ramifications throughout probability theory, are the binomial distribution, the normal distribution, and the Poisson distribution [Feller, 1968: 156].

All other stochastic distributions (e.g. the Weibull, Rayleigh, Yule–Greenwood, Markov processes, and so forth) are more complex than the Poisson, and as such the Poisson distribution serves as a baseline against which alternative stochastic and deterministic explanations of a behavior can be tested. If data fit a Poisson distribution, then those data are statistically indistinguishable from data produced by a random process involving no information beyond the expected value for the occurrence of the event per unit of time.

A finding of Poisson randomness in a set of data could be explained in one of three ways:

(1) The data are generated by a process that is actually Poisson.

(2) There is a non-Poisson process operating which produces events at a frequency which appears to be Poisson at the level of temporal aggregation.

(3) There is a non-Poisson process operating but the data are sampled randomly and thus appear to be Poisson-distributed because of measurement.

The third possibility will not be dealt with in detail in this paper, though it has been considered extensively elsewhere in discussions of events data (e.g. Vincent, 1983; McClelland, 1983). The choice between the first and second is more difficult and our research design will include a variety of controls to attempt to differentiate between these possibilities.

Since most theories of international behavior assume that events are intentional, and hence presumably follow some type of pattern, the Poisson distribution is important as a baseline against which to ascertain that any observed patterns are not generated purely by chance. The Poisson distribution will not fit constant levels of interaction, slowly increasing or decreasing levels, cyclical patterns of interaction, and concentrated bursts of activity. Each of these patterns has been suggested in the theoretical literature. The first pattern is implicit in most "steady-state" theories of international behavior, in particular most realist and balance-of-power models, though it is rarely explicitly stated as an assumption. The cyclical pattern is found in some grand "rise and fall" theories, most notably Toynbee's and perhaps Wallerstein's, and more recently in world systems theories linking international behavior to economic cycles (e.g. Thompson and Zuk, 1982). The fourth possibility is implicit in most crisis studies, which argue that most important events in international affairs occur in relatively short-lived crisis periods.

If the Poisson distribution cannot be rejected as a description of the observed interactions, then there is statistical evidence that any alleged patterns which are observed are simply due to chance. Perhaps the key difference between the Poisson and other processes which might generate interactions is that the Poisson process has no "memory." To produce any non-Poisson distribution, some type of systematic memory is needed, either to maintain the current level of the system (constant level), to change the level to match past levels of the system (cyclical), or to keep the activity of the system concentrated in short intervals (crisis). This memory can be expressed in a variety of mathematical forms — for example, a differential equation or a Markov chain — but, to generate a non-Poisson distribution, some characteristic of the system must determine subsequent levels with sufficient regularity for a pattern to be obtained. The simplest explanation for such a memory is doubtless the human memory of decision-makers, though memory incorporated into economic cycles (e.g. Kondratieff waves) is another possibility. The Poisson is a null model in the sense that most theories of international behavior assume that memory is a factor in behavior; yet the Poisson is a plausible model because a surprisingly large variety of international behavior has been shown to fit the model.

Finally, to place our work in a broader perspective, it is useful to compare it to a similar debate taking place in the field of quantitative ecology (see Lewin, 1983). For years a variety of formal models has been proposed to explain the distribution of species on the basis of competition and other interactions. Recently Simberloff and his associates (Simberloff, 1978; Connor and Simberloff, 1979) showed that many of these distributions can be accounted for by simple random processes without requiring the more complex interactive processes found in existing ecological theories. These studies, like ours, deal with the general question of determining the extent to which Poisson random behavior alone can explain an observed phenomenon.

Hypotheses and Design

H1: The occurrence of inter-nation interactions is Poisson-distributed over time.

On the basis of earlier studies showing that specific types of international behavior are Poisson-distributed, we wish to see whether or not international interactions generally are Poisson-distributed.

H2: The extent to which interactions are Poisson-distributed is a function of the level of interaction among nations.

Since international interactions involve a heterogeneous set of activities, we hypothesize that a Poisson distribution may fit data on some types of interactions (e.g. physical conflict) but not others (e.g. verbal cooperation).

H3: The extent to which interactions are Poisson-distributed varies across actors and across target nations.

There is no particular reason to assume that all actors behave identically toward all targets. For example, nations may engage in nonrandom behavior with their principal targets and random behavior with all others. Thus, we would like to test whether the Poisson distribution of interactions varies across actors and targets or whether the distributional pattern is universal.

H4: The extent to which interactions are Poisson-distributed varies with the level of temporal aggregation.

As noted above, the Poisson distribution depends on the unit of time used to aggregate the data. Thus, for example, it may be the case that behavior is Poisson-distributed when aggregated by year but is not Poisson-distributed when aggregated by month. The shorter period of aggregation also reduces the value of the intensity parameter m and makes it more likely that condition (1) of the Poisson process will be satisfied.

To study these hypotheses, we examined the proportion of cases where dyadic distributions of international events follow a Poisson distribution using a number of aggregations. For hypotheses H1 and H2, we looked at all dyads — 30 (6×5) for the Middle East set and 20 (5×4) for the NATO set — using different levels of aggregation of the events reported in the COPDAB set (all events, cooperative only, conflictual only, nonverbal cooperative, verbal cooperative, verbal conflictual, and nonverbal conflictual). For hypothesis H3, we looked at the distribution for each nation as target or actor for each of the four specific types of events (nonverbal cooperative, verbal cooperative, verbal conflictual, and nonverbal conflictual), which yielded a total of 20 distributions for the Middle East and 16 for NATO. For hypothesis H4, we did all the analyses at both monthly and yearly levels of temporal aggregation.

The correspondence of the observed observations and the expected distributions was tested using the following goodness-of-fit tests:

(1) *The chi-square test.* This test has been widely used in previous research when comparing Poisson-like distributions with empirical distributions of events (see e.g. McGowan and Rood, 1975; Job, 1976; Siverson and Duncan, 1976). In testing the null hypothesis that the observed distribution is not significantly different from the Poisson distribution, we shall reject the null hypothesis only if the calculated chi-square value is greater than the critical chi-square value at the 0.01 level or greater, and shall conclude that the Poisson does not fit the data. Expected k were aggregated to a minimum of 3 (see Hines and Montgomery, 1980).

(2) *A comparison of the mean with the variance* (which should equal 1.00 if the data are Poisson-distributed). If the ratio $s^2/\bar{x}$ is large, then the data suggest departure from the Poisson distribution. Since $(n-1)(s^2/\bar{x})$ approximates a chi-square distribution with $n - 1$ degrees of freedom, we were able to assess the magnitude of the $s^2/\bar{x}$ ratio.

The lowest degree of freedom allowed in the chi-square table is one. In the few cases (especially in the Western European data set) where this number equals zero, we evaluated goodness of fit by relying solely on the magnitude of the $s^2/\bar{x}$ ratio.

Note that in both cases our statement that the data fit the Poisson distribution means that we did not reject the hypothesis that the data were Poisson-distributed. Thus the Poisson is our null hypothesis rather than any alternative hypothesis.

Data

The hypotheses were tested using the Conflict and Peace Data Bank (COPDAB) events data set for the period 1948–78 (Azar, 1980a, 1980b). COPDAB is an extensive, machine-readable, longitudinal collection of daily international and domestic "'events'. . . reported in over 70 sources" (Azar, 1980b: 146). These sources include such major newspapers as the *New York Times* and *Washington Post* and regional publications such as *Middle East Affairs* and *Middle East Economic Digest*.

COPDAB was used for several reasons. Compared with other data sets (WEIS and others available from the ICPSR at the time we started the research), COPDAB reports more Middle Eastern events (Vincent, 1983:164), relies on multiple sources, including some from the Middle East and Europe, and covers a longer time period. At the same time, we are cognisant of the possible limitations of the data set (see, e.g., Azar and Dak, 1975; Howell, 1983; McClelland, 1983;

Vincent, 1983). We thus consider this study a test of the workability of the events data set as well as a test of international behavior in the abstract.

Although events data sets such as COPDAB appear at first to contain considerable information, data at the dyadic level are often very sparse. For example, while we examined over 16,000 interactions, this works out to only about 10 interactions per dyad-year. A data set of 16,000 interactions sounds sizable, and chews up considerable computer time, but it is still very far from a day-by-day account of international behavior. Even at the level of only a single interaction per day, such an accounting would involve (for the data sets being considered here) some 547,500 interactions (50 dyads × 30 years × 365 days). As a consequence, it is clear that COPDAB is a sample rather than a universe of the activity in the international system, though it is not a random sample. Activities which are more conspicuous, such as wars, or which somehow catch the attention of a newspaper editor are included in the set; other activities are not.

The COPDAB scale for international events consists of 15 points, or levels, ranging from the most cooperative event (1) to the most conflictual event (15). For much of the analysis, we aggregated the interactions (following Hopple et al., 1980) into four categories and analyzed each separately:

> *Nonverbal cooperation* (levels 1–4):
>> Examples: unification into one state, strategic alliance, military and economic support;
> *Verbal cooperation* (levels 5–7):
>> Examples: cultural and scientific support, verbal support of goals, values, and regime, and official exchanges, talks, and policy expression;
> *Verbal conflict* (levels 9–10):
>> Examples: verbal expression displaying discord in interaction and hostility in interaction;
> *Nonverbal conflict* (levels 11–15):
>> Examples: hostile diplomatic, economic, and military actions, small-scale military acts, limited wars, and extensive wars.

The analysis was done for two international subsystems: one in the Middle East and the other a part of NATO. They were chosen for two reasons. First, both are extensively covered in the COPDAB data set. COPDAB focused originally on the Middle East, and hence, we suspect, coverage of that area is more thorough than is that of Asia or Latin America. Second, there is a general bias in the international news media toward coverage of Western Europe, and the densest events set

TABLE 11.1 Number of Events by Nation, 1948–1978

Nation	Cooperative Events			Conflictive Events			
	Non-verbal (1–4)	Verbal (5–7)	All Coop. (1–7)	Verbal (9–10)	Non-verbal (11–15)	All Confl. (9–15)	Total Events[a] (1–15)
Middle East							
Iran	69	170	239	71	36	107	348
Iraq	177	601	778	225	98	323	1,110
Kuwait	124	289	413	44	33	77	493
Jordan	104	598	702	96	50	146	849
Saudi Arabia	156	488	644	33	6	39	688
Syria	171	583	754	220	66	286	1,048
Total	801	2,729	3,530	689	289	978	4,536
Western Europe							
France	439	1,725	2,164	472	55	527	2,702
W. Germany	465	1,417	1,882	307	29	336	2,293
Italy	349	787	1,136	107	12	119	1,268
UK	375	1,789	2,164	372	18	390	2,577
USA	564	1,778	2,342	355	60	415	2,757
Total	2,192	7,496	9,688	1,613	174	1,787	11,597

a. Includes level 8, a neutral category.

was found in that region. Since the Middle East set is about twice as conflictual as the NATO set (in terms of conflict as a proportion of total interaction), the two sets provide some additional control for the effects of whether the interactions within the region are conflictual or cooperative.

The analysis looked at interaction only within each subsystem. For the Middle East set, this involved 4,536 interactions; for the NATO set, 11,597 interactions. The number and type of interactions for each nation are reported in Table 11.1.

Results

The results of the analysis, reported in Tables 11.2 and 11.3, generally support the Poisson model. For the Middle East, when the data are aggregated annually (Table 11.2), 18 of the 30 distributions analyzed (60 percent) are sufficiently random that the Poisson distribution cannot be rejected. Analyzing the cooperative and conflictual dimensions separately yields an identical figure for cooper-

TABLE 11.2 Percentage of Dyads Obeying the Poisson Distribution: Annual Data

	Middle East[a] (%)		Western Europe (%)
Level of interaction			
Cooperative events (1–7)	60		15
Nonverbal cooperation (1–4)	100		90
Verbal cooperation (5–7)	63		25
Conflictive events (9–15)	72		75
Verbal conflict (9–10)	72		80
Nonverbal conflict (11–15)	88		100
All interactions (1–15)	60		15
Actor[a]			
Iran	89	France	75
Iraq	68	West Germany	75
Jordan	79	Italy	88
Kuwait	89	UK	69
Saudia Arabia	89	USA	63
Syria	70		
Target[a]			
Iran	89	France	69
Iraq	60	West Germany	63
Jordan	83	Italy	94
Kuwait	83	UK	50
Saudi Arabia	89	USA	69
Syria	70		

a. Seven Middle Eastern cases with zero frequencies excluded from the analysis.

ation (60 percent) and a somewhat higher one for conflict (72 percent). Nonverbal cooperation, and to a somewhat lesser extent, nonverbal conflict are Poisson-distributed in almost all cases, while distributional analysis of levels 5–7 (verbal cooperation) and 9-10 (verbal conflict) produce only a moderate fit to the data (of less than two-thirds and almost three-fourths of the distributions).

Table 11.2 shows moderate support for the hypothesis that the fit of the Poisson distribution is a function of the actor: compare, for example, the figures for Iran versus Syria and Kuwait or Saudi Arabia versus Iraq. The results also indicate differences with respect to the target: compare, again, the percentages for Iran and Syria or for Saudi Arabia and Iraq. Furthermore, it is rather striking to note that in the Middle Eastern region the nations that initiate most of the Poisson interactions are also the nations to which most of the Poisson reactions have been targeted, while nations which initiate the least number of Poisson interactions are also the nations to which the least number of Poisson interactions have been targeted. This is consistent with the findings of Schrodt (1983), using arms transfer behavior for the Middle East, of a high degree of similarity in actor and target behavior in COPDAB correlations.

Data on the NATO allies substantiate our findings in the Middle East, with some important exceptions. While not supporting the Poisson model with respect to all types of interactions, the results reveal that three-fourths of all conflictual interactions are Poisson-distributed over time, while only 3 of 20 distributions analyzed with cooperation data (15 percent) are Poisson-distributed. Table 11.2 also shows strong variations, depending on the specific type of interaction, in the percentage of Western European dyads that obey the Poisson distribution. In particular, we found strong evidence for the assertion that physical conflict interactions (levels 11–15) are Poisson distributed, and no support for the thesis that verbal cooperation events (levels 5–7) are Poisson-distributed. We thus find again considerable support for our second hypothesis concerning the Poisson patterns as a function of the level of interactions.

The NATO interactions also show variations with respect to actor and target. Compare, for example, the figures for Italy versus those for all other nations in Table 11.2, and the target Italy versus all the other nations. Again, as in the Middle East, the results suggest that the same nations that initiate most of the Poisson-like distributions in their respective regions are those to which most of the Poisson interaction has been directed.

Overall, there are significantly more Poisson distributions in the Middle Eastern data set than in the NATO set. This finding, suggesting some political differences, holds for all types of interactions combined as well as for the various types of cooperative behavior. At the same time, however, more verbal and nonverbal conflictual interactions were Poisson-distributed in Western Europe than in the Middle East.

The general hypothesis that the Poisson model fits the distribution of international events thus finds support for two geographical regions with different environments. Moreover, these results are consistent with previous results, which suggest that international conflicts are Poisson-distributed (see Richardson, 1945; Moyal, 1949; Singer and Small, 1972) and that nonverbal cooperative events such as alliance formation and defense agreements are stochastically distributed over

**TABLE 11.3 Percentage of Dyads Obeying the Poisson Distribution:
Monthly Data**

	Middle East[a] (%)		*Western Europe* (%)
Level of interaction			
Nonverbal cooperation (1–4)	83		45
Verbal cooperation (5–7)	27		0
Verbal conflict (9–10)	60		55
Nonverbal conflict (11–15)	77		75
Actor[a]			
Iran	74	France	31
Iraq	26	West Germany	25
Jordan	74	Italy	68
Kuwait	68	UK	56
Saudi Arabia	67	USA	44
Syria	50		
Target[a]			
Iran	74	France	31
Iraq	55	West Germany	38
Jordan	28	Italy	56
Kuwait	61	UK	44
Saudi Arabia	72	USA	50
Syria	65		

a. Seven Middle Eastern cases with zero frequencies excluded from the analysis.

time (McGowan and Rood, 1975; Siverson and Duncan, 1976). Our analysis nevertheless indicates that most verbal events (especially cooperative) are not Poisson-distributed. Such events have not been analyzed previously for this property, and it appears that the applicability of the Poisson model is partly a function of the type of event.

The results presented above use the year as the unit of aggregation. The analysis was repeated on monthly data, with the results reported in Table 11.3. Generally, we would expect monthly aggregations to reduce the value of the Poisson intensity parameter m (i.e. events are less likely to occur in a given month than in a given year), and hence to increase the likelihood of a Poisson distribution, but it is also possible that the shorter time scale will reveal other characteristics of the data.

For the Middle East, the analysis of monthly data basically verifies the findings in the annual data. The major difference in the statistical results is that the total number of Poisson-like distributions found is substantially lower for almost all nations and all levels analyzed.

Nonetheless, inferences based on both data sets are almost identical, with a number of important exceptions.

Some exceptions pertain to the level of interaction and the actors themselves. In terms of level of interaction, variations in the percentage of monthly data on dyads which obey the Poisson distribution provide even sharper contrasts between verbal cooperation and other types of interaction. In terms of cross-national variation, monthly data again show considerable differences between Iran and Iraq based on the target nations, and the figures for Jordan and to a lesser extent Kuwait are substantially lower for the monthly data than for the annual observations.

We should point out again that in both regions the percentages of dyadic interactions fitting the Poisson model are considerably lower in the monthly than in the yearly aggregations. This was contrary to our expectations and probably is significant. *Ceteris paribus*, the monthly aggregations should have a lower intensity parameter m and hence be more likely to fit the Poisson model, and yet the opposite occurs. This may indicate that the nonrandom features of the interactions occur at short time intervals.

The monthly NATO interactions show less congruence with annual data than do the Middle Eastern ones. In particular, the share of nonverbal cooperative events obeying the Poisson model drops from 75 to 45 percent. The analysis still finds that nonverbal conflictual events are Poisson-distributed. In terms of actors and target nations, here again, the percentage of Poisson-distributed cases is substantially lower than for annual aggregations but clearly shows sharp cross-national differences according to the nation involved in the interaction.

While the results we have reported seem fairly consistent, two notes of caution are in order. First, the figures reported in Tables 11.2 and 11.3 rely only on the chi-square test (and, in cases where the number of degrees of freedom equals zero, only on the ratio $s^2/\bar{x}$). While the analysis we did is consistent with the techniques used in most studies of the Poisson distribution, the chi-square at the 0.01 level is a conservative procedure and the Poisson distribution might be rejected if a less conservative significance level were to be used. In addition, we looked only at the distribution of events and did not consider other indicators (such as inter-arrival times) which would be necessary to show conclusively that the data were Poisson-distributed. For example, in cases where we looked at the ratio $s^2/\bar{x}$, it did not support some of the findings.

Second, in a number of instances, particularly in the Middle Eastern data set, the dyadic events are very rare (i.e., the frequency of their occurrence is sometimes less than ten for the entire period) and therefore the data fit the Poisson distribution almost by default. This by itself biases some dyadic interactions toward fitting the Poisson model. We did, however, exclude from the analysis seven cases (all in the Middle East) with zero frequencies for the entire period. Conversely, in some of the NATO dyads (e.g. UK/USA) the number of interactions is so large that the normal distribution is probably more appropriate than the Poisson. We did not formally test this hypothesis, but the data for these dyads appear roughly normally distributed.

We controlled experimentally for cases with low levels of interaction. When cases with fewer than ten interactions for the entire period are excluded from the analysis, then the results for the impact of interaction level on interaction pattern are about the same for Western Europe, but are reduced by about 20 percent for each of the two conflictual categories of Middle Eastern interactions. When the impact of the actors on the interaction pattern is assessed, significant changes appear only for the United States, which now drops to 40 percent, while all Western European countries drop by only 3–4 percent. In terms of the impact of the targets on the pattern, only the figure for the UK changes, while in the Middle East there are no significant changes except for Iraq, where the probability increases slightly.

Despite these limitations of our analysis, we can state with considerable confidence that we have detected the following distributional properties:

(1) There is at least moderate support for the thesis that Poisson-like processes operate in the subsystems analyzed.
(2) There is strong support for the assertion that the extent of Poisson behavior is a function of the type of interaction.
(3) Most nonverbal cooperative events in the Middle East and most physical conflictual events in Western Europe are Poisson-distributed.
(4) The hypothesis that there are cross-national variations in terms of the Poisson behavior of actors and targets finds moderate support.
(5) The data appear more random when aggregated at the yearly than at the monthly level, despite the intrinsic bias of the monthly data toward fitting better the Poisson distribution, so that nonrandom features of the interaction appear to be occurring over relatively short periods of time.

Conclusions

The basic hypothesis presented here is that the frequency of international interactions between a pair of nations can be described by a Poisson random process. This hypothesis is supported by the data in the majority of the cases we examined. The analysis suggests, however, that there are substantial differences in the percentage of cases obeying the Poisson distribution. It depends on the level of interaction, the nation initiating the action, and the target nation. Interactions are also less likely to be Poisson-distributed for data aggregated by months rather than years. These findings hold for two very different regional subsystems.

The finding that the distribution of international events is in many cases indistinguishable from that generated by a simple stochastic process is troublesome, since virtually all theories of international behavior assume that international events are patterned in ways different from the Poisson law. We share this assessment, and feel that our results indicate not so much intrinsic randomness as indications of the characteristics of those interactions. For example, the Poisson distribution of wars over time is a well-established result, but this does not mean that the events leading up to a war are random or that wars are totally unpredictable. The result merely means that, based on the time scale being used (decades, in most studies) and the information available (e.g. average frequency of war), a Poisson model is a good description of the behavior. A war which appears as a random event in a large time frame may appear determined in a different time and information frame. For example, the wars of German unification in the nineteenth century are not sufficiently aberrent to invalidate a Poisson fit of war in the interval of 1815–1945, but in the short period of 1860–75, and given the motivations of Otto von Bismarck, they can scarcely be called random events.

We suggest that there are at least four possible explanations for these results. First, the COPDAB data may be randomly sampled from a larger set of patterned data. Second, the distributions may be artifacts of deterministic processes which happen to match the Poisson distribution. Third, the nonrandom processes may occur at time intervals shorter than those which we studied. Fourth, nations may focus their patterned behavior on some dyadic relationships, leaving others as essentially random. We feel that the latter pair of explanations is more likely than the former.

The first possibility is that our findings are simply artifacts of the COPDAB data set. As noted earlier, COPDAB is problematic in terms of the density of the data, but generally our findings are the opposite of what one would expect if the data collection were the sole cause of randomness. Specifically, the data about which we are most confident are also those most likely to show a Poisson distribution.

In any events data set, the nonverbal events (levels 1–4 and 11–15) are probably not significantly affected by data collection, and hence any randomness detected in those events is a function of behavior and not a data artifact. With few exceptions, wars, alliances, unifications, and the like are conspicuous and unlikely to be missed. In verbal events, data quality is more problematic. For a verbal event to be recorded in the events data set, it must be sufficiently conspicuous and extraordinary that it is reported in the international media and thereby picked up in the events data collection. This is probably as dependent on the context of an event as on the event itself, and on essentially random circumstances such as a slow news day or a reporter in the right place at the right time. Nonetheless, our study indicates that verbal events are *less* likely to be Poisson-distributed, so any random sampling that occurs has the opposite effect of what would be expected.

Second, there is the possibility that a deterministic process operates to produce behavior that appears to be Poisson-distributed. Houweling and Kuné (1984) provide an example of this, and the "chaotic" behavior of the finite-difference logistic equation (May, 1976) is another example. While it may be possible to construct and justify such models, in general they have not been proposed and in their absence the stochastic explanation is preferable on the grounds of parsimony.

A third possibility is that events are nonrandom but are determined on a shorter time scale than those we have studied. Our analysis would support this explanation. The smallest level of aggregation we considered was a month, and monthly aggregations were less likely to be Poisson-distributed than were yearly aggregations.

It is simple to construct situations in which the unit of temporal aggregation significantly affects the observed degree of randomness in the data. Suppose, for example, that there existed a set of circumstances which, upon simultaneous occurrence, uniquely guaranteed that a war would break out within two weeks. Suppose further that those circumstances were themselves randomly determined (e.g. weather-related economic dislocations, deaths of leaders, garbled communications and machine failures, mixed strategy plays in zero-sum games, and so forth). In such a case, events would seem random on the scale of a month, but deterministic on the scale of two weeks. The converse is also possible: a long-term deterministic process could operate to change the value of the intensity parameter of a Poisson process, so that the short-term aggregations would appear random but the long-term would not. It is possible that, if the level of aggregation were smaller (e.g. a week or day) or, what is less likely, given our analysis, larger, the Poisson model would be less applicable.

A fourth possibility, also supported by our research, is that some but not all behavior is random. The most likely mechanism driving this explanation is the fact that individuals and organizations have finite capabilities for processing information. These are focused on high-priority issues; lower-priority issues only sporadically achieve the prominence that gets them into an events data set. This possible explanation is supported by most anecdotal accounts of organizational decision-making, which indicate that many low-level activities occur in addition to those reported in the newspapers. This might explain, for example, the high level of Poisson behavior in NATO with respect to Italy. Mintz and Schrodt (1984) explore this possibility in considerably greater detail by looking at the conditional distributions of dyadic events; Schrodt (1984) has looked at patterns of events on a purely sequential basis and found evidence that randomness depends in part on the extent to which a dyad is engaged in ongoing interaction.

In summary, our analysis indicates that a majority of the dyadic interactions in the Middle Eastern and NATO subsystems is distributed sufficiently randomly that the Poisson distribution cannot be rejected as an explanation. Nonetheless, the extent of this randomness varies systematically with the level of interaction and the unit of temporal aggregation, and also varies across nations. As a consequence, we suspect that these findings are not simply artifacts of the data, but instead indicate that nonrandom patterns of interaction occur over short time intervals, and are more likely to be found in low-level interactions such as verbal cooperation than in highly visible interactions such as nonverbal conflict.

REFERENCES

AZAR, E. E. (1980a) COPDAB Codebook. Chapel Hill: University of North Carolina at Chapel Hill, Conflict and Peace Data Bank (mimeographed).

AZAR, E. E. (1980b) "The conflict and peace data bank (COPDAB) project." Journal of Conflict Resolution 24 (March): 143-152.

———and J. BEN DAK (1975) Theory and Practice of Events Data Research. New York: Gordon and Breach.

CHAN, S. (1978) "Temporal delineation of international conflicts: Poisson results from the Vietnam war, 1963–1965." International Studies Quarterly 22 (June): 237–265.

CINLAR, E. (1975) Introduction to Stochastic Processes. Englewood Cliffs, NJ: Prentice-Hall.

CIOFFI-REVILLA, C. (1985) "Political reliability theory and war in the international system." American Journal of Political Science 29 (February): 47–68.

CONNOR, E. F. and D. SIMBERLOFF (1979) "The assembly of species communities: chance or competition?" Ecology 60 (December): 1132–1140.

DAVIS, W. W., G. T. DUNCAN, and R. M. SIVERSON (1978) "The dynamics of warfare, 1816–1965." American Journal of Political Science 22 (November): 772–792.

FELLER, W. (1968) An Introduction to Probability Theory and Its Applications (3d ed.). New York: John Wiley.

HINES, W. W. and D. C. MONTGOMERY (1980) Probability and Statistics in Engineering and Management Science (2d ed.). New York: John Wiley.

HOPPLE, G. W., P. J. ROSSA, and J. WILKENFELD (1980) "Threat and foreign policy: the overt behavior of states in conflict," pp. 19–53 in P. J. McGowan and C. W. Kegley, Jr (eds.), Sage International Yearbook of Foreign Policy Studies, vol. 3: Threats, Weapons, and Foreign Policy. Beverly Hills, Calif.: Sage.

HORVATH, W. J. and C. C. FOSTER (1963) "Stochastic models of war alliances." Journal of Conflict Resolution 7 (June); 110–116.

HOUWELING, H. W. and J. B. KUNÉ (1984) "Do outbreaks of war follow a Poisson-process?" Journal of Conflict Resolution 28 (March): 51–61.

HOWELL, L. D. (1983) "A comparative study of the WEIS and COPDAB data sets." International Studies Quarterly 27 (June): 149–159.

JOB, B. L. (1974) The Alliance Formation Behavior of Nations in the International System. Unpublished PhD dissertation, Indiana University.

——— (1976) "Membership in inter-nation alliances, 1815–1965: an exploration utilizing mathematical probability models," pp. 74–109 in D. A. Zinnes and J. V. Gillespie (eds.), Mathematical Models in International Relations. New York: Praeger.

LAEMMLE, P. (1977) "Epidemiology of domestic military intervention: evaluation of contagion as an explanatory concept." Behavioral Science 22 (September): 327–333.

LEWIN, R. (1983) "Santa Rosalia was a goat." Science 221 (12 August): 636–639.

LI, R. P. Y. and W. R. THOMPSON (1978) "The stochastic process of alliance formation behavior." American Political Science Review 72 (December): 1288–1303.

MAY, R. M. (1976) "Simple mathematical models with very complicated dynamics." Nature 261 (10 June): 459–467.

McCLELLAND, C. A. (1983) "Let the user beware." International Studies Quarterly 27 (June): 169–177.

McGOWAN, P. J. and R. M. ROOD (1975) "Alliance behavior in balance of power systems: applying a Poisson model to nineteenth-century Europe." American Political Science Review 69 (September): 859–870.

MIDLARSKY, M. I. (1970) "Mathematical models of instability and a theory of diffusion." International Studies Quarterly 14 (March): 60–84.

——— (1981) "Equilibria in a nineteenth-century balance-of-power system." American Journal of Political Science 25 (May): 270–296.

MINTZ, A. and P. A. SCHRODT (1984) "A conditional probability analysis of regional interactions in the Middle East." Unpublished paper presented at the 25th Annual Convention of the International Studies Association, Atlanta, Ga. (March).

MOST, B. A. and H. STARR (1980) "Diffusion, reinforcement, geopolitics, and the spread of war." American Political Science Review 74 (December): 932–946.

MOYAL, J. E. (1949) "The distribution of wars in time." Journal of the Royal Statistical Society 112, 4: 446–449.

PARZEN, E. (1962) Stochastic Processes. San Francisco, Calif.: Holden-Day.

RICHARDSON, L. F. (1941) "Frequency of occurrence of wars and other fatal quarrels." Nature 148 (15 November): 598.

——— (1945) "The distribution of wars in time." Journal of the Royal Statistical Society 107, 3–4: 242–250.

———— (1960) Statistics of Deadly Quarrels. Pittsburgh, Pa.: Boxwood Press; and Chicago, Ill.: Quadrangle Books.

Chicago, Ill.: Quadrangle Books.

SCHRODT, P. A. (1983) "Arms transfers and international conflict in the Arabian Sea area." Int. Interactions 10, 1: 95-123.

————(1984) "Artificial intelligence and international crisis." Unpublished paper presented at the 80th Annual Meeting of the American Political Science Association, Washington, DC (August).

SIMBERLOFF, D. (1978) "Using island biogeographic distributions to determine if colonization is stochastic." American Naturalist 112 (July–August): 713–726.

SINGER, J. D. and M. SMALL (1972) The Wages of War, 1816–1965: A Statistical Handbook. New York: John Wiley.

SIVERSON, R. M. and G. T. DUNCAN (1976) "Stochastic models of international alliance initiation, 1885–1965," pp. 110–131 in D. A. Zinnes and J. V. Gillespie (eds.), Mathematical Models in International Relations. New York: Praeger.

THOMPSON, W. R. and L. G. ZUK (1982) "War, inflation, and the Kontratieff long wave." Journal of Conflict Resolution 26 (December): 621–644.

VINCENT, J. E. (1983) "WEIS vs. COPDAB correspondence problems." International Studies Quarterly 27 (June): 161-168.

WEISS, H. K. (1963) "Stochastic models for the duration and magnitude of a 'deadly quarrel.'" Operations Research 11 (January–February): 101–121.

ABSTRACTS/RÉSUMÉS

1

Communication and Interaction in Global Politics
Claudio Cioffi-Revilla
Richard L. Merritt
Dina A. Zinnes

Understanding the complexities of global politics requires more systematic analysis of the interplay of two core elements, communication and interaction. Important foci include the dynamics of interaction in an essentially anarchic world, bargaining behavior of international actors, and international integration. Relevant analytic research is proceeding at various levels, from formal modeling using mathematics to data-based statistical studies. Increasingly, analysts in all these traditions are applying their models to real-world issues.

Communication et interaction en politique mondiale

La compréhension des complexités de la politique mondiale exige plus d'analyse systématique de l'influence mutuelle de deux éléments centraux, la communication et l'interaction. Parmi les points de concentration importants: la dynamique de l'interaction dans un monde essentiellement anarchiste; le comportement dans la négotiation d'acteurs internationaux; l'intégration internationale. La recherche analytique relative à cela se fait à divers niveaux, de la formation formelle de modèles qui se servent des mathématiques, à des études statistiques sur base de données. De plus en plus les analystes de toutes ces traditions appliquent leurs modèles à des cas réels.

2

Transaction Flows and Integrative Processes
Dina A. Zinnes
Robert G. Muncaster

Building on the earlier work of Karl Deutsch, this study translates into mathematical form a number of Deutsch's assumptions concerning transaction flows and cooperation. The resulting mathematical model describes how the *volume* of interaction, together with the extent to which the interaction between two nations is balanced, produces varying degrees of cooperation. Although the complexity of the model does not permit a complete analysis, it is possible to show a set of conditions which produces complete cooperation — integration — and another set which makes cooperation decrease.

Mouvements des transactions et processus d'intégration

A partir des travaux antérieurs de Karl Deutsch, cette étude traduit en forme mathématique un certain nombre de postulats de Deutsch sur les mouvements des transactions et sur la coopération. Le modèle mathématique qui en résulte décrit la façon dont le *volume* d'interactions, joint au degré d'équilibre de l'interaction entre deux nations, produit des degrés variables de coopération. Bien que la complexité du modèle ne permette pas d'analyse complète, il est possible de montrer un ensemble de conditions qui produisent une coopération complète — intégration — ainsi qu'un autre ensemble qui réduit la coopération.

3

Crises, War, and Security Reliability
Claudio Cioffi-Revilla

In his "crisis theory of war," Quincy Wright conjectured that the probability of war is a function of the probability of crisis escalation during an arc of time containing n crises. Using the theory of political reliability, a formal restatement of Wright's argument is presented and his conjectured equations are formally derived. Although Wright and others have noted that the probability of war converges toward certainty as $n \to +\infty$, this study shows that convergence occurs much faster, and security reliability is therefore far more sensitive than might be intuitively expected. Moreover, a theorem shows that the probability of war is more sensitive to p than it is to n.

Crises, la guerre, et fiabilité de la sécurité

Dans sa "crisis theory of war," Quincy Wright a émis l'hypothèse que la probabilité de guerre est en fonction de la probabilité d'accroissement de crise pendant une courbe de temps qui contiendrait des crises n. En nous servant de la théorie de la fiabilité politique, l'argument de Wright est exposé de nouveau d'une manière formelle, et ses équations hypothétiques en sont formellement dérivées. Bien que Wright et d'autres aient remarqué que la probabilité de guerre se rapproche de la certitude lorsque $n \to +\infty$, notre étude témoigne du fait que cette convergence a lieu bien plus rapidement, donc la fiabilité de la sécurité est bien plus délicate que l'intuition ne le laisserait supposer. En outre, un théorème montre que la probabilité de guerre est plus sensible à p qu'à n.

4

Modeling an International Trade System
Brian M. Pollins
Grant Kirkpatrick

In seeking to incorporate political determinants into a model of bilateral flows that reflects current, accepted trade theory, the chapter specifies the estimating model in a way which closely fits its continuous-time theoretical form. An empirical exploration of the viability of key economic assumptions relating to the elasticity of substitution and speed of adjustment precedes an estimation of the parameters on political determinants. Preliminary estimations yield results conforming to theoretic expectations.

Modélisation d'un système internationale du commerce

En poursuivant l'incorporation de déterminants politiques dans un modèle de mouvements bilatéraux qui reflète la théorie du commerce courante et acceptée, ce chapitre spécifie le modèle d'estimation d'une façon qui s'ajuste de très près à sa forme théorique de temps continu. Une exploration empirique de la viabilité de postulats-clé économiques par rapport à l'élasticité de substitutions et la rapidité d'ajustements, précède une estimation des paramètres sur des déterminants politiques. Des estimations préliminaires donnent des résultats qui se conforment aux attentes théoriques.

5

Social Time
Pierre Allan

The clocks we use are physical ones. Analyzing and modeling social processes according to the time durations of physical clocks may be too stringent a requirement in some cases. A general procedure for developing social time referentials in a formal way is presented. It is based on the intensity and magnitude of social processes. Two concrete formalizations of alternative social time scales are presented and compared: diplomatic time and event time.

Le temps social

Les horloges que nous utilisons nous viennent de la physique. Analyser et modéliser des processus sociaux selon les durées temporelles fournies par des horloges physiques pourrait être une condition trop contraignante dans certains cas. On présente une procédure formelle générale pour développer des référentiels temporels sociaux. Celle-ci est basée sur l'intensité et la grandeur des processus sociaux. Deux formalisations concrètes d'échelles alternatives de temps social sont présentées et comparées: le temps diplomatique et le temps événementiel.

6

Misperception and Satisficing in International Conflict
Michael Nicholson

A modified game theory model, in which opponents misperceive the acts available to the opponent, and the utilities attributed to the various possible consequences, is applied to the Falklands conflict — a classic case of misperception.

Fausse perception et "satisficing" en conflits internationaux

Une forme de la "théorie des jeux" est appliquée, selon laquelle chaque combattant a une fausse perception des stratégies dont dispose l'adversaire; et la guerre des Iles Malouines/Falkland — un exemple classique de fausses perceptions — est analysée pour illustrer les divers enseignements qui découlent de cette méthode.

7

The Verification Problem in Arms Control:
A Game-Theoretic Analysis
Steven J. Brams
Morton D. Davis

A two-person, non-constant-sum game of imperfect information, called the "Truth Game," in which a signaler must choose between telling the truth and lying, and a detector must respond by believing or not believing the signaler, is used to model the verification problem in arms control. Optimal "inducement" and "guarantee" strategies, which are always mixed (random), are calculated, and their relevance to strategic and normative choices in a world of uncertainty are evaluated.

Le problème de vérification dans le contrôle des armements: analyse suivant la théorie des jeux

Afin d'établir un modèle du problème de vérification en matière de contrôle des armements, nous nous servons d'un jeu à deux personnes, de somme non-constante et d'information imparfaite, "Le Jeu de la Vérité." Un signaleur devra faire le choix entre vérité et mensonge, et un détecteur devra réagir en croyant ou non le signaleur. Les stratégies optimales d'"incitation" et de "garanties," toujours determinées au hasard, sont calculées et évaluées par les auteurs, ainsi que leurs rapports à des choix stratégiques et normatifs dans un monde d'incertitudes.

8

Ambiguous Information and the Arms Race and Mutual Deterrence Games
Raymond Dacey

If a superpower uses ambiguous rhetoric as a manipulative device in a play of the arms race or mutual deterrence game, then bribes, threats, and tit-for-tat are all risk-free to the user. The analysis rests on (1) the usual lottery notion of ambiguity, (2) formal notions of a probabilistic bribe, probabilistic threat, and probabilistic tit-for-tat, and (3) decision-theoretic (as opposed to game-theoretic) play of the game. Bribes, threats, and tit-for-tat are risk-free in the sense that, if ambiguity induces a change in the adversary's choice, then it will induce a change toward cooperation. Formal analysis establishes the result, which is illustrated by the mechanics of probabilistic tit-for-tat as a manipulative device.

Information ambiguë et la course aux armements et le jeu de dissuasion mutuelle

Si une superpuissance se sert de rhétorique ambiguë à des fins de manipulation dans un duel tel que la course aux armements ou bien le jeu de dissuasion mutuelle, la corruption, les menaces, et la riposte "oeil pour oeil" sont sans risques pour l'utilisateur. Notre analyse s'appuie sur la notion habituelle d'ambiguïté et de hasard, et introduit les notions formelles de corruption, menace et riposte probabilistes. Elle s'appuie aussi sur l'aspect théorique de la décision (par opposition à la théorie du jeu). Corruption, menaces, et ripostes sont sans danger au sens où, si l'ambiguïté entraîne un changement dans le choix de l'adversaire, elle entraînera un choix dans le sens de la coopération. L'article présente l'analyse formelle qui aboutit au résultat et donne un exemple du fonctionnement de la riposte "oeil pour oeil, dent pour dent" en tant que moyen de manipulation.

9

Language and Communication: The Rise of the Monolingual State
J. A. Laponce

It seems likely that a century-old trend — the increase in the number of spoken languages — has been reversed. After an era of expansion by divergence, languages have, it seems, entered a period of negative growth rate. At the beginning of what is likely to be a new era, this chapter does some stocktaking by measuring the cultural, demographic, and military power of the major competitors and speculates on the consequences for national and international politics of the increased coincidence of state and language boundaries.

Langage et communication: la montée de l'état monolingue

Il semblerait qu'une évolution séculaire — l'accroissement du nombre de langues parlées dans le monde — ait été renversée à l'époque contemporaine et que les langues soient entrées dans une phase de régression numérique. Au début de ce qui est vraisemblablement une époque nouvelle, ce chapitre fait un inventaire de la puissance démographique, culturelle et militaire des principaux acteurs et se demande ce que seront vraisemblablement les conséquences de la coïncidence accrue des frontières étatiques et des frontières linguistiques des politiques nationales et internationales.

10

European Community and Intra-European Communications:
The Evidence of Mail Flows
Cal Clark
Richard L. Merritt

International mail flows, analyzed using the RS^t statistic ("relative sending," a modification of the Savage-Deutsch RA statistic), indicate that the "Six" enjoyed an inchoate communications network before they formed the European Economic Community, and that economic union strengthened the network. Distance plays an important role in these patterns, as does trade; language similarity is more important for trade than mail flows. Changing communication habits contributed to attitudinal shifts that provided a "permissive consensus" for steps toward formal unity.

Communauté européenne et communications intra-européennes:
l'évidence du mouvement du courrier

Les mouvements internationaux du courrier, analysés selon la statistique RS^t ("relative sending" — envoi relatif, une modification de la statistique RA de Savage et Deutsch), indiquent que Les Six possédaient un rudimentaire réseau de communications avant la formation de la CEE, et que l'union économique a renforcé ce réseau. Les distances jouent un rôle important dans ces schémas, ainsi que le commerce; les similarités de langage sont plus importantes pour le commerce que pour la circulation du courrier. L'évolution des coutumes en communications a contribué à modifier des attitudes qui créèrent un "consensus permissif" de mesures en direction d'une unification formelle.

11

Distributional Patterns of Regional Interactions:
A Test of the Poisson Process as a Null Model
Alex Mintz
Philip A. Schrodt

International interactions reported in the COPDAB events data set are examined for two international subsystems: the Arab Middle East and the North Atlantic region. A Poisson model of interaction is supported in the majority of the dyadic interactions studied, indicating that the hypothesis of random interaction cannot be rejected at the monthly and yearly levels of aggregation. The extent to which the data follow a Poisson distribution varies systematically with the type of interaction, the actors, and the targets of the interactions, and seems less prevalent at the monthly level of aggregation than at the yearly level.

Schémas de distribution d'interactions régionales: un test du processus de Poisson comme modèle nul

Les interactions internationales rapportées dans le dossier d'événements COPDAB sont examinées par rapport à deux sous-systèmes internationaux: le Moyen Orient et la région Atlantique du nord. Un modèle Poisson d'interaction est confirmé dans la majorité des interactions en dyade que nous avons étudiées, et indique que l'hypothèse d'interaction prise au hasard ne peut être rejetée aux niveaux d'agrégations mensuelles ou annuelles. Les données suivent une distribution Poisson à des degrés qui varient systématiquement, selon le type d'interaction, d'acteurs, et de cibles des interactions. Il semble prévaloir moins au niveau des agrégations mensuelles qu'à celui des agrégations annuelles.

INDEX

ABOUT THE
CONTRIBUTORS

PIERRE ALLAN was George A. Miller Visiting Scholar at the University of Illinois at Urbana-Champaign when he wrote this contribution. His main research interests are methodology, international relations, and political economy. He is the author of *Crisis Bargaining and the Arms Race* (1983) and is presently professor of political science at the University of Geneva, Switzerland.

STEVEN J. BRAMS is professor of politics at New York University, with research interests in applications of game theory and social choice theory. His most recent books are *Biblical Games: A Strategic Analysis of Stories in the Old Testament* (1980), *Superior Beings: If They Exist, How Would We Know?* (1983), *Approval Voting* (1983), with Peter C. Fishburn, and *Superpower Games: Applying Game Theory to Superpower Conflict* (1985).

CLAUDIO CIOFFI-REVILLA is associate professor of political science and Beckman Fellow in The Center for Advanced Study (1985) at the University of Illinois at Urbana-Champaign. In 1983 he was elected to the International Medici Academy for his work on mathematical models of conflict.

CAL CLARK is professor of political science at the University of Wyoming. His principal research interests include comparative communism and international interactions. He is the co-author of *The Communist Balkans in International Politics* and co-editor of *Studies in Dependency Reversal.*

RAYMOND DACEY received the B.S. degree in Mathematics from Pennsylvania State University, the Ph.D. in Economics and Management Science from Purdue University, and was a postdoctoral fellow in Philosophy at Johns Hopkins University. He has been on the faculties of the University of Iowa and the University of Oklahoma, and is now dean of the College of Business and Economics at the University of Idaho. He is also involved with the Institute for the Study of Conflict Theory and International Security.

MORTON D. DAVIS is professor of mathematics at City College of New York, with primary interests in game theory and mathematical modeling. He is currently working on problems of artificial intelligence and computer learning of parlor games. He is author of *Game Theory: A Nontechnical Introduction* (rev. ed., 1983) and several professional papers in game theory.

GRANT KIRKPATRICK is a research scientist on the staff of the Institute for World Economics in Kiel, West Germany. His work is in the area of open economy macroeconomics, particularly in multi-country modeling of open economies. Relevant work has been published in *Weltwirtschaftliches Archiv*.

JEAN A. LAPONCE is professor of political science at the University of British Columbia, Vancouver. His main interests are the study of political perceptions, ethnic conflict, and experimentation on small groups. His most recent publication relevant to the present chapter is *Langue et territoire* (1984).

RICHARD L. MERRITT, professor of political science and research professor in communications, University of Illinois at Urbana-Champaign, has focused his research on international political communication and West German politics. He has been vice-president of the International Political Science Association and the International Studies Association.

ALEX MINTZ is assistant professor of political science at the Hebrew University of Jerusalem (Israel). He has authored *The Politics of Resource Allocation in the US Department of Defense* (1985) as well as several articles on Israel's military–industrial sector and on conflictual interactions in the Middle East.

ROBERT G. MUNCASTER is associate professor of mathematics at the University of Illinois at Urbana-Champaign, specializing in applied mathematics and rational mechanics. His current interests include the study of international conflict, with recent work published in the *Journal of Conflict Resolution*.

MICHAEL NICHOLSON is a member of the Department of Decision Theory, University of Manchester. His research uses formal modeling, particularly to study the beginning and ending of war. His most recent publication is *The Scientific Analysis of Social Behaviour: A Defence of Empiricism in Social Science* (1983).

BRIAN M. POLLINS is currently assistant professor in the Department of Political Science at the Ohio State University. He also maintains an affiliation with the Science Center Berlin as an associate member of the GLOBUS team. Related work has been published in *International Studies Quarterly* and *International Political Science Review*.

PHILIP SCHRODT is an associate professor of political science at Northwestern University. His primary research work is in mathematical models of international politics. His past work includes studies of the Richardson arms race model, the cube law, and arms transfers; he is currently working on applications of artificial intelligence models to international relations.

DINA A. ZINNES, Merriam Professor of Political Science at the University of Illinois at Urbana-Champaign, has focused her research on the construction, analysis, and empirical testing of mathematical models of international relations. Her research has appeared in, inter alia, *Journal of Conflict Resolution*, *International Studies Quarterly*, *World Politics*, and *American Political Science Review*. She has also edited a number of volumes devoted to the presentation of mathematical models in international relations and has written a survey of the quantitative research literature in this area, *Contemporary Research in International Relations* (1976).